Double Agent Celery

Double Agent Celery

MI5's Crooked Hero

Carolinda Witt
Foreword by Nigel West

Pen & Sword
MILITARY

First published in Great Britain in 2017 by
Pen & Sword Military
an imprint of
Pen & Sword Books Ltd
47 Church Street
Barnsley
South Yorkshire
S70 2AS

ISBN 978 1 52671 614 9

A CIP catalogue record for this book is
available from the British Library.

Printed and bound in England
By CPI Group (UK) Ltd, Croydon, CR0 4YY

Pen & Sword Books Ltd incorporates the Imprints of Pen & Sword
Archaeology, Atlas, Aviation, Battleground, Discovery, Family History,
History, Maritime, Military, Naval, Politics, Railways, Select, Transport,
True Crime, Fiction, Frontline Books, Leo Cooper, Praetorian Press, Seaforth
Publishing, Wharncliffe and White Owl.

For a complete list of Pen & Sword titles please contact
PEN & SWORD BOOKS LIMITED
47 Church Street, Barnsley, South Yorkshire, S70 2AS, England
E-mail: enquiries@pen-and-sword.co.uk
Website: www.pen-and-sword.co.uk

'It is not the critic who counts; not the man who points out how the strong man stumbles, or where the doer of deeds could have done them better. The credit belongs to the man who is actually in the arena, whose face is marred by dust and sweat and blood; who strives valiantly; who errs, who comes short again and again, because there is no effort without error and shortcoming; but who does actually strive to do the deeds; who knows great enthusiasms, the great devotions; who spends himself in a worthy cause; who at the best knows in the end the triumph of high achievement, and who at the worst, if he fails, at least fails while daring greatly, so that his place shall never be with those cold and timid souls who neither know victory nor defeat.'

Theodore Roosevelt

Contents

Dramatis Personae

Adair, George 'Robin'	Eldest son of Walter Dicketts and his 1st wife Phyllis Hobson
Adair, Mike	Grandson of Walter Dicketts, son of Rodney Adair
Adair, Rodney	Second son of Walter Dicketts and his 1st wife Phyllis Hobson
Bade, Lily	Arthur Owens' 27-year-old mistress
Biscuit	MI5 double agent Sam McCarthy
Boyle, Archie	Director of Air Intelligence
Brown, Jack	Abwehr codename for Walter Dicketts
Burton, Maurice	Snow's radio operator
Butcher, Harry	Alias for British writer who met Georg Sessler after the war
Canaris, Wilhelm	Chief of the Abwehr
Caroli, Gösta	MI5 double agent Summer
Celery	MI5 double agent Walter Dicketts
Chapman, Eddie	MI5 double agent Zigzag
Charlie	MI5 double agent Eschborn, a photographer
Cowgill, Felix	Deputy head of SIS's Section V
Del Pozo, Miguel	Spanish journalist and Abwehr spy, MI5 codename Pogo
Denker, Walter Anton	Name on Walter Dicketts' German passport
Dicketts, Alma Farquhar	Walter Dicketts' 16-year-old 2nd wife Alma Wood
Dicketts, Arthur Skinner	Walter Dicketts' father
Dicketts, Effie 'Tonie'	Daughter of Walter Dicketts and mistress Dora Guerrier

Dicketts, Eric 'Dick'	Son of Walter Dicketts and mistress Dora Guerrier
Dicketts, 'Judy' Rose	Walter Dicketts' 4th wife, Judith Rose Kalman
Dicketts, Kay	Mistress of Walter Dicketts when married to 3rd wife Vera, real name Kathleen Mary Holdcroft
Dicketts, Phyllis	Walter Dicketts' 1st wife, Phyllis Hobson
Dicketts, Robert	Son of Walter Dicketts and 4th wife Judith Kalman
Dicketts, Vera Nellie	Walter Dicketts' 3rd wife, Vera Nellie Fudge
Dicketts, Walter	MI5 double agent Celery
Dierks, Hans	Abwehr officer
Dobler/Doebler, Herbert	Gestapo agent alias H Duarte in Lisbon
Eschborn C	MI5 double agent Charlie
Fudge, Vera Nellie	Walter Dicketts' 3rd wife
Gagan, Inspector	Special Branch detective
Guerrier, Dora Viva	Mistress of Walter Dicketts when married to 1st wife Phyllis
GW	MI5 double agent Gwilym Williams
Gwyer, John	MI5 officer and peacetime lawyer
Haylor, Ronnie	MI5 officer
Hinchley-Cooke, Edward	MI5 officer and interrogator
Heydrich, Reinhardt	Brutal Nazi Chief of the SS or SD (Sicherheitsdienst)
Hobson, Phyllis	Walter Dicketts' 1st wife
Holdcroft, Kathleen Mary	Walter Dicketts' 2nd mistress when married to 3rd wife Vera Dicketts
Horsfall, 'Jock' St John	MI5's discreet chauffeur and famous racing driver
Jarvis, Ralph	SIS officer in Lisbon
Johnny	Abwehr codename for Arthur Owens
Kalman, Judith 'Judy'	Walter Dicketts' 4th wife
Krafft, Mathilde	Abwehr paymaster in England
Lahousen, Erwin	Senior Abwehr officer and member of German resistance

Stopford, Richman	MI5 officer
Summer	MI5 double agent Gösta Caroli
Tate	MI5 double agent Wulf Schmidt
Tricycle	MI5 double agent Dusko Popov
Tudhope, Richard	Son of Walter Dicketts' 3rd wife Vera Nellie Fudge
Trautmann, Werner	Head of Communications Ast. Hamburg
Wein, Richard	Owens' Abwehr radio operator at Wohldorf-Hamburg
White, Dick	MI5 officer and future Director General of both MI5 and SIS
Williams, Gwilym	MI5 double agent GW
Wilson, Thomas	An alias occasionally adopted by Snow
Witt, Effie 'Tonie'	Daughter of Walter Dicketts and mistress Dora Guerrier
Wood, Alma Farquhar	Walter Dicketts' 16-year-old 2nd wife
Yule, Colonel J.F.	MI5 radio expert
Zigzag	MI5 double agent Eddie Chapman

Abbreviations

Abwehr	The German armed forces intelligence service
Abteilung I	Espionage department, Abwehr
Abteilung II	Sabotage department, Abwehr
Abteilung III	Counter-intelligence department, Abwehr
Ast.	Abwehrstelle. District or section of the Abwehr, subordinate to Berlin
BI (a)	MI5's German double agent section
BP	Bletchley Park, British codebreaking centre in Buckinghamshire
BUF	British Union of Fascists
C	Title of the head of SIS
Camp 020	British interrogation camp in South London for captured enemy agents
Cipher	A cryptographic system in which letters or numbers represent plain-text units (generally single letters)
Code	A cryptographic system generally set out in a code in which groups of letters or numbers represent plain-text words or phrases
CSDIC	Combined Services Detailed Interrogation Centre, Bad Nenndorf, Germany
DG	Director General MI5
DMI	Director of Military Intelligence
DNI	Director of Naval Intelligence
ENIGMA	German electrical cipher machines
ISK	Machine-generated signals (Illicit or Intelligence Service Knox) after codebreaker Dilly Knox
ISOS	Decrypted Abwehr hand cipher wireless traffic (Illicit or Intelligence Service Oliver Strachey) after cryptographer Strachey

GC&CS	Government Code and Cypher School
MI5	British Security Service
MI9	Escape and Evasion, SIS
NID	Naval Intelligence Division
RSLO	Regional Security Liaison Officer
RSS	Radio Security Service
SD	Sicherheitsdienst, the Nazi Party's internal intelligence service (civilian intelligence) which took over the functions of the Abwehr in 1944
SIGINT	Signals intelligence
SIS	Secret Intelligence Service, also known as MI6
SO2	Special Operations 2
SOE	Special Operations Executive
ULTRA	British military intelligence gained by decrypting enemy communications
W/T	Wireless Telegraphy
XX	Double cross, double agents or the Twenty (double cross) committee

Walter Dicketts Family Tree

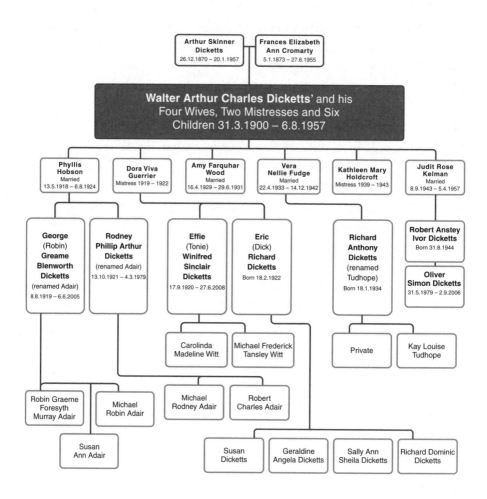

Author's Note

Walter Dicketts is my grandfather. He had six children to four different women, and my mother Effie 'Tonie' was his only daughter, but she didn't even know his name, as she had been lied to by the woman she believed to be her mother, who was really her grandmother.

Just ten days after my mother's death in 2008, I discovered the truth that had eluded her for her whole life – the name of her father and what he did. Remarkably, he was one of MI5's more notorious British double agents in the Second World War called Celery. His family didn't know he was a spy, and by the time his top-secret file was released by the British National Archives, Walter Dicketts had been dead for forty-four years.

Dicketts' life outside of spying was equally remarkable – almost unbelievable. No one in his family knew about the existence of the other, except two half-brothers who hadn't seen each other since they were kids. My mother, who had grown up as a single child, had five brothers she never knew about, including her younger brother who had been given away at birth.

It was very poignant to realize that the one person to whom this information would have meant so much, would never know, and I would never feel the joy of sharing it with her.

I soon realized that the remarkable story of how Walter Dicketts entered Germany as a British spy in the middle of the Second World War and got away with it, belonged to history.

Foreword

Wartime intelligence personnel rarely conform to a particular type, and much the same can be said for their agents. Some are foolhardy, others are egotists, sociopaths, ideologues and gamblers, but it takes a very special category of double agent to work convincingly for two masters, and then willingly place their lives on the line.

During the Second World War, there were plenty of double agents run by both sides. The Abwehr and Sicherheitsdienst ran very successful penetration operations against the Allies in France, Belgium and the Netherlands, while MI5 and SIS (the Secret Intelligence Service) created extensive networks across the globe, run by dedicated organizations set up for the purpose in London, Cairo and Delhi. With the benefit of recently declassified files, it is now possible to take a fresh and more informed view of these hitherto classified clandestine operations.

What distinguishes Celery in particular was his willingness, along with only a handful of others, to put himself in jeopardy by agreeing to travel to the Continent and confront his German controllers face-to-face. For most double agents, in contact with the enemy by wireless transmitter or the mail, the personal risks were small and they could terminate their links unilaterally, without suffering too many adverse consequences, but Walter Dicketts - like Snow, Tricycle and Zigzag - agreed to a rendezvous in neutral Lisbon, and then was escorted to the heart of the Reich, far beyond MI5's reach should he be compromised. From the moment an agent stepped ashore in Portugal, subject to the Gestapo-trained PVDE secret police, and under the ubiquitous surveillance masterminded by Axis agencies represented by the Bulgarian, Hungarian, Italian and Vichy services, there was unrelenting danger. Abduction was not unusual, and the large Abwehr and the Sicherheitsdienst presence both operated unfettered. The loneliness and vulnerability of anyone on a secret assignment in such adverse conditions can only be imagined.

Four remarkable men – Walter Dicketts, Arthur Owens, Dusan Popov and Eddie Chapman – stand out from the rest of MI5's impressive stable of 'controlled enemy agents', partly because each in their own way was a bit of a scoundrel, but mainly because they willingly agreed to stroll into the lion's den, their life utterly dependent on their initiative and sense of self-preservation. None of them was under any obligation to undertake these missions, and all fully understood their likely fate if the true scale of their duplicity was even suspected. They may have been rogues, but being mildly villainous offered precious little protection against the power exercised so ruthlessly by the Nazis and their co-conspirators.

In retrospect, it may seem surprising that the Abwehr was duped so comprehensively by MI5 and SIS. Of course, hostile penetration, defection and untraceable leaks are occupational hazards for all security and intelligence agencies, but the Germans suffered from all these disadvantages quite consistently. They began the war handicapped by a paucity of assets already *in situ*, but this was the result of a conscious policy which had been forced on the organization following the arrest and imprisonment of Dr Hermann Goertz in 1938. This very public exposure of German espionage, involving an agent who had been caught while conducting a survey of RAF airfields in Kent, caused much political embarrassment in Berlin and prompted a ban on further similar adventures so as to avoid damaging diplomatic relations at a particularly sensitive time when the ambassador, Joachim von Ribbentrop, was seeking to cultivate the British government.

In the relative information vacuum relevant to the British Isles, the Abwehr was forced to grasp almost any opportunity, and in this challenging environment Snow and his recruit Celery offered the chance to build a reliable, well-connected spy-ring apparently based on Nazi sympathizers, nationalists and members, like Dicketts, of a supposedly disaffected officer class. It may be that the Abwehr was insufficiently discriminating in its choice of agents, but, devoid of alternatives, the Hamburg *Abstellen* took the bait.

In many ways, one can comprehend why Celery appeared to be such an attractive prospect. He had served as an RAF officer, had a first-hand knowledge of intelligence, had friends in the Air Ministry, and his well-documented brushes with the law showed him to be ingenious but greedy, manipulative and resourceful. These were all attributes that might be associated with someone who, having fallen foul of the police, might be thought to be potentially disloyal to his country. The Germans would later make a similar misjudgment about Eddie Chapman, a career criminal who convincingly portrayed himself as a man with a grudge against the British authorities. In both examples, Celery and Zigzag persuaded their German contacts of what they were self-delusionally predisposed to believe, that there was a criminal sub-class that owed no loyalty to anyone but themselves, and that these ex-convicts were essentially mercenaries, available for hire.

It should also be said, with the benefit of defector interviews and the interrogation of captured Abwehr officers, that the organization suffered from two institutional disadvantages. Firstly, staff who recruited agents were not routinely rotated to prevent them from becoming too closely associated with their sources. A new pair of eyes as a handler is good tradecraft and avoids the trap of case officers tending to overlook contradictions, and tying their own careers to the performance of their agents. Secondly, complete candour was not always encouraged and it was widely believed within *KriegsOrganisations* that anyone who confided legitimate doubts about a recruit's continued integrity might be rewarded with a transfer to the Russian Front, or worse. Therefore, almost inevitably, it was in the best interests of those harbouring concerns, to remain silent about them, even to their closest colleagues.

Reading the files in isolation often fails to convey the drama and the deeply personal crises that these double agents endured. All had tangled love-lives, families that had little or no idea of their wartime activities, and descendants who found themselves astonished at the previously unsuspected and undisclosed exploits. Individual declassified dossiers, released to the National Archives at Kew, provide a fascinating glimpse of the covert activities, but it is only when the framework revealed by the archives is overlain with the intensely human dimension of broken hearts, betrayed loyalties and twisted morals that the full picture emerges.

Nigel West
www.nigelwest.com
January 2016

Prologue

26 March 1941, Lisbon

At the Hotel Metropole in Lisbon at dawn, two British spies known to the Germans as Johnny and Brown were packing their bags for the flight back to England for the third day running. The adverse weather conditions which had twice delayed their departure were gone.

Brown was worn out and anxious to return to England. He had survived three weeks in Germany being interrogated and treated with great suspicion by officers who came from every section of the Abwehr to try their hand against the alleged British traitor. Brown was threatened, tricked, plied with alcohol and even drugged, before he was accepted as a German agent who was willing to sell out his country as a means to ending the war. In reality, he was a double agent working for MI5. His real name was Walter Dicketts and his codename was Celery.

Dicketts was well aware how dangerous his mission was before he went into Germany. If he slipped up he would be executed as a spy. There could be no escape. All he had to protect him was his photographic memory, his skills in deception and the implausible word of Nikolaus Ritter, a vain and self-aggrandizing officer of the Abwehr. Incredibly, he managed to outwit the Nazis and return safely to Lisbon, carrying vital intelligence he had obtained in Hamburg. He carried this information inside a large envelope officially sealed at the British Embassy and addressed to his employer, Major Thomas Argyll Robertson, Room 055, at the War Office.[1]

His co-spy Johnny was ill. He too was a British double agent – a Welshman by the name of Arthur Owens, whose codename was Snow. Owens' role had been to introduce Dicketts to his pre-war contact, Major Ritter of the Abwehr. When Ritter refused to allow him to accompany Dicketts into Germany, he had become consumed with jealousy. Forced to remain behind in Lisbon, he had spent the last three weeks worried, to the point of breakdown, that his fellow spy might have been executed.

Having practically drowned himself in alcohol during his long and arduous wait for news, Owens became bitter and suspicious when a triumphant Dicketts returned with cash and instructions to operate a triple-cross. Envious of Dicketts' accounts of being wined and dined in the best restaurants and accommodated in the finest hotels in Hamburg and Berlin, Owens wondered if his own position with the Germans had been usurped, and, if so, was his ongoing value to MI5 also at risk? And worse, had Ritter revealed compromising information about the true nature of their relationship? Perhaps his former friend and sidekick was now more dangerous to him alive than dead.

Aboard their Dutch-owned DC3 aircraft, they ordered a gin fizz and settled down for what they hoped would be an uneventful journey home. They wore gold watches given to them by the Germans and carried gold bracelets for their girlfriends. Dicketts wore an ersatz overcoat purchased in Germany, with the label carefully removed, and the contents of his new suitcase included two new shirts and two new sets of underwear. Inside his pockets he carried the proof of his journey: receipts for meals he'd eaten, tickets, menus, match books from bars and letterheads from the famous Adlon Hotel in Berlin and the Vier Jahreszeiten in Hamburg. Owens' pockets contained something altogether more ominous – explosives hidden inside two fountain pens and a great deal of money – '£10,000 in notes'.[2]

A fellow passenger carrying a sealed embassy bag waved his glass of Scotch in front of them laughing.

'That's no drink,'[3] he said, in the cultured English accent redolent of the school halls of Eton. Dicketts wondered if he had been sent to spy on them. Could Owens' earlier warnings about the poor treatment he would receive in England be true after all?

Several hours later they touched down safely at Bristol's Whitchurch Airport, relieved the monumental stress of the last few months was over. Dicketts expected to be closely questioned by MI5 and even disbelieved at times, but he knew he had done all they had asked of him and more. I've put my life on the line for my country, and obtained important information, he thought. Surely I've more than repaid my debt to society and they'll grant me a commission in the RAF or MI5 now?

He didn't know it yet, but Owens had betrayed him to the Abwehr before he even went into Germany and it was a miracle he was still alive.

Chapter 1

A Fateful Meeting

'I've always wanted to play a spy, because it is the ultimate acting exercise. You are never what you seem.' Benedict Cumberbatch

In late January 1940, the River Thames froze over in the severest winter since 1894. As the temperatures began to rise in March, Londoners felt an increasing sense of impending doom. They knew the improved weather conditions meant a greater risk of invasion by the Germans and their city would experience the first real shocks of the war.

On the morning of Saturday, 16 March, a tall man in his late 30s with 'black hair, well-greased' and neatly brushed back, strode purposefully down Friars Style Road in leafy Richmond and entered the brick arches of the Marlborough public house.[1] He was casually dressed in a light brown tweed sports coat, grey flannel trousers and a light raincoat. He shoved open the saloon doors in front of him and entered. After his eyes had adjusted to the dimly lit interior, he made his way to the bar and ordered a gin.

His name was Walter Dicketts. He was an ex-RNAS officer who ran away from school at 15, enlisted in the First World War, became a pilot and worked in Air Intelligence towards the end of the war. When he tried to enlist again in the current war, his application had been rejected due to some fraudulent activities in his past – despite having been clean for over a decade. Dicketts was frustrated by the whole business, as he knew himself to be an experienced and useful man who desperately wanted to do his bit for his country – if only the authorities would give him a chance. In the meantime, he was running very short of cash.

He and a small thin man with brown hair exchanged polite greetings at the bar and began a casual conversation. The other man's face was bony and he had large, wide-set brown eyes, with one eye slightly higher than the other, giving him a rather shifty-looking appearance. His ears were small and 'almost transparent' and his fingers were stained with nicotine.[2]

Speaking softly, without any discernible accent, he introduced himself as Thomas Wilson.

Their conversation began like that of most strangers with small talk and casual discussion. They discovered they had both travelled widely to places like America, Canada and most of the countries in Europe, and from then on their interest in each other was genuine. They swapped anecdotes about the places they had seen and the cuisines they had tasted, and for a moment the reality of war seemed very far away.

In many ways, theirs was a meeting of like minds. They had so much in common, including the flaws in their personalities which would soon become apparent. Dicketts was nearly 40 and Wilson a year older. They were opportunistic survivors in a world where wealth and influence remained largely in the hands of the upper classes. Consummate salesmen, they loved money and took the sort of risks to obtain it that most people wouldn't even consider. Even in their private lives there were parallels - both their marriages had ended with a great deal of bitterness and they were currently living with younger women they referred to as their wives.

There were differences too; Dicketts was well-educated and the son of a successful stockbroker's clerk, who commuted to London from their comfortable, white-painted seaside home, a short stroll from the beach at Southend-on-Sea. Wilson was the son of a master plumber from Cilybebyll, a small rural village nestled in the coal-mining valleys of South Wales, surrounded by mountains, beautiful countryside, spectacular views and winding country lanes.

Physically, they couldn't have been more different. Dicketts was tall and handsome, with a pronounced dimple on his chin and a charming smile. He had a deep, rather loud voice and was a totally convincing, erudite and interesting companion – a combination of traits which had duped many others in the past. Wilson was small and thin, and he was an equally engaging and entertaining companion who could also be boastful, indiscreet, shrewd and artful.

Wilson insisted on paying for everything and ignored Dicketts' protestations to the contrary; by the time it came to leave, he was calling his new friend Dick, and Dicketts was calling him Tom. They lived within walking distance of the pub and agreed to return later that evening, bringing their wives with them. The attractive young women in their mid-20s made an immediate impression when they arrived. Wilson's mistress Lily was tall and blonde with a 'natural sex appeal',[3] and Kay Dicketts had brown wavy hair, dark eyebrows and painted red lips.[4]

At 10 pm, Wilson invited the Dicketts to play darts with them at his flat in Marlborough Road, where they stayed until 1.00 am the following morning. By this stage they had drunk a considerable amount of alcohol. Wilson asked Dicketts to meet him back at the pub later that day, where they discussed general business matters. Wilson told him he had a large amount of money which he kept fluid in several bank accounts, and was currently buying gold and diamonds as the pound was bound to fall later. 'What do you do for a living, Dick?'

Dicketts said he was surviving on very small means, but he had a pro-posed patent for ready-made mustard in tin containers similar to toothpaste. Wilson immediately said, 'That's an excellent idea and if my partner agrees I'll finance it.'[5]

Dicketts was surprised by his quick response. It sounded too good to be true, but he was running very short of funds and Wilson appeared to have a lot of cash lying around. He was right to be suspicious – his new friend was not all that he was pretending to be. Even the name Wilson was false. His real name was Arthur Owens and he was Snow, Britain's first double agent. As for the likelihood of his ever being truly interested in the mustard tube idea, the chances were very small indeed. Owens' unprofitable battery busi-ness was a front for his clandestine activities as a spy, and both he and his partner William Rolph worked for MI5.

A more likely prospect is that he thought Dicketts' background as a dis-enfranchised ex-RAF man from the last war was exactly the type of man his German spymaster, Nikolaus Ritter, would be interested in. Owens knew he would have to play him very carefully. First he would boost his ego and spend lots of money on him. Once Dicketts knew there was plenty of cash available, Owens would see if he could be bought - and then if he could be trusted. In the meantime, he would dig into Dicketts' past to see if he could compromise him in any way.

It was an interesting game, as both men were well-matched. Owens didn't realize it yet, but Dicketts wasn't whom he appeared to be either. He was a serial confidence trickster with a string of convictions behind him for obtaining money by false pretences. He was a charming shape-shifter who could appear to be anything or anyone he wanted. The whole mustard tube concept could have been a ploy to get Owens to part with all that money he was throwing around so generously.

Owens began the process of recruitment. He took Dicketts and Kay to see a show at the theatre, and then back to his and Lily's flat for drinks and supper. When the meal was over, he pulled Dicketts aside and said he had taken a great liking to him: 'I'd like to invite you and Kay to join us on a five-day motor trip to Devon and Bournemouth over Easter – at my expense.'

'That's very kind of you to ask, but I'm afraid I'll have to decline as I haven't got the funds to do so,' Dicketts said.

'Don't be silly, you can have whatever money you like from me.'

Dicketts refused again, so Owens suggested they sign an agreement with regard to the mustard patent and wrote him a cheque for £25 as a preliminary payment. The sharp-eyed Dicketts immediately noticed his signature was in a different name to Wilson, but before he could say anything, Owens quickly pointed to it and said, 'I'll explain that another time.'

Dicketts had to keep his smile and suspicions to himself. His new friend was adopting a strategy he was more than familiar with, and it was amusing to be on the other side for once. He had used twenty-two aliases at the high point of his criminal career. What did Wilson want, he wondered? After all, he didn't have any cash or assets, so why was he being so generous? He must be involved in something murky and wanted Dicketts to do something he couldn't - or wasn't prepared to do.

During their time away, the foursome became very friendly and stayed at the mansion-like Lansdowne Hotel in Bournemouth, the iconic Castle Hotel in Dartmouth with its picture-postcard views of the harbour, and Boltons in the ancient fishing village of Brixham in Devon. Dicketts noticed that on each occasion, he signed the registration forms as T. Wilson.

The day after their return, Owens took Dicketts to meet his partner at their office in Sackville Street, near Piccadilly Circus, who told him the mustard patent was already on the market. Dicketts became very upset at this and said he knew it wasn't true.

'Don't worry. I can use you in other ways. Money is no object,' Owens reassured him.

The following day, having succeeded in getting Dicketts to depend on him for money, Owens moved onto the next part of his plan– collusion. He told him in the strictest confidence that he was the key man in the British

Secret Service; the whole house where he lived belonged to him and he had a bodyguard of three men living in the ground-floor and basement flats.

'How much money do you need to come and work for me, carrying on normal business under my direction as a cover?' Owens asked. 'But before you answer, you mustn't alter your standard of living or move to a better address – and you mustn't say anything to anyone.'[6] It was almost too easy; Dicketts readily agreed and was given a salary of £10 a week plus expenses and £50 to pay off some of his debts.

Although Dicketts needed the money, he had another agenda too. If Owens really was working for British intelligence, he might get the opportunity to work for SIS again. He would have been shocked to discover that he already had the attention of MI5, Britain's secret police and counter-espionage division, who were listening to their conversations through a hidden microphone in agent Snow's apartment. They had observed his comings and goings, and wondered who he was and whether his sudden appearance was as innocent as it seemed.

They already knew a great deal about Snow, as he was the first British double agent to be recruited at the beginning of the war. He had initially come into contact with British intelligence during 1936 when, in the course of running his battery business, he travelled widely throughout Europe. When he returned from his trips, he reported any intelligence he had gathered to SIS on an informal basis. When his business began to fail, Owens decided to become a paid spy and received payments from both the German and the British Secret Service until the outbreak of the Second World War, when he was arrested by MI5.

Owens' relationship with both SIS and MI5 was characterized by mistrust and usefulness. Owens was a difficult character whose 'principal characteristics were vanity and inherent untruthfulness'.[7] At the time of his meeting with Dicketts in March 1941, the fledgling British double-cross team had very few agents – and of those, Snow was the most important. His German radio had been confiscated by MI5 on the outbreak of war, and they were now controlling it. As far as the Germans were concerned, they believed the radio was still being operated by Snow and continued to send him requests for information. This was a godsend for MI5, who could deduce from the Germans' questions what information they needed and what they already knew. It was like having an open window into the headquarters of the Abwehr, and to lose it would be disastrous.

If Dicketts was a German spy sent to check up on Snow, then their entire double-cross system was at risk and they would have to start again from scratch. MI5's watchers gave Dicketts the codename Celery, and told Special Branch to find out who he was and why he was in contact with Snow.

MI5 discovered a great deal of information about Dicketts' criminal background between the years 1920-1931. But they knew nothing of his early background or his struggle to adjust to normal life, having served as a boy soldier during the First World War. They knew nothing of his work in the social services, or his efforts and success in going clean in the decade leading up to the Second World War. Any view they formed of Dicketts was based on the limited information they had about him, and none of that was good. Yet there was so much more to him than that.

* * *

At midnight on 4 August 1914, there were crowds standing outside the offices of the *Southend Standard*, waiting for news of England's declaration of war against Germany following the latter's unprovoked invasion of Belgium. Britain's newly appointed Secretary of State of War, Lord Kitchener, warned the government that the outcome of the war would be decided by 'the last million men that Britain could throw into battle'.[8]

The war that many believed would be over by Christmas began that day and ended four years later, with the signing of the Armistice on the eleventh hour of the eleventh day of the eleventh month of 1918.

On 6 August 1914, Kitchener issued his first call to arms for 100,000 volunteers, aged between 19 and 35. The scale of the response was astounding: around 30,000 men enlisted every day, swamping the military recruiters, who were forced to enlist local dignitaries and magistrates for assistance. By the end of September, over 750,000 men had volunteered, and by January 1915, nearly a million.

Walter Dicketts was living with his parents at Southend-on-Sea, where he attended the local grammar school and witnessed the troops taking up station in the area and practising 'parades and drills in the local parks'.[9] The wounded began to pour in from the battlefields in France, local hotels were turned into hospitals and the town came under attack by Zeppelins. When news reached Britain that its professional soldiers, the British Expeditionary Force, were in retreat following the Battle of Mons, there was a spike in recruiting numbers as men realized their homes, families and country might now be at risk. It wasn't just men who enlisted; many young boys desperate to be one of the lads lied about their age, and sometimes even their names so their parents couldn't track them down and make them return home.

Walter Dicketts decided to join their ranks immediately following his 15th birthday on 31 March 1915. His biggest problem was how to convince the recruitment officers that he was 18. On 5 April, he absconded from school and nervously took his place in line at the recruitment centre. When his turn came, he drew himself up to his full height and lowered his voice to appear older than he was. Affecting a confidence he didn't quite feel, he managed to keep his voice steady as he lied about being three years older than he actually was.

'Languages?' asked the enlistment officer, without bothering to look up.

'French, German and Swahili,' Dicketts replied, with just the right degree of certainty.[10] The only Swahili he spoke was a few lines taught to him by one of his school friends, whose parents lived in the British colony of Kenya. In reality, Dicketts didn't need to try and bluff his way in by trying to appear older than he was, as proof of age or even identity wasn't required at this stage of the war. The rule of thumb was that if a volunteer wanted to fight for his country and was physically fit enough to do so, why stop him? It is thought that as many as 250,000 'boy soldiers' were recruited in this way.[11]

After his measurements were taken, he was given his King's Shilling and accepted into the Royal Naval Air Service (RNAS) as Petty Officer Air Mechanic First Class (Driver) for the 'Duration of the Hostilities'.[12] It all seemed like a grand adventure to Dicketts, but his enthusiasm was tempered by the thought of his parents' reaction; they would be shocked and upset by his news – particularly his mother, Frances, who'd be terrified that her only child could get killed or injured. But it was too late now, and he couldn't back out even if they wanted him to.

After completing his initial training, Dicketts was sent to France as a dispatch rider with an RNAS armoured car division.[13] At a time when telecommunications were limited and insecure, dispatch riders were used to deliver urgent orders and messages between headquarters and military units. Racing against time, they hurtled along all kinds of terrain, from slippery tracks to stony cliffsides, often using back roads away from the enemy's line of sight. To prevent their messages getting through, dispatch riders were often targeted by the enemy, and had to avoid being captured, injured or killed.

Dicketts became a personal messenger between Captain French of the RN Mobile Battery Section at Admiralty and Colonel Houberdun at the French Arsenal, and was just 15½ when he brought back plans of the French 75in artillery gun to England.[14] Little did he realize that he would soon be using these guns, mounted on trucks, to fire upon the giant Zeppelin bombers which were terrorizing British citizens at the time.

From February to September 1915, Dicketts was a driver with an RNAS armoured car division in France. Civilian cars like the Lanchester and Rolls Royce Silver Ghost model were fitted with armour plating and machine-gun mountings in the turret, and used to provide speed and protection for communications and to rescue stranded airmen from dangerous areas. They were also put to good use in combat, working closely with the aircraft overhead who reported sightings of enemy troops or vehicles, which were immediately followed up by the armoured cars, which sped into the attack.

Dicketts' division was disbanded in September due to the static nature of trench warfare and the inability of the cars to cross muddy terrain pockmarked with shell holes, and he was transferred to the RNMB Anti-Aircraft Corps.[15] Their role was to try and shoot down enemy aircraft, or at least prevent them carrying out aerial reconnaissance. Pilots from both sides flew over each other's trenches, mapping them and pin-pointing their artillery placements so they could be targeted later. Once the artillery barrage began, the pilots would take to the air again and watch where their shells were falling, so they could report back to base and the guns be adjusted accordingly.

Back home, war came to ordinary British citizens in the terrifying form of German Zeppelins, giant, cigar-shaped behemoths which prowled the night skies, striking fear and alarm into all those below. On 8 September 1915, the ominous shadow of Zeppelin *L.13* passed over the dome of St Paul's Cathedral and unloaded a 3-ton bomb, the largest ever dropped at the time, on the city's financial hub, then proceeded east, dropping the remainder of its bombs on other targets throughout central London.[16] The bombs caused more than half a million pounds of damage and killed twenty-two people, six of them children. The public was outraged and demanded protection from the 'baby killers', and the government responded by instituting blackouts and installing massive searchlights. Precious air and anti-aircraft defences, including Dicketts' squadron, were diverted from the front lines in France, and positioned around the capital and the East Coast,[17] to try to shoot down any Zeppelins trying to sneak silently into Britain from over the North Sea. Despite their vast size, the Zeppelins were almost impossible to shoot down as anti-aircraft guns had little effect on airships above 10,000ft, and the solid bullets fired from British aircraft did little more than punch small, ineffective holes into the gas bags of the airships.

In the spring of 1916, the Army took over the responsibility for home defence and the RFC (Royal Flying Corps) was given the new explosive and incendiary bullets that turned the tide against the Zeppelins. Lieutenant William Leefe Robinson used these new weapons to shoot down a Zeppelin on 3 September, and became an instant hero in the process.

Dicketts' anti-aircraft division returned to the battlefields in France and in January 1917 he became a driver with the newly developed landships (tanks),[18] which the British hoped would end the deadlock of trench warfare by breaking through enemy lines. Dicketts and his fellow tank crews suffered from the appalling conditions inside the early tanks: the heat was suffocating, and deadly carbon monoxide fumes filled the interior from the exhaust pipe located behind the driver.[19] Tank crews wore chainmail masks, complete with goggles and helmets to protect themselves from the dangers of bullet splash, or fragments being knocked inside the tank – a more uncomfortable mix cannot be imagined.

After six months in the hellish conditions of the tanks, Dicketts became a Probationary Flight Officer and began his initial, three-week flight training at Crystal Palace in July 1917.[20] His flying instruction took place at the Naval Flying School in Eastbourne, which was a busy and vibrant place, full of young men like him who were learning to fly. Now going by the nickname 'Dickie', Dicketts completed his flight training and was sent to Cranwell to learn cross-country navigation, aerial gunnery, bombing, photography and wireless training. Unknown to the authorities, who believed him to be 20 years old, Dicketts was only 17 when he graduated as a flight sub-lieutenant on 5 December, rated as 'a good officer, and a fair pilot' and recommended for bombers.[21]

Until later, Dicketts' experience with women was extremely limited. And yet he had experienced things most adults never would; he had seen the full horror of war - young men, the cream of Britain, lying dead and dying. He had heard the screams and groans of the wounded as they struggled to live, and wondered when his time would come. He was so young and had so much life ahead of him, if he could only make it out alive. But if he had to die, he decided, then at least he would have known what it was like to be in love.

The object of his affection was his girlfriend, Phyllis Hobson, the elder daughter of the wealthy proprietor of the silver cutlery firm, Henry Hobson and Sons. She and her sister worked for the Women's Land Army and took care of the king's prize-winning livestock at his magnificent estate at Sandringham, about an hour away from the RNAS Training Establishment in Cranwell.[22] With so many men away at war, the Hobson girls, like women all over the country, had taken over roles normally carried out by men - working on the land, in factories, in offices, driving trucks and buses and undertaking tasks denied to them before the war.

Phyllis knew her time with Dicketts could be very short and that she would be heartbroken if he were killed, but like other young women in the unique circumstances of war, she decided to live for today as tomorrow might never come.

Dicketts was badly injured in an aeroplane accident on 12 March 1917, which may well have saved his life. The Naval Medical Board declared him 'permanently unfit for further flying'[23] on 3 April; a month that would come to be known as 'bloody April', during which the Allied forces experienced the highest casualty rate in British aviation history. German superiority in terms of aircraft, equipment and the better training and greater experience of their pilots was at a high point at this stage of the war. The British lost 50 per cent of their forces during the month, and the average life expectancy of a British flyer at the front fell to just 'ninety-two hours flying time'.[24]

It is remarkable how these young pilots took to the air at all in their flimsy and unreliable aircraft made of thin strips of wood, linen cloth and wire. Learning to fly was dangerous; 'more than half of the 14,000 British pilots who died in WWl were killed during training'.[25] They were freezing cold inside their open-air cockpits, and the castor oil and unmuffled exhaust fumes from their engines blew straight towards them, making them nauseous. They had no hearing protection against the noise of the engine and machine-gun fire, and the lack of oxygen at higher altitudes affected their ability to judge space, time and distance. They suffered from airsickness, vertigo and fainting from the rapid changes in motion and gravitational pressure, and if anything went wrong, they had no parachutes.

Their commanding officers had made the decision not to supply them with parachutes, in the misplaced belief that they would jump out at the first sign of danger and they would lose too many aircraft. The statistics were appalling. Fighter pilots could expect to last about 'forty to fifty hours' before being killed, and the average fatality rate in non-combat flying was 'one for every sixty-five hours of flying'.[26] It wasn't until the end of the war that they finally realized that pilots were more valuable and harder to replace than aircraft.

On 1 April 1918, the RNAS and RFC were amalgamated to form the Royal Air Force (RAF). Dicketts was reassigned to the Air Intelligence section of the Air Ministry and sent to No 4 Group in Felixstowe as a Naval Base Intelligence Officer at the end of April.[27]

He and Phyllis married in Felixstowe on 13 May, against the wishes of her family. Her brothers believed he was a gold-digger, and tried in vain to stop her marrying him, but Phyllis was determined to do so, with or without their approval. She may have felt a degree of satisfaction when, six months later, he was promoted to Temporary Staff Officer at the Air Ministry in London, with the rank of captain.[28] The newly married couple left Felixstowe and moved into her family's large and elegant house, Hassendean, in Tulse Hill, South London, previously the home of the famous British tenor, Edward Lloyd.

Whether Phyllis knew it or not, her husband perjured himself on their wedding licence, saying he was 23 when in fact he had just turned 18.[29] Dicketts was born on 31 March 1900, and had added three years to his age to enlist, and a further two to marry.[30] In 1918, when he married Phyllis, the authorities believed he was 21, and he risked losing his commission if they found out the truth. Given her family's strong opposition to their marriage, it would have made matters much worse had they discovered that Dicketts was two years younger – not three years older – than his 20-year old wife. Regardless of whether Phyllis was complicit in the deception or misinformed, it was a decision she would later come to regret.

* * *

On 11 November 1918, the Germans agreed to a ceasefire and the First World War was over. The Allied victors set a date to meet in Paris during

January 1919 to establish the peace terms for Germany and the other defeated nations. The peace treaties they came up with reshaped the map of Europe and the world, and imposed guilt and stiff financial penalties on Germany – so severe, in fact, that Hitler would later rise to power on the basis that the terms of the Versailles Treaty were the cause of Germany's economic woes.

Dicketts' report on secret German seaplane bases[31] was well received at the peace conference, and with the signing of the treaties in June, his commission was relinquished on 7 March 1919 and he was placed on Special Reserve and retained.[32]

On 8 August 1919, Captain W.A. Dicketts and Phyllis proudly announced the birth of their son, George Graeme Blenworth Dicketts, in *The Times*.[33] Three days later, Dicketts travelled to Amsterdam to represent the Air Ministry at the First Aviation Exhibition (ELTA) on 12 August.[34] The event featured around a hundred aircraft from Allied countries and ran for forty-two days. There were flying demonstrations, acrobatics and joy rides, and an estimated 500,000 spectators visited the exhibition. It was a meeting point for many Allied pilots who had heard about each other but had never met.

In an interesting aside, given Dicketts' later role with MI5, one of the British pilots attending was Major Christopher Draper DSC, who became Britain's first double agent during the Second World War. Draper, also known as 'The Mad Major' for his daredevil penchant for flying under bridges, was an outspoken critic of the way the British government treated its Great War veterans at the end of the war.[35] His views brought him to the attention of the Nazi Party as a potential sympathizer, and in 1933 the German Secret Service contacted him in London and asked him to spy for Germany. Draper agreed to do it, then dutifully reported the approach to MI5, where he was put in touch with Lieutenant Colonel Edward Hinchley-Cooke. Under the thinly disguised pretext of buying postage stamps, Draper and Hilmar Dierks from the Abwehr wrote to each other, using PO Box 629, Hamburg, as a cover address.[36]

From February 1936 onwards, MI5 intercepted all mail sent to and from this address, giving them the heads-up on any British citizen who was in contact with the Abwehr. Then, in September 1936, a letter to a man called Arthur Owens, aka Snow, was intercepted – the same man whose chance meeting with Dicketts at the Marlborough pub in Richmond in March 1940 resulted in Dicketts' recruitment as double agent Celery. The letter asked

Owens to meet a Mr L. Sanders at the Minerva Hotel in Cologne.[37] The return address was PO Box 629.

When Dicketts returned from ELTA, Air Commodore Maurice West asked him if he would be interested in doing some 'special work'.[38] Dicketts immediately agreed and was sent to see Sir Mansfield Smith-Cummings, the first head of SIS, more commonly known as MI6 (Military Intelligence, Section 6), who recruited the notorious spy Sydney Reilly among others. Cummings told him to find out where the Germans were hiding the aircraft engines they still hadn't surrendered to the Allies, which he succeeded in doing. With the help of Anton Blowett, a communist from Amsterdam, he discovered 6,000 engines.[39] Despite his success, the war was officially over and soon there would be less work for many young men like him. As the post-war recession set in, cuts were made across all government departments, including the intelligence services.

Captain Dicketts' final role in Air Intelligence was ADC (aide-de-camp) to distinguished foreign visitors. He 'entertained and conducted the Argentine Military Air Mission'[40] during this period, although the only record of this event is a photograph of him standing in a group of seven uniformed men; two are officers of the Argentine Military Air Force.[41]

Dicketts' absences from home became more frequent, which Phyllis put down to his workload. She was preoccupied with caring for the needs of their new baby boy and didn't realize her husband was seeing another woman – someone completely different to her in almost every way.

* * *

In March 1919, the 20-year-old Dora Viva Guerrier was appearing with other Tiller dancers in the ninth Hippodrome Revue in a West End Albert de Courville production called *Joy Bells*.[42] As an added attraction, the all-white, five-piece Original Dixieland Jazz Band was brought over from New Orleans and their performance received a rapturous response from the audience. It was the first time that live jazz had been heard in London, and contributed to the jazz craze that followed. The show was so popular that it ran for 723 performances.

The Tiller Girls were the most famous dancers of the 1920s and 1930s; to buy a ticket to one of their shows, one literally had to join a queue that stretched all the way around the block.[43] They performed at the best theatres around the world, such as the Wintergarten in Berlin, the Folies Bergère in Paris and the

London Palladium. Diana Vreeland, the former editor-in-chief of *Vogue*, was a Tiller Girl from 1929. At the end of a performance, 'stage-door Johnnies' would hang around outside the theatre with gifts of flowers, chocolates and even jewellery, hoping to meet a Tiller Girl. Captain Dicketts was one of them.

Dora was a very attractive young woman - tall, toned and slim. She had striking big blue eyes, perfectly offset by her fashionable peroxide blonde bob, and vivid red lips shaped in a cupid's bow. She was assertive and energetic, and lived life to the full. Like all the Tiller Girls, she had many suitors, and despite Dicketts' good looks and charm, she had no need to choose a married man.

She, like most young women of her generation, had gained a new-found independence during the war, but was naïve when it came to men. There were no role models to guide them, as their mothers' generation had only very limited choices before the war; just 24 per cent of them worked outside of home, usually as domestic servants or labourers in the textile and clothing industry. Equal rights for women wouldn't exist for almost fifty years, and you had to be 30 years old before you were allowed to vote.[44]

It was also a time of great change. So many men had been killed in the Great War that it had shifted the balance between men and women. The 1921 Census figures revealed there were 1,720,802 more females than males in the population: 1,209 single women for every 1,000 men. [45] The tragic reality was that men were in very short supply, particularly for women aged between 25 and 29, and the men who survived found themselves in the unique position of being able to pick and choose the woman they wanted. Ugly men could find themselves going out with pretty women, and some women would do almost anything to keep a man. To complicate matters further, working women were forced to give up their jobs to returning soldiers, and with so many options available, some men 'became selfish and ruthless'. Judging by his future actions, it is possible Dicketts may have been one of them.[46]

In January 1920, Dora became pregnant with my mother. It couldn't have come at a worse time, as Dicketts' discharge had taken place nine months earlier and he had no skills other than those he had learned in the war.[47] There was stiff competition for jobs, as so many people were unemployed and around two-and-a-half million British workers were involved in strike action after staple wartime industries like coal mining, shipbuilding and steel contracted.[48]

Dora tried to abort their baby by drinking bottles of gin and taking extremely hot baths, and when that failed, Effie Winifred Sinclair Dicketts was born on 17 September 1920. Dora, who was 22 years old at the time, persuaded her mother Euphemia and stepfather Bill to raise Effie as their own, but made them promise that they would never tell her the truth about her identity.

It took Dora four months to register Effie's birth. Did she hope Dicketts would somehow manage to pull a rabbit out of the hat, or perhaps he wasn't around to ask? Around the same time as Effie's birth, an unknown creditor had petitioned a receiving order against Dicketts, whose liabilities were 'over £1,000 [around £40,000 today] and his assets nil'.[49] Dicketts didn't turn up to court for his public examination in bankruptcy on 8 December 1920, and a warrant for his arrest was issued. If he had gone on the run, then Dora would have been left alone to perjure herself on Effie's birth registration document. She called herself Dora Dicketts, despite never having married Dicketts, and said Effie's father was called Arthur Dicketts instead of Walter Arthur Charles. As for his profession, she wrote 'unknown (deceased)'.[50] The upshot of this ensured that if Effie ever tried to trace her father, she would fail.

Effie grew up believing her grandmother Euphemia was her mother, and Dora her older sister. In the early 1930s, when Effie was a teenager, she tried to find work, only to be told she needed an identity card and to obtain one of those, she would need to produce her birth certificate. To Effie's surprise, Euphemia became very distressed when she asked her for it – begging her not to say anything to anyone as she had forgotten to register Effie's birth and would get into terrible trouble with the police if they found out. Naturally, Effie believed her, but it put her in a shocking position. She was a person without identity until she married my father, Freddy Witt, at 19 and became Mrs Effie 'Tonie' Witt.

Shortly after their marriage, my father needed her birth certificate for an insurance policy and Euphemia was forced to confess. With tears pouring down her face, Euphemia told Effie she wasn't her mother, she was her grandmother - and Dora was her real mother. The news shattered Effie to the core. Everything she had believed about her identity wasn't true at all, and the sense of betrayal by every member of her family cut her deeply; it seemed that everyone knew the truth except her. 'So, who is my father then?'

she asked Euphemia, once she realized it couldn't be the man she knew as Pater, Euphemia's second husband, Bill. 'I don't know,' said Euphemia. 'He was just some stage-door Johnny Dora met at the theatre.'

* * *

The very much alive Walter Dicketts had returned to his wife Phyllis, who became pregnant to him with their second child in January 1921. In early April, without providing any explanation, Dicketts suddenly disappeared. Phyllis and his parents didn't hear from him again until July.

Unknown to them, Dicketts had returned to Dora, who became pregnant to him a month later. Phyllis and Dora were now both pregnant to him at the same time. It was a disaster and appears to have tipped him over the edge. In July, he went to the hydro (water therapy) at Ashover, Derbyshire, where, calling himself Major Ashton-Dell, he became friendly with Mr Maynard Cook of H.J. Cook's outfitters in Chesterfield. After gaining Mr Cook's confidence, he told him he was almost running out of cash and wondered if he could help him out. It was only temporary he said, as he had recently opened an account at Barclays Bank and was waiting for his funds to clear. 'Suppose I pay £50 into your account and you let me have £15 until my account is cleared?' he asked.[51]

Mr Cook agreed and Dicketts wrote him a cheque in the name of Ashton-Dell. None of that money found its way to his pregnant wife and mistress. Instead, that same day Dicketts went to H.J. Cook's outfitters and purchased a pair of silk pyjamas, two pairs of socks and a pair of trousers – paying for them with another fictitious cheque in the name of Dell. When the cheques were returned marked 'no account', Cook alerted the police and Dicketts was taken into custody and charged with obtaining money by false pretences.

Dicketts contacted his father, who hadn't heard from him since he walked out on Phyllis in April, and said he had been arrested in Derbyshire. It was the first time someone in the Dicketts family had been in trouble with the law, and his shocked and rather disbelieving father, Arthur, travelled to Chesterfield to give evidence at his trial. On 8 August 1921, he told the court that he had noticed a distinct change in his 21-year-old son's behaviour during the last twelve months. 'Previously he had been a most lovable boy and an excellent husband,' he said. 'I will do whatever I can for him, and am willing to make full restitution for any money he owes.'

Mr Mather, Dicketts' defence lawyer, submitted that his 'was not a case for punishment but a case for medical treatment, as he had never received proper medical attention since he went strange in his mind'.[52] Mather described Dicketts to the court as a young ex-captain of the RAF who had also been a King's Messenger (the equivalent of a despatch rider in the Great War, not the courier role attached to the Foreign Office) and a member of the Intelligence Department of the War Office. 'He is well educated and comes from extremely good stock. His father holds an important position as a London businessman.' Given his exemplary background and the foolhardy way he had gone about forging the cheques, his recent actions were so out of character that it was clear he was 'not at times mentally responsible for his actions', said Mather.

Mather went on to describe the injuries which may have led to the change in Dicketts' behaviour. At 14, he had sustained a serious head injury after colliding with a wall while riding his bicycle in Westcliffe-on-Sea. He had fallen for 30ft before striking his head on an iron railing. 'Shortly after recovering from a three months' illness', he joined the RNAS and was badly injured in an aeroplane accident eighteen months ago. 'He was instructing a pilot in a difficult "stunt" at Cranwell when the pilot fainted and the machine crashed to the ground. Dicketts was thrown out and received such severe injuries that his legs and arms were paralysed and his eye sight affected. The accused was obliged to undergo three months' electrical treatment as every nerve in his body was shattered. His behaviour had never been the same since,' said Mather.[53]

It was a convincing argument and the judge agreed to give Dicketts another chance. He was bound over for twelve months in his own recognisance – a promise in writing that he would show up for future court appearances and not engage in illegal activity during this period. If he breached the conditions, he would be fined £50. His father agreed to act as surety and would be obliged to pay the fine if his son wasn't able to do so.

Phyllis gave birth to their second son, Rodney, on 13 October 1921,[54] the same day that Dicketts appeared in front of the Recorder at Westminster Court, where it became clear his misdemeanour at Ashover was just the tip of the iceberg. Any parent reading the newspaper articles that followed a few days later would have despaired. Why was their son behaving like this and what, if anything, could they do about it? The following appeared in the *Daily Mirror*:

Ex-Officers' Joy Rides:

Summer Tour of Expensive Hotels Without Paying for It.

Two young married ex-officers of the Royal Air Force, Walter Dicketts and Percy Doland – both of whom had severe crashes while flying – pleaded guilty at the Old Bailey yesterday to obtaining credit by fraud and sentence was postponed. They hired cars in fictitious names, it was stated, and stayed during the summer at expensive hotels in various parts of the country without paying their bills.[55]

Dicketts' counsel tried to obtain leniency in his sentence by informing the court that he 'had two children, the younger being three days old, and that his wife was seriously ill', to which the Recorder pointedly retorted, 'That makes it worse and shows what a thoroughly heartless, selfish man he is.'[56] Who knows what the Recorder would have said, had he discovered the existence of his mistress Dora and their two children?

Worse was to come. A month later, on 17 November 1921, *The Times* described Dicketts' and Doland's latest exploit under the headline:

Ex-Airman's Wholesale Dissipation.

At the Central Criminal Court yesterday, Walter Arthur Charles Dicketts, 22, was sentenced by the Recorder to nine months' imprisonment, with hard labour … Dicketts yesterday pleaded 'Guilty' to stealing as a Bailee £475 [£10,075 today] belonging to Mr George Gibson. Mr Abinger, for the prosecution, said Dicketts represented that the Army Canteen Board had several million cigarettes which he could procure at the price of £1 [£21.20 today] per thousand, and having obtained the £475 from the prosecutor in respect of the purchase of 500,000, he disappeared. Mr Laskey, for the defence, said that the defendants had both done good service in the Flying Corps, which Dicketts, who rose to the rank of flight-commander, joined at the age of 15 … They had been found wanting in moral restraint and plunged into wholesale dissipation.

On 18 October 1921, Dicketts received two sentences of nine months to be served concurrently at Wormwood Scrubs prison.[57] Rodney was only a baby when his father was sent to jail, and Dora gave birth to Eric on 18 February 1922 when he was still in prison.[58]

Having already given one child to her mother to raise, Dora had no option but to give her baby son Eric away at birth to Mrs Chickie Perrins, a dressmaker at the theatre, who already had two children of her own. One can only guess at the pain this separation caused Dora. She registered his birth six weeks later, and by the time she had finished falsifying his birth certificate, the only thing Effie and Eric had in common, other than their genes, was her bogus name, Dora Dicketts. This time his father wasn't deceased after all, but was a 'music hall artiste'.[59] He had a different name too: William Walter Arthur Dicketts. Sadly, mother and son would never see each other again.

Three months later, on 28 June 1922, she married Cable Boville 'Bo' Clark, a Canadian barrister,[60] while Dicketts was still in prison, and a month later boarded the ship to take them to her new home in Canada, when she got cold feet and promptly carted her luggage back down the gangplank, leaving her 25-year-old husband to return home alone. She had since joined a dance troupe in France and wouldn't be home any time soon.

None of this was revealed to Dicketts, who went to see her at her mother's house after his release from prison. He was met at the door by her grandmother, Agnes, a cantankerous old battleaxe who told him Dora and the children had gone, and sent him packing 'with a flea in his ear'. Years later, Dora discovered that Agnes – whom she called 'the old bitch' – had hidden all his letters to her, but by then it was too late.[61]

Dora wasn't unintelligent, but she was headstrong and opinionated. She was also statuesque, funny and elegant. Her wealthy father, George Guerrier, had abandoned her mother and two siblings when she was a child, and Dora had seen firsthand how hard it had been for her mother to raise three children on her own. She found love again with Fin Olsen, a wealthy Danish wine merchant she met in Bordeaux, but she never told him or their twins, Pouza and Axel, about her other children, Effie and Eric. She continued to maintain the illusion that she was Effie's sister throughout her life, and took her secrets with her to the grave.

Phyllis remained with Dicketts for the sake of their children, but would soon tire of his behaviour. She sued for divorce, citing adultery, and when she married again, changed the name of her children to that of her new husband, Adair. She told them, 'Never, never, try and contact your father, he's very bad news.'[62] They, too, never saw their father again, who was always referred to in their family as 'Dickie Dicketts, the Rotter'.[63]

As for Dicketts, his actions caused repercussions that would last a lifetime. Along with his sentence, he was 'deprived of the rank of captain' and with it, his respectability.[64] The professional disgrace of losing his rank for dishonesty was irreparable and would impact negatively upon him for the rest of his life. Officers who had served with him in the RNAS and the Air Ministry suddenly turned their back on him; doors that were once open became closed and invitations ceased. Men he respected now wanted nothing to do with him, and he, the son of a good family, had become a common criminal who would soon have a string of convictions behind him.

MI6's founder, Mansfield Cummings, who had tasked Dicketts with finding the Germans' hidden aircraft engines at the end of the Great War, believed a special agent should be 'a gentleman, and a capable one, absolutely honest with considerable tack and at the same time force of character … experience shows that any amount of brilliance or low cunning will not make up for a lack of scrupulous personal honesty. In the long run it is only the honest man who can defeat the ruffian.'[65] Dicketts would never again be fully trusted by members of the intelligence services, no matter how brave his actions during the Second World War.

Dicketts' father, Arthur, whose profession as a stockbroker in the City also demanded the highest levels of honesty and respectability, could only hope his peers didn't realize the young man appearing in all the papers was his son. If he and his wife Frances cherished any thought that prison would reform their son, they would soon be disappointed - it appeared to have done the opposite.

Chapter 2

From Batteries to Spying

'Honesty is for the most part less profitable than dishonesty' Plato

' Snow has picked up a crook called Celery,' wrote Guy Liddell, head of counter-espionage at MI5, in his ultra-secret war diary on 7 April 1940.[1] Within days of meeting Arthur Owens (Snow) at the Marlborough pub in Richmond, MI5 managed to find out who Dicketts was, along with his criminal record, but it still didn't shed any light on the nature of his relationship with Owens.

Major Tommy Robertson, Owens' boss at MI5, was worried that he may have already told Dicketts a tremendous amount about what he was doing, as he'd done this before with his other friends. Robertson wondered if they couldn't find some way to 'frighten' Owens to stop him doing the same thing again.[2] Robertson's concern was warranted, as within a short time of their meeting, Owens took Dicketts up to a locked room at the top of his house and showed him a powerful radio device, which he demonstrated by tuning into several countries.

Dicketts' response was muted and wary, which Owens picked up on immediately. In what was a veiled threat, he told Dicketts he already knew all about him and there was no need for Dicketts to be concerned. However, Dicketts was concerned: was Owens bluffing, and if so, why? Did he really have information about him, and if so, where did he get it and how much did he actually know?

Owens clearly had a plan in mind for Dicketts, and things were beginning to move very quickly in that direction. Owens needed to know if he could trust Dicketts, who could be very useful to him as a fellow spy, obtaining secret information and carrying out covert activities on his behalf. Owens needed to establish what would motivate Dicketts to become a spy – was it money, ideology, compromise or ego (commonly known by the anacronym MICE) that would turn Dicketts into a willing sidekick?

In fact, Dicketts had already become a spy – one who was spying on Owens himself. What Dicketts needed to find out for certain was whether Owens was a bona fide British spy or a German agent pretending to be a British spy. Dicketts would have been surprised to learn that both MI5 and SIS were asking themselves the same thing, and in the not so distant future, Dicketts would be asked to risk his life to find out.

Dicketts decided to stick around and gather the proof he needed, so he accepted Owens' invitation to go to Brighton with their wives to celebrate his 40th birthday on 31 March, where once again Owens insisted on paying all their expenses. Dicketts later recalled:

> When we returned that night he was very tired and the great amount of liquor he had consumed somewhat overcame him. He told me that Germany was certain to win the war and that he and his wife were going there to live as soon as his work was completed in England, adding that he was Chief of the German Secret Service over here with unlimited [word unreadable] and resources.[3]

Dicketts realized it was probably the drink talking, and took advantage of Owens' inebriated state to try to get him to open up even more. 'You wouldn't want to do anything against the British Empire,' Dicketts said, to which Owens replied he was out for peace and that nationality didn't come into it. Aware that Owens responded well to flattery, Dicketts agreed with him and said, 'Any thinking man would sacrifice anything to stop the war.'

Dicketts realized if he could expose a German spy ring in wartime, it would restore some of his lost respectability amongst his peers and perhaps regain him a commission in the RAF. He was strongly motivated to find out if Owens and his cohorts were enemy agents working clandestinely from within Britain, and get paid for it by Owens himself. Owens was paying him £10 per week plus expenses to purchase cheap whisky and gin, which he planned to repackage and sell on the black market. Owens told Dicketts he was going to stop importing batteries from Belgium if he could obtain enough gin.

He told Dicketts he was going to Germany on Thursday, 4 April, and would have plenty of work for him to do when he got back. Two days before his departure, Dicketts was driving Owens home from the office in Sackville

Street when Owens asked him to go to an address in Queen's Road, Norwood, and wait for him in the car. As soon as Owens was inside, Dicketts took out a pencil and notepad and sketched a diagram of the street and their location on a map, as he was certain this was the house where Owens' boss lived. Dicketts guessed correctly that Owens had come to receive his last-minute instructions before he left for Germany. This was confirmed when Owens reappeared forty-five minutes later and said he had to keep a special appointment at 8.30 pm, and 'it was most important his wife went with him'.[4] It was an odd thing to say, as Owens hadn't said anything to him about it earlier in the day, and Dicketts realized it had something to do with what had taken place inside the house.

What Dicketts didn't know at the time was that MI5 had decided to pull Owens firmly back into line, and Dicketts with him. Dicketts couldn't have known how important Owens was to British intelligence at the time, as Owens' pre-war relationship with Major Nikolaus Ritter was to lead to the formation of the British double-cross system of the Second World War. Owens was the double agent from which all others stemmed, and the messages he sent over his German radio transmitter allowed British codebreakers to read the Abwehr's secret communications for twenty-four hours until the Enigma settings were changed the following day.

* * *

Arthur Graham Owens was also the man against whom Walter Dicketts would soon be pitched in a life and death struggle to be believed over the other. Owens was a year older than Dicketts, born in Wales on 14 April 1899, the son of William, a master plumber who was also an inventor, and his wife Ada.[5] Owens and his wife Jessie had moved to Canada in 1921 with their young son, Robert, where they lived for thirteen years. Owens inherited some money after his father's death but 'squandered' it on developing and marketing his own battery-related inventions.[6]

The family returned to England in 1933, where Owens found work as a consulting electrical engineer with the Expanded Metal Company, which had several contracts with the British Admiralty. The millionaire owner of this company, Hans Hamilton, was impressed with Owens and backed him in forming the Owens Battery Company 'to market his inventions' to do with battery accumulators and separators.[7]

Owens travelled regularly to Holland, Belgium and Germany on business, and shared any technical information he gathered with Naval Intelligence on his return. The British were interested in businessmen like Owens who travelled throughout Germany, whose information could help them estimate the growth rate and developments of the Nazi regime. Hitler had continued to expand Germany's military power in secrecy, in direct contravention of the terms of the Treaty of Versailles, signed at the end of the Great War. In 1935, Hitler went public and Europe was appalled to discover that Germany's Luftwaffe now had 2,500 warplanes and its army would soon number 550,000 men.

Owens' business had begun to struggle financially by January 1936, so he came up with the bright idea of asking British intelligence if he could get paid for the information he brought them, instead of just giving it away. Owens approached his contact Mr Fletcher at the Admiralty, and said he wanted to work for the British Government. He was put in touch with Colonel Edward Peal from SIS, who told him what type of naval and air information they wanted from Germany, but didn't give him 'anything in writing' – in other words, Owens was not 'officially' employed by British intelligence.[8]

That month, Owens returned from a trip to Germany and gave Peal some important information 'about German coastal motor-boats'. It was a great start, but Owens was getting paid for intelligence twice – by the Germans as well as the British. When Owens told Peal six months later that he had made friends with a German chemical engineer called Konrad Pieper, who was willing to provide information on gas and metals, Peal became suspicious. He wondered if this man was the same person as Kapt-Leutnant Pfeiffer of the German Secret Service; if so, he was probably trying to recruit Owens as a German spy.[9]

Owens said he had only encouraged this friendship with Pieper so he could obtain information on behalf of SIS, and showed Peal some drawings of German submarine batteries which Pieper had given him. Was Owens aware that he was in touch with the German Secret Service, thought Peal, and if so, what information did Owens have about SIS that he might be encouraged to pass onto the Germans? Peal decided to place Owens under observation and see what he got up to.

'Pieper's going to Italy,' said Owens. 'Is there any information you would like Pieper to obtain for you?' Peal was too seasoned a spy to fall for that one. Questions revealed what you didn't know, and the enemy would simply provide false or misleading information in return. So he could find out what information Owens brought him, Peal gave Owens a verbal questionnaire and some money to cover Pieper's expenses.[10] The moment Owens left, Peal got in touch with MI5's Lieutenant Colonel Edward Hinchley-Cooke, who arranged for Owens' mail to be intercepted.

Despite this and several other payments for information, nothing of value was ever received, and in September 1936, Owens admitted to Peal 'that he didn't think Pieper was going to be of any use, as he was so nervous'.[11]

In fact, Owens knew perfectly well Pieper was a recruiter for the Abwehr, Germany's military intelligence service, and claimed to have met him through his boss, Hans Hamilton of the Expanded Metal Company.[12] Owens said he asked Pieper for information in such a way that he could have had no doubt Owens was a British agent. 'You'd do better to work on behalf of the Germans, as they pay more,' Pieper had replied.[13]

The two of them had then discussed various ways of making money, including forming 'a pool' whereby they would sell information to different countries, and share the takings between them.[14] Owens had no qualms about using SIS to pay for his developing relationship with German intelligence, and persuaded Peal to part with £20 so he could rendezvous with Pieper in Brussels to obtain information on SIS's behalf. However, Owens' real motive for this trip was to go with Pieper to the German Embassy to be introduced to a Dr Hoffmann, who asked him why he wanted to be a German spy.[15] Owens said he was a Welsh Nationalist who hated the British, and was willing to provide information on the British naval and aviation industry.[16]

Owens heard nothing from the Germans for several months, until a letter arrived from a Mr L. Sanders, suggesting a meeting in Cologne in mid-October 1936.[17] MI5 intercepted this letter and immediately recognized the return address - Postfach (Post Office box) 629, Hamburg - which they knew to be a collection address for the German Secret Service. It had already been compromised by another British spy, the daredevil pilot Major Christopher Draper, who used the same address to communicate with Hilmar Dierks from the Abwehr. The Germans had no idea the British knew all about it.

MI5 intercepted Owens' reply accepting Mr Sander's invitation, and decided to let him go to see if Owens reported the meeting on his return. If he didn't, it was solid proof that Owens was intentionally misleading SIS.

Owens travelled to Cologne, where he met Mr Sanders, whose real identity was 'Captain Hilmar Dierks'[18] from the Abwehr, whose primary role was to gather naval and air intelligence about the UK and USA. Owens offered his services to Dierks and was accepted. Owens – agent No. 3504, or 'Johnny' as he was better known – was to continue with his electrical business as it provided an excellent cover for their regular *treffs* (meetings). If Owens needed to report anything between meetings, he was to disguise the sensitive information using a basic code and send his letter to Post Office box 629 in Hamburg.

When Owens returned to England, he got in contact with Peal, who arranged to meet him at the St Ermin's Hotel on 14 October. Hinchley-Cooke from MI5 arranged for two of his men to sit at the table next to Peal and Owens so they could listen in to their conversation. 'Your men were so close, I could almost hear them swallowing their drinks,' Peal quipped afterwards.[19]

During the meeting, Peal asked Owens several times if he wished to disclose any further information, but Owens didn't take the bait and merely replied, 'No, thank you.' The fact that Owens didn't admit he was in contact with German intelligence made him an immediate espionage suspect, and any information he gave SIS from now on would be considered highly suspect.

Peal got in touch with the Admiralty and warned them that Owens was double-crossing.[20] He said extreme care must be taken with Owens, or the Germans would learn more about British intelligence-gathering methods through Owens than SIS would learn about the Germans. The one person Peal didn't inform was Owens himself. If he shut down Owens' operation, SIS would learn nothing at all. Far better to keep Owens under close observation to see who he contacted, and to find out what kind of information the Germans were interested in. The trick was to do it without Owens noticing.

Peal sent a thorough description of Owens to Lieutenant Colonel Hinchley-Cooke, a German-speaking expert in counter-intelligence at MI5, saying he was a 'typical Welsh underfed, Cardiff type'.[21] MI5's Watcher Service was ordered to keep Owens under intense surveillance, 'but it was essential that Owens did not become aware he was being observed', ordered Hinchley-Cook. If the watchers thought Owens had spotted them, they were to drop it at once.

Owens' early attempts at gathering intelligence were amateurish and unlikely to satisfy the Germans. The watchers logged him entering an aircraft camera manufacturing business, from which he re-emerged carrying a catalogue. Owens also visited several other businesses, where he tested binoculars, purchased an aviation magazine called *Popular Flying*, obtained a pamphlet from a Communist shop and another from the War Office containing photographs of vehicles and weapons in service during 1936.[22]

Despite their caution, Owens had spotted the watchers and went to see Peal on 16 November in a state of great agitation, to report his contact with German intelligence. 'I can't stand it any longer, being followed about wherever I go,' said Owens. Peal refused to see him and told Owens to put it in writing instead.

Two days later, Peal and Hinchley-Cooke interviewed Owens, who was telling so many lies that they asked him to submit a full report in writing by Monday. They examined Owens' report and knew immediately that his visits to Brussels, Cologne and Hamburg were for the single purpose of making contact with Pieper or his German connections – and the only reason he had admitted it was because he knew he was being followed, and thought it would disarm suspicion. Owens may have thought he had outsmarted British intelligence, but Peal thought Owens was hiding something. He had referred to his first meeting with Pieper but hadn't given them a date.

'What date did you meet Pieper,' asked Peal.

'September 1935,' replied Owens. It was exactly the proof Peal needed – Owens had been in touch with German intelligence before he offered his services to the Admiralty.

'Your services are no longer required,' Peal told Owens afterwards.

Shortly after this meeting, Owens showed up with a letter from Hamburg feigning innocence: 'You had better have this letter as it was sent off on the 9th and I've only just received it. It's very mysterious but my mail is always arriving late. You people probably know all about it.'

SIS knew Owens was trying to outwit them by admitting he had received a letter from German intelligence before they could arrest him, and was attempting to convey that despite his contact with the Germans, he was really working for British interests only. Although it was plain as day what Owens was up to, it was a clever strategic move that Owens could use as evidence of his loyalty to Britain, should SIS try to prosecute him. But it worked two ways, and now SIS could have no doubt that Owens thought he could surpass them.

The letter Owens gave SIS was from Mr Sanders (Dierks) in Germany, making it plain that he was not a man to be fooled:

> The newspapers of your country as well as ours, are much quicker than your letters. Since a number of years, I am also in possession of the magazine pictures you sent me and you will understand that this is rather disappointing; I don't own a museum, you know. Kindly take notice therefore, that henceforth your letters will have to be a little more up to date.[23]

Owens would have to lift his game considerably if he wanted to continue being paid by the Germans.

* * *

In early January 1937, Owens met the man against whom MI5 and the Double Cross Committee would match their wits in the early part of the Second World War.

Owens had gone to meet Dierks in Cologne as planned, and was introduced to Dr Rantzau, a tallish man in his late 30s, with blond wavy hair and blue eyes. Dierks explained that Rantzau was the representative of an import/export firm that specialized in aviation matters. In reality, he was Captain Nikolaus Ritter, head of the Abwehr's newly formed Air Intelligence Division in Hamburg.

'I thought he might be useful to you,' Dierks told Ritter beforehand. 'He is a Welshman who offered his services to our embassy in Brussels when I was stationed there.'[24]

Ritter, who spoke fluent English with an American accent, invited Owens to dinner and asked him why he wanted to spy for Germany. Owens said he and his father had invented a special anti-aircraft shell to destroy the Zeppelins that bombed England during the Great War, and had been cheated out of the money they were entitled to by the British authorities. 'The whole experience has made me very bitter,' said Owens.

It was a convincing argument, but it wasn't the truth, as Owens would admit many years later: 'It was a sudden improvisation on my part and had no basis in fact.'[25]

Owens and 'The Doctor', as he would soon call Ritter, got on surprisingly well. Certainly far better than he did with SIS's Colonel Edward Peal. Ritter made little of Dierk's dissatisfaction with Owens' intelligence gathering, and said he viewed it as a simple lack of training on Dierk's part. Next, Ritter set about creating a legitimate cover for their relationship to fool British intelligence, by writing a letter to Owens on his 'company stationery, using the name Dr Rantzau', asking if he would be interested in importing a new kind of dry battery to England, and could he come to Hamburg to discuss it?[26] MI5 intercepted this letter and were very interested in this new correspondent who wanted to discuss 'technical matters'.

Captain Nikolaus Adolf Fritz Ritter was a 38-year-old ex-Army officer who had been made chief of Air Intelligence in Hamburg despite a complete lack of experience in intelligence, or even as an aviator. He spoke English fluently with an American accent, having spent ten years in the United States, where he married an American woman and with whom he had two children, a boy and a girl.

Ritter came from a prominent aristocratic Prussian family who had moved to New York in 1924, after his paternal uncle offered him a way out of an impoverished Germany, reeling under enormous debt repayments after the Great War. He met his first wife, Aurora, a classmate at Columbia University, whose daughter Katharine reveals in her book, *Aurora*, that her father went through twenty-two different jobs during his first year of marriage, and 'considered himself as upper-class nobility and was not keen on taking orders from individuals whom he considered of subordinate social standing'.[27] It was Aurora who paid all the bills and put food on the table.

When Ritter's father became gravely ill in 1936, he took his American grandchildren to Germany so they could meet their grandfather before he died. After several months, Ritter had to return to America so he could send money for his family to return. While he was gone, Ritter's mother told Aurora that she was not going to support an American and two children indefinitely, and literally put her out onto the street in Bremen with two babies and no money. Germans were suspicious of foreigners back then, particularly those who couldn't speak any German, and Aurora was forced to take on the most menial of tasks in order to survive. Eventually, her children were taken from her by the German social services until she could earn enough money for them to have a place of their own.

Meanwhile, Ritter, who had found no permanent work in New York, began liquidating all her assets. He sold Aurora's 'Coca-Cola stock, her property on the New Jersey Turnpike, and all of her Miami land, as well as her car'.[28] He implored Aurora to approach one of his contacts, a Captain Klevermann, to give him a chance to prove himself in the German Army. It was an extraordinary request from an American at the time, but the stunned Klevermann finally agreed, and Ritter immediately returned by ocean liner. Aurora waited and waited for him to disembark with all the other passengers, scanning the decks to see if she could recognize him. She thought he must have missed his voyage, until finally she spotted him on the top deck with the first-class passengers. Aurora was speechless. 'We hardly had food to eat or money to keep a roof over our heads, and Vati [father] was coming back in luxury,' writes Katharine.[29]

The German military soon recognized Ritter's proficiency in French and English, particularly as he spoke American English, with all its idioms and slang. To his astonishment, he was given a commanding role in the Abwehr, where in July 1937 he was instructed by Admiral Canaris, the head of the Abwehr himself, 'to extend intelligence work immediately to cover the air force and aviation of the United States'.[30]

Informed that the Luftwaffe was keen to obtain plans for America's top secret Norden bombsight, which was considered to be the most accurate system of delivering bombs to their targets at the time, Ritter returned to the United States to enroll German spies. In what was to be his most successful mission during his time in the Abwehr, Ritter recruited Hermann Lang, a German-born naturalized American who worked as the inspector in charge of the assembly of the Norden bombsight. A loyal German, Lang took his company's blueprints home, section by section, and painstakingly copied them by hand after his wife had gone to bed. He returned the originals the next day with no-one the wiser. His copies were smuggled out of America by German stewards, who took them aboard their ships and straight into the hands of Ritter in Hamburg.

In this way, the complete set of drawings for the Norden bombsight was in German hands by the beginning of 1938. As a result, Owens' new spymaster's standing within the Abwehr was extremely high when they met before the war.

Owens contacted Peal again in September 1937, to tell him he had made a very good contact in Germany. Peal already knew this of course because they had been intercepting his mail for months, but agreed to meet him with Hinchley-Cooke later that week.

'Why do you want to see us?' asked Peal. 'We've already told you we no longer require your services.'[31]

'Why?' asked Owens.

'Because your information isn't of any value, and besides your contact with German intelligence is precisely why we don't want to work with you. There can be no question of you running with the hare and hunting with the hounds. If you choose to continue contact with German intelligence on your own behalf, and get into difficulties, you will not be entitled to claim compensation from the British Intelligence Service,' said Peal.

The idea of prosecuting Owens under the Official Secrets Act had already been dismissed because he would simply use his previous paid relationship with SIS for his defence. Instead, they insisted he sign an agreement stating, 'I fully realise that I am not employed and have not been employed since November 1936 by any British Intelligence Service.'[32]

As far as the Germans were concerned, Ritter was very happy with the information he received from his Welsh spy. In his post-war autobiography, Ritter wrote that over the next two years, Johnny (Owens) visited Hamburg almost once a month, reporting on the missions which he had been given. He proved to be an outstanding spy, and as war came ever closer, the Abwehr chiefs in Berlin became increasingly impressed by 'Johnny, the Master Spy'.[33]

Owens visited Hamburg so regularly that he became close friends of Ritter and his second wife, Irmgard, and wanted to bring Lily and the baby and live in Germany.[34] Owens spent most of his evenings at the Ritters' apartment, where he enthralled everyone by singing Welsh folk songs in a 'fine tenor voice'.[35] At other times, closely monitored by the Abwehr, he would go on alone to Hamburg's famous nightclub district, the Reeperbahn. He was a regular visitor at the Valhalla Club, where he became rather too attached to a blonde girl who was quietly arrested and told to get out of town. The Abwehr replaced her with one of their trusted agents, Ingrid, another fascinating blonde who became his regular girlfriend in Hamburg, and he spent most of his free time with her.

It was not all fun though. Owens received training in the most up-to-date German spycraft: wireless transmission (using Morse code), codes, microphotography, meteorological observation, identification of aircraft, description of airfields and sabotage. According to Ritter, who was captured and interrogated at CSDIC (Combined Services Detailed Interrogation Centre) at the end of the Second World War, Owens' mission was to report detailed information on airfields, aircraft factories and special devices used by the RAF.[36]

The war diary of senior Abwehr officer General Lahousen reveals that each time Owens left Hamburg, 'he carried a considerable sum in pound notes, so that by the summer of 1939, the Welshman was enjoying an income of something like two thousand pounds a year [around £113,800 today], tax free, from his activities as a spy in England'.[37]

At one point, acting on the instructions from the Abwehr, Owens made contact with the British Union of Fascists (BUF) to propose a scheme whereby they would place four secret transmitters in Britain, to transmit black propaganda in the event of war. MI5 received a report of his blatant solicitations, which revealed his flair for the dramatic. Apparently, Owens had openly bragged of his association with British intelligence, for whom he said he was engaged in espionage abroad. Through them he had learned of plots to engage in war against Germany, and said that everything possible must be done to prevent this crime. He also claimed to be a direct personal agent of Hitler, and was returning to Germany on 26 July to attend a conference.

The leading officials of the BUF regarded him with considerable suspicion and quashed his ideas, making it very clear that they would never betray their country in wartime. They described Owens as 'an agent-provocateur and a fool'.[38]

The Germans believed Welsh Nationalists could be used for sabotage in the event of war, and sent Owens to recruit them. MI5 were never certain if the dozen or so sub-agents Owens told the Germans he controlled were real or existed only in his imagination.[39] This state of affairs continued until March 1938, when Owens called upon his old contact Mr Fletcher at the Admiralty, and offered him films and photographs he had recently taken of German ships and dockyards. Fletcher immediately contacted Hinchley-Cooke, who warned him to have nothing to do with Owens.

When Owens arrived, Fletcher got him sign a document stating that he fully understood that the Naval Intelligence Division of the Admiralty wished to have no dealings with him whatsoever. Then Owens was conducted out of the Admiralty and told not to return.

Two months after his visit to the BUF, Owens appeared to have had a change of heart. He contacted Special Branch in September 1938 and said he wanted to get in contact with Lieutenant Colonel Hinchley-Cooke from MI5. When asked, Owens refused to give any details over the telephone, so a meeting was arranged at Scotland Yard, with Hinchley-Cooke and two police officers in attendance.

Hinchley-Cooke, a long-serving operative of MI5 who was awarded an OBE at the end of the war for his contribution in catching spies, had an unrivalled reputation as an interrogator. He spoke German fluently and was a strong man with a friendly nature. At the beginning of their meeting, he warned Owens that whatever he said would be taken down and used against him in evidence, and that whatever he said, he did so voluntarily.

'You have been in touch with the German Secret Service?' asked Hinchley-Cooke.[40]

'Yes, I have. At least they have been in touch with me.'

'Were you a paid spy?'

'Yes, I was.'

Despite having just admitted to being a paid German agent, Owens tried to convince Hinchley-Cooke that his true loyalty lay with Britain. He said that even though he was fully aware of the danger he was in, he had always done everything he could for this country:

> Probably my system is different from yours but I have always had one object [*sic*] in view and that was to help the country when I could. I can now. I risked my life to get it for you, at least I deserve a little thanks. I am prepared to go on and I will take further chances if you wish it, but I will do no more – it isn't worth it.

'You wish to go on and you know our view?' asked Hinchley-Cooke.

Owens agreed and said he was about to receive a secret transmitting set and codes so he could communicate directly with German headquarters. He was to have sole charge of all the secret addresses of German agents in European countries, and would be in charge of a bureau in England whose purpose was to distribute information. At this announcement, Hinchley-Cooke became very interested: wireless technology was still in its infancy and the opportunity to get hold of a German set was highly desirable.

Owens said he had openly been shown the Luftwaffe's plans to attack British aerodromes in preparation for an invasion. The Germans were sending him a portable transmitting device which would arrive before 17 January, and he was to immediately take this device to various aerodromes and report on the number of machines and men that were concentrated there.

If that was the case, then the Germans were paying lip service to the 'peace in our time' settlement British Prime Minister Neville Chamberlain thought he had agreed with Hitler at Munich. It was vital intelligence, but MI5 weren't sure Owens could be trusted.

'Do you know of any German spies operating in the UK?' asked Hinchley-Cooke.

Owens said he had met two men in Hamburg – one of them was the most dangerous German agent in Britain and the other was the tobacconist where they would send Owens' mail in future. MI5 immediately realized Owens had established other means of communication with the Germans that they were completely unaware of.

Aware that he had thoroughly gained MI5's attention, Owens asked what he should do now? In what was their first tacit approval of Owens' activities, Hinchley-Cooke replied:

'Just carry on in the way you intended to.'

Having finally managed to gain MI5's interest, Owens went all out to ingratiate himself to the British authorities. A few days after this meeting, he warned MI5 that the Germans had received leaked information about secret artillery developments and British troop movements. Most worrying was the fact that the Germans already knew about British tactical plans to funnel attacking German aircraft towards British fighters. Owens said he was to provide information to the Germans by radio that would to some degree govern where the attack would take place on London.

Owens asked for some advice on how to handle the matter, and was told to keep in regular contact with Inspector Gagan from Special Branch. Meanwhile, MI5 checked to see if Owens' information was correct, and when they found it was, set about urgently finding the leak.

They were still very wary of Owens, so his regular meetings with Special Branch were usually held in public places. Before every meeting, he was reminded that he was not in any way working for the English authorities; they could take no responsibility for anything that he might do, they could give him no instructions as to how he should work, and whatever he did was 'entirely on his own initiative'.[41]

This informal relationship between Owens and British intelligence continued until the outbreak of war in September 1939, with Owens imparting information he considered important on a somewhat regular basis. However, MI5 remained sceptical about his loyalties, and the feeling was mutual.

In October 1938, Owens asked Hinchley-Cooke to give him his assurance that MI5 had not tipped him off to the Germans. Playing a double game was dangerous work, and Owens wanted confirmation that he had not been compromised. At first sight it was a reasonable request, but MI5 were aware that Owens was continuing to receive payment from the Germans, ostensibly so he could continue to provide them with valuable information. For the time being, Owens was in the unique position of being able to play off one side against the other.

Ritter wrote in his memoirs that he had once suggested to Owens 'that he should offer himself to the Secret Service to guarantee his freedom of movement'.[42] Ritter would provide Owens with forged documents to convince British intelligence that he was really working for them, so he could continue to travel around with their consent.

As far as MI5 were concerned, the benefits of stringing Owens along offered a direct link to Ritter and the upper echelons of the German Secret Service. When the Second World War broke out, it was a dividend that paid countless times over.

On 16 January 1939, Owens contacted Special Branch to arrange an urgent meeting with Hinchley-Cooke. His German wireless set had arrived as promised, via diplomatic pouch to the German Embassy in London. It had been concealed in a harmless-looking suitcase which was hidden in a cloakroom at London's Victoria Station.[43]

He was met by Inspector Gagan, who went with him to his office to look at a letter he had just received. Inside the envelope was a cloakroom ticket, some pages of technical instructions and the key to a small attaché case. Gagan saw the envelope had no postal marks on it, and immediately suspected the involvement of German agents operating within the United Kingdom.

Aware that Owens' visit to the cloakroom might be being watched, Gagan followed him at a discreet distance, as Owens collected the wireless and then took it back to his office. Once there, Owens transferred the contents into another case to disguise it, and then gave it to Gagan to take to Hinchley-Cooke. He also gave Gagan the code he had been given to operate the wireless and a list of questions for information the Germans wanted him to obtain.

When British intelligence received the transmitter, and took it apart, they realized it was both smaller and more technologically advanced than their own British sets. Despite their mistrust of Owens, MI5 gave him back the radio so they could observe what he and the Germans did with it. The use of radio transmitters (not voice, just wireless telegraphy using Morse code) for spy communications was relatively new, and MI5 decided they would learn more from having access to a known wireless device than none at all.

Owens was concerned about being seen in the company of Special Branch officers, as he knew there were German spies operating in Britain. If they discovered what Owens was doing, he risked losing his lucrative income from the Germans, and worse, he might also lose his life. Owens' concern appears to have been warranted, as the day after the wireless was returned to him, he was stopped by an unknown man at Morden Underground Station who showed him a letter signed by Dr Rantzau, which said he was authorized to give Owens a message. Owens played ignorant for a while, until the man – who looked like an American - told Owens to expect a telegram shortly from Dr Rantzau saying 'Require samples immediately'.[44] This message meant that the frontiers with Germany would be closed within forty-eight hours, and Owens was to hire a car immediately and go to specific aerodromes to report 'which machines were filled with petrol, whether the crew were standing by, and whether the machines were loaded with bombs or not'.

Unknown to Britain, the Abwehr was on full alert. Hitler had instructed its head, Admiral Canaris, to prepare for his final offensive against Czechoslovakia in March. It was a breach of his peace pact with Chamberlain, and the Germans didn't know how Britain would react.

Finally, Owens was providing information that was of real value to MI5. Owens said he would go to West Hartlepool, one of his regular business haunts, and reply to this message from the Grand Hotel. So that Ritter knew he was in place and standing by, Owens would send a message saying, 'Regarding the samples, I have a car ready to call on all your customers.'[45]

Just as things looked as if they were going well, MI5 received a letter from the Air Ministry. A retired squadron leader had come in to report Owens' suspicious behaviour, saying he had met him in a pub, where he talked openly of his connection with a certain 'Colonel of the CID at Scotland Yard'.[46] Not only that, Owens had bragged to him that he was partly responsible for the arrest of a woman agent in Aberdeen, and later when he was worse for drink, said he worked for Germany as well. Owens said he held an SS badge and was paid £5 per week from German sources, but couldn't bring his pay with him out of Germany when he came back to England.

Shortly after Owens' arrived in West Hartlepool, the Air Ministry received another letter, which it immediately forwarded onto MI5. Apparently, Owens had turned up at the airbase with a camera, saying he was going to take some photographs, and when he was asked what for, he had replied, 'To take over to the other side.'[47]

Owens turned up again the following day armed with a portable German transmitter, and had refused to let it out of his hands. Completely in the dark as to what was going on, 'x' from the airbase (name redacted) wrote to the Air Ministry, saying, 'I hope you do not think that I am making an unnecessary fuss, but I have never yet heard of a genuine agent talking so much about his job and knowing the man to be a very considerable perverter of the truth has aroused some very grave suspicions in my mind.'[48]

MI5's reply reveals how delicately they were handling Owens at the time. 'This office has a considerable adverse record of Snow. There is no objection to x being told, in strictest confidence that we know Snow is a bad lot, requiring very discreet handling. At the same time x should be warned not to try and draw Snow, or display undue interest in his story, but to simply pass on to Squadron-Leader Plant anything he hears.'[49]

Unfettered, Owens travelled around taking photographs of the South Durham Steel and Iron Works, the coastline at Hartlepool and the new civil aerodrome at West Hartlepool, and took the negatives to Hinchley-Cooke to be developed. When he came to collect them a week later, he was met by Inspector Gagan, who warned him that the sending of photographs abroad may be considered an offence under the Official Secrets Act.

When the implications of what he had been told sank in, Owens said that under those circumstances, he would not be taking any further action with regard to the photographs, and neither would he be sending them abroad. Clearly rather miffed by this experience, Owens 'expressed his regret that the authorities did not wish to utilise his services'.[50]

This episode appears to have had a profound effect on Owens' behaviour, as three months later, Gagan reported that Owens appeared to have plenty of money and was travelling everywhere by cabs: 'He makes no secret of the fact that he is paid by the Germans with whom he is working and speaks very highly of them in every way.'[51] Owens said he wasn't worried about the British authorities anymore, and said his attitude was due to the fact that he, his father and brother had been cheated out of hundreds of thousands of pounds to do with their invention of an anti-aircraft shell to be used against Zeppelins. It was the same story Owens had told the Germans.

According to German records made public at the end of the war, Owens was very active on behalf of the Germans during this period, and was paid very handsomely for it.[52] Despite this, Owens continued to meet with Inspector Gagan, and told him what information the Germans required of him. In March 1939, Owens told Gagan that the Germans were very anxious to receive information on political scandals involving people such as Churchill and Eden, which they could use for propaganda purposes in Germany. But what was more worrying was the Germans appeared to have quite up-to-date, top secret information, as revealed in their questions to Owens. He was to try to obtain details on the latest developments to a new British anti-aircraft gun, and the results of recent experiments carried out on a new form of 'wireless cloud'. MI5 were alarmed by these latest requests, as it proved Germany had highly placed informants in Britain.[53]

As Owens' involvement with the Germans continued to grow, his marriage began to suffer. In the summer of 1938, Owens had taken his wife to Hamburg with him, having warned Ritter that Jessie was becoming suspicious of his activities there. Indeed, Ritter noticed immediately how little affection there was between the two of them, and that Jessie acted as if she was completely uninterested in their conversations.

It was during this trip that Owens began his wireless training with Lieutenant Colonel Trautmann, head of the Abwehr's secret radio station in Stettin.[54] As there was no wireless station in Hamburg at the time, Ritter arranged for Owens to be taught in the elegant apartment of his secretary's (and future wife Irmgard Von Klitzing) grandmother, which was also the cover address for their written correspondence, which bypassed Britain's mail interception service.

A year later on 11 August 1939, shortly before the outbreak of war, Owens brought his new girlfriend, Lily Bade, to Hamburg. Lily was a 27-year-old dressmaker who had been born in Britain to a German mother, and the only thing she had in common with Owens' wife was that they were both blonde. Whereas Jessie was short, calm and neat, Lily was tall and sturdy, a whole head taller than Owens. She was carefree, intelligent and had a natural sex appeal, and Ritter could see that Owens was madly in love with her.[55]

The news Owens had to impart during this *treff* was sensational. He told Ritter about a new British process for hardening armour plating and that a British airfield had been fitted with gas tanks for loading poison gas onto bombers. The German High Command in Berlin was incredulous, and didn't believe Owens. It was Owens' and Ritter's last peace-time meeting; the next time they met, their countries were at war.

Back home in England, Jessie was on the warpath. Convinced her husband had taken Lily with him to Germany, Jessie took her revenge the moment they left. She got in touch with Scotland Yard and reported her husband for trying to recruit their 18-year-old son Robert, her brother's step-daughter and various friends as German spies. Jessie said she had wanted to report Owens for 'this despicable business' for some time, but had not done so for the sake of their children.[56]

She described how during their holiday in Ostend the year before, Owens had received a letter from Ritter asking him to come to Hamburg. Unaware that her husband and Ritter had orchestrated the whole sequence beforehand, Jessie and Owens went to Hamburg, leaving their teenage children behind with the hotel manager, where Ritter made 'a feeble and amateurish attempt' to recruit her as a German agent. Upon returning to their hotel, Jessie discovered that their children had been approached by none other than Konrad Pieper, who attempted to blackmail them for money he believed was owing to him, and were only rescued through the intervention of the hotel manager.

Jessie told the police Owens had a group of agents working under him, and travelled to sensitive military sites with his transmitter, then reported back to his German masters, using the key word of 'CONGRATULATIONS', the letters of which stood for numbers. She said she had destroyed some RAF codebooks she found in their house to prevent them falling into German hands.

She warned the police that her husband was very clever, carrying coded messages covered in tin foil either in his mouth or in the petrol cavity end of a cigarette lighter. On a recent return trip from Germany, he had become very 'scared' after a railway employee warned him that he was likely to be searched and followed. Jessie watched as Owens put some incriminating evidence into his mouth, chewed it up and then spat it out of the carriage window, telling her he was going to reveal all to the British authorities. Owens had been sober for weeks, she said.

Clearly furious, Jessie had also written to Ritter, telling him that his prize agent was working for British intelligence. Owens managed to explain this away by telling Ritter that Jessie had been motivated by jealousy, using his previous connection with SIS in order to discredit him. Ever the wily fox, Owens reminded Ritter that he had voluntarily disclosed this information to him at the very beginning of their relationship, and Ritter had accepted his explanation and never referred to it again.

Although M15 knew most of the information that Jessie had given them, it did clarify the depth of Owens' involvement with the Germans, and he would soon feel the repercussions.

* * *

On 1 September 1939, detention orders for Arthur Owens and Lily Bade were issued under Regulation 18b:

> This individual was originally employed by our Foreign Intelligence Section. It was subsequently discovered that he had betrayed his trust and gone over to the German Espionage Service operating against this country and that he was in fact double-crossing. On his own admission he is still in the pay of the Germans and makes frequent journeys to Germany, no doubt taking with him any information he can get hold of. As he is a most untrustworthy individual, his activities should be curtailed immediately on the outbreak of hostilities.[57]

On 3 September, Britain declared war on Germany. Special Branch detectives were sent to arrest Owens and Lily, but couldn't find them.

In Hamburg, Owens' significance to the Germans increased exponentially with the discovery that his was the only transmitter in the entire Abwehr Air Intelligence section – and Owens 'was their only direct contact'.[58]

Chapter 3

About Turn

'The battles after the wars are over can be the toughest; there's no longer the public interest that accompanies, for good and for ill, the start of combat.' Nancy Gibbs

On the outbreak of war, MI5's rapidly expanding staff soon ran out of office space at Thames House - they knew they would have to allow for even greater expansion as the war progressed, and their new premises would have to be secure. The solution to their dilemma was a most unlikely premises: Wormwood Scrubs, a convict-built Victorian prison in West London. All the prisoners were evacuated under the Emergency Orders Act, and the cells were made ready for ninety-two members of staff, complete with desks, safes, filing cabinets and various other office equipment. Officers were given a cell each, and two secretaries shared a cell. MI5's massive card-index system known as 'The Registry', containing information on the citizens of the country as far back as the Great War, was guarded in the prison and a photocopy of all its data was stored at Blenheim Palace, near Oxford. As soon as German bombs began to fall on the prison during the London Blitz in September 1940, most of the staff were transferred to Blenheim.

Housed amongst the cells at Wormwood Scrubs was a secret intelligence network set up by Vernon Kell, the head of MI5, called the Radio Security Service (RSS), or MI8, whose role was to detect and close down illicit wireless stations operated by enemy spies in Britain. Working alongside a team of experts who demonstrated a keen grasp of Morse Code, language and cryptology was MI5's John Masterman and Major Tommy (Tar) Robertson, who ran the double agent XX System. Robertson already controlled Snow and would later employ Walter Dicketts as double agent Celery.

If someone had told Walter Dicketts, whilst he was serving his first prison sentence inside Wormwood Scrubs in August 1921, that fifteen years later he would be employed by members of MI5 operating from within this very prison, he would never have believed them. Back then, he was an energetic 22-year-old, who like most prisoners was struggling with the loss of liberty, the enforced silence and the hours spent in meaningless time. He missed the sights and sounds of life outside the prison walls, going for a drink in the pub, a stroll down the street and the company of women, friends and family. He thought constantly about his future and spent many hours alone, mining his memories over and over until eventually they became stale and uninteresting.

Inside a prison cell, there was no escape from himself and he had many memories he would have preferred to forget – the violence and brutality of war, the constant fear of injury or death and the loss of his rank and respectability. On the home front, he faced his parents' disappointment at his behaviour, the anger of Phyllis – whose family had been right about him after all – the disappearance of Dora and the loss of all four of his children. Whatever plans or dreams he may have had, all of them were now at risk. Society had condemned him as a common criminal, and it was up to him what he made of it.

Dicketts was released in August 1922, and at first things appeared to have been going relatively well. He found work with a Mr Rose from Southampton, upon whom he created a positive impression, and Phyllis agreed to give their marriage a second chance for the sake of the children.

Unfortunately, he soon went back to his philandering ways, and according to Phyllis's divorce petition a year later, her husband frequently committed adultery with a girl called Annette Benson, with whom he cohabited at her apartment in London's Edgware Road.

A year after his release, in late August 1923, Dicketts returned to crime. He put on his smartest clothes, tightened the knot of his tie, smoothed back his hair and placed his hat at the right angle, before making his way to Cheapside, the former gold and jewellery manufacturing centre of medieval London. Gems sparkled from the shop windows of the famous jewellers, Mappin & Webb, holders of a royal warrant since 1897, where Dicketts entered and told the shop assistant what he was looking for. He said he was the secretary of a local tradesman who required the goods for presentation purposes, and items were brought out and placed on velvet for his inspection. He examined them carefully, peering expertly at hallmarks and testing clasps before deciding upon a gold cigarette case and a diamond wrist watch, today worth around £2,000. The goods were gift-wrapped, and Dicketts paid for them with a bogus cheque and left the shop. No-one suspected a thing.

The goods were sold the next day before the cheque could be dishonoured, but something went wrong and he was arrested shortly afterwards. He appeared before Sir Ernest Wilde, the senior Circuit Judge, at the Old Bailey on 5 September and pleaded guilty.[1] Detective-Sergeant Giles told the court that Dicketts was living with a young woman 'of expensive tastes' who was responsible for his downfall.[2] 'It was probably to gratify her that he acted as he did,' Giles said.

He described Dicketts' war record as excellent and said his nerves had been shattered as a result of an aeroplane crash. 'With his gratuity money he ran wild and travelled all over the country in motor-cars for which he never paid. He has also been associated with the film world.'[3]

The next day, under the leadline BRILLIANT YOUNG AIRMAN'S DOWNFALL. GIVEN HIS LAST CHANCE, the *Guardian* said:[4]

> Ordering Dicketts to be kept in custody until next sessions, the Recorder [judge] said: 'I know that shell-shock is absolutely true. People who say it is not do not know anything about psychology. At the same time, I cannot allow you to go about defrauding people. I hear that restitution has been made and that your employer is willing to be bound over with you. I shall give you what will be the last chance you will ever receive.'

Dicketts avoided a jail sentence and was bound over in his own recognisance – a legal promise that he would show up for future court appearances and not engage in illegal activity during the terms of the agreement. Dicketts must have been doing good work for his employer, as Mr Rose agreed to act as his guarantor; perhaps Rose shared the same view as the judge, that Dicketts' behaviour was due to his experiences during the war. The reality was that so many young men were suffering from shellshock, what is now called PTSD (Post-Traumatic Stress Disorder), that the legal system was initially sympathetic to offenders who had seen violent and brutal action on the front lines.

Shellshock was the signature injury of the First World War, with an estimated 2 per cent of men who had seen active service identified as suffering from it. Shellshock wasn't well understood in those days, and was described in 1919 by Philip Gibbs - one of five official British reporters during the war – as follows:

> Something was wrong. They put on civilian clothes again and looked to their mothers and wives very much like the young men who had gone to business in the peaceful days before August 1914. But they had not come back the same men. Something had altered in them. They were subject to sudden moods, and queer tempers, fits of profound depression alternating with a restless desire for pleasure.[5]

Many returning veterans lost faith in the values of the society that had sent them to war, and struggled to make sense of it all. Having witnessed the true horror of war, they were somehow expected to simply return to normal life. Far from being a land fit for heroes, as they had been promised, there was little help for them in terms of employment, housing, pensions and welfare. According to Richard Van Emden's *The Soldiers' War*,[6] survivors generally had nothing but 'contempt and suspicion for the leaders of the nation for which they had fought so hard'.[7] The way the medals were handed out after the war compounded the bitterness, when officers who had never seen a shell unless it was being loaded onto a truck, received the same medals as those who had seen furious, bloody warfare in the trenches.

At his 1921 trial in Chesterfield for attempting to defraud H.J. Cook's outfitters, Dicketts' counsel submitted to the court that his client's offence was partly attributable to 'the reckless character and heedlessness of tomorrow which were needed for a successful airman'.[8] Cecil Lewis, a fellow Great War pilot, would have agreed with those characteristics, and described the young men he met between 1914 and 1918 in his autobiography *Sagittarius Rising*:

> The Royal Flying Corps [and the RNAS] attracted adventurous spirits, the devil-may-care young bloods of England, the fast livers, the furious drivers – men who were not happy unless they were taking risks. This invested the Corps with a certain style (not always admirable). We had the sense of being the last word in warfare, the advance guard of wars to come, and felt, I suppose, that we could afford to be a little extravagant.[9]

Lewis's description seems to describe Dicketts 'to a t'. It is almost as if he lived a large part of his life straight out of the pages of this book.

There was a big difference though – most First World War veterans did not resort to crime, and Dicketts made a career out of it. Between the years 1923 and 1931, his primary source of income appears to have been confidence trickery. He travelled widely to France, Spain, Greece, Canada, the USA and South America and used multiple aliases, including Richard Blake, Christopher Arthur Welfare, Richard Moreton, Charles Mills, Major R. Carberry, H. Dichetter, R. Ashtondale, Fox, Lessingham, Blackey, Rockdorf, Lohr, Colonel Woodhouse and even George Washington.[10]

Police described him as a very elusive, well-educated and clever swindler, and by 1941 his skills of deception were so highly developed that he was able to dupe the German Abwehr that he was a British traitor, when he was actually working for MI5.

Scamming people became second nature to Dicketts and he got away with many crimes, disappearing before he could be arrested. He obtained a British passport by forging a solicitor's signature, and in January 1925 was 'caught swindling' in France.[11] Going by the name Christopher Welfare, Dicketts entered a French bank and brazenly opened an account using a worthless cheque drawn on an English bank. Although he received a large sum of money from the bank, Dicketts was quickly captured by police and sentenced to four months' imprisonment. By the time he was released, Dicketts was fluent in French.

Unfortunately for him, he was met by two British detectives who extricated him from France and took him back to England to face three charges in the name of Richard Blake. In one charge, Dicketts had placed advertisements in the daily papers, saying he was the owner of some 'Automatic Advertising Clocks, which were to be installed at railway stations in London and the provinces'.[12] Dicketts claimed various firms had already agreed to place advertisements on the clocks, and he was looking for people who were willing to invest £200 each to be part of his exciting new business opportunity, which proved to be completely fictitious.

Dicketts pleaded guilty before the magistrate in London in June, and was sentenced to nine months' hard labour.[13] The entire year of 1925 was spent in jail or in custody awaiting sentencing. For a young man of 25, it was a waste of time and life, and from the moment he was released in early

January 1926, Dicketts seemed to have been intent in making up for it. He did film stunt work for Elstree Studios and Cricklewood Studios, whose silent adventure film *The Qualified Adventurer*, based on the novel by Selwyn Jepson, was in production around the time of his release. If Dicketts had hopes of becoming an actor, he would have realized very quickly that with so few British films being made, his chance of success was very slim and he would need another source of income. So he became involved in a number of businesses – Belgravia Properties Ltd, Supreme Radiator Co. Ltd and W.J. Berry & Co Ltd – which failed during the economic recession Britain experienced during the 1920s.[14] Although this period is sometimes referred to as the 'roaring twenties', for the British economy it was a period of depression, deflation and a steady decline in Britain's former economic pre-eminence. Unable to survive in this economic downturn, Dicketts' businesses failed in September 1926 and he was left almost penniless.

What Dicketts did next is remarkable. At a time when international travel was rare and limited to businessmen, the wealthy and the adventurous, Dicketts set out to see the world without a penny to his name. He planned to find work along the way and knew he could persuade most people to employ him.

If Dicketts kept a diary of his travels or wrote letters home describing his experiences, they no longer exist. And if it wasn't for a 1933 job reference written on his behalf, by Mr R. Willoughby Piggott of the Hampshire Prisoner's Aid Society, Dicketts' activities during this period would have remained a mystery.[15] Since the source of Piggott's information could only be Dicketts himself, and given his propensity for deception, it is likely Dicketts embellished the importance of his role to secure the position.

Dicketts sold everything he had to pay off his debts and travelled to Greece, where he assisted in the inauguration of the 'Grecian Island Air Postal Service'.[16] Although records of his involvement are yet to be found, Dicketts was a qualified seaplane pilot from his time with the RNAS in the First World War, and Greek postage stamps with seaplane images do exist from 1926. Dicketts said he left Greece 'after the Pangalos Revolution in September 1926 when the drachma crashed to 600 and consequently payment was almost worthless', and these facts are correct: the drachma did fall to 55 per cent of its value in the period following Pangalos' bloodless coup and his subsequent dictatorship in 1926, giving credence to Dicketts' claim that he was in Greece at the time.

When Dicketts left Greece in 1926, he crossed the Atlantic by sea and made his way to Mexico, where he 'served seventeen months as an officer in the Mexican Air Force until the revolution of 1928'.[17] Since Dicketts didn't possess a Mexican passport or speak Spanish, this seems unlikely. However, given his role as ADC (aide-de-camp) to distinguished foreign visitors with the Air Ministry during the Great War, it is possible Dicketts either knew someone or talked his way into some sort of advisory role. Once again, Dicketts' facts are correct: there was a revolution in Mexico in 1928, follow- ing Álvaro Obregón's election as president for a second term.

From Mexico, he travelled north and crossed the US border into San Diego, then headed east to the San Felipe Valley, where he found work as secretary to a rancher for four months. That ended after 'the wells ran dry' and an 'alkali substance made the land unsaleable'. Dicketts' information is probably genuine as much of the San Felipe region was under seawater for millions of years, and local soils are more alkaline than other soils.[18] Dicketts travelled around America finding work wherever he could. He did 'sports and lecture work' for various YMCA clubs, and was offered 'an excellent position in the West Coast Development Corporation, where he put a lot of hard work and was promoted'.

In August 1928, Dicketts said he failed to comply with US 'immigra- tion formalities', and returned to the UK, travelling first class aboard the Hamburg-America Line's SS *New York*. His profession as listed on the pas- senger manifest is 'author'.[19] This is the first indication of Dicketts' desire to earn a living as an author, which he would pursue intermittently until his death.

Dicketts remained in England for a matter of weeks, and then made his way to Spain, where he approached HM Consul-General at Barcelona in October 1928 'with a story that he was representing the Gladstone Corporation of New York and intended to arrange for the representation of this and other American firms at the forthcoming exhibition at that place'.[20] Having gaining the confidence of a number of persons at the British Club, Dicketts managed to persuade the director of a bank to advance him a sum of money, and then disappeared from Spain.

On 14 January 1929, the British Foreign Office sent a warning letter to all His Majesty's Consular and Passport Control Officers stating that Walter Arthur Charles Dicketts, 'alias Richard Moreton, alias Christopher Arthur

Welfare who is 6 ft. tall with brown eyes and black hair, has a criminal record, both in his country and France, for obtaining money by fraud and false pretences'.[21] Going by the name of Moreton, he had obtained financial assistance by false pretences from the Social Services Bureaus of Chattanooga, Tennessee, in February 1928, and later from various societies in Detroit, 'where His Majesty's Consul placed him in contact with a prospective employer. He however, failed to put in an appearance.

'He is of good appearance and plausible manner, and Consular officers are accordingly warned to exercise caution in any dealings with him,'[22] warned the Foreign Office.

* * *

With his pockets full from his latest exploits in Spain, Dicketts returned to England and moved into his parents' home in the pretty fishing village of Leigh-on-Sea at the mouth of the River Thames in Essex. At low tide, the foreshore at Leigh is covered in a wide expanse of mud flats and creeks, and a fresh salty ocean smell pervades the air. The village is a fondly remembered place of fun and family time for locals and holidaymakers alike; visits to the cockle sheds, hot chips, ice-cream, walks on the promenade and happy children digging, throwing and playing in the mud, filling buckets and making mud castles while their parents kept one eye on them and the other on the tide.

Arthur and Francis Dicketts lived in a large white house, just one road back from the sea. Its regular rail service made Leigh an ideal commuter town for people like Arthur, who travelled daily to his stockbroking job in the city. The London Stock Exchange was the largest in the world at that time, listing almost one-third of all the public and private securities. It was a distinguished profession, and membership to the Exchange was strictly controlled. The fact that his son had a criminal record was embarrassing enough, but soon a scandal would erupt from which there would be nowhere to hide.

In the small community of Leigh-on-Sea, Walter's parents found themselves in the middle of intense media and public scrutiny as news of their son's elopement with a 16-year-old local girl was reported in the local newspapers. The story grabbed the interest of readers all over the world, as police tried to find the 30-year-old Walter Dicketts before he could marry the innocent Alma Wood. There were sightings all over the country as the general public tried to assist the police, and the media, aware that they had a hot story, published endless updates on their progress.

On 20 May 1929, under the headline MISSING SOUTHEND GIRL, *The Times* reported:

> The police at Southend are making inquiries with a view to tracing Miss Alma Wood 16 ½ who has been missing from her home at Leigh-on-Sea since April 30th, and a man known by the name of Dicketts to whom she was to have been married in London. Miss Alma Farquhar is described at 5ft 4 inches tall, with light brown bobbed hair, grey eyes, and when last seen was dressed in a navy blue three-piece suit of silk with a brown tweed coat and scarf. [23]

And the *Daily Express* reported on 26 May, under the headline SWINDLER WHO MARRIED A GIRL OF SIXTEEN:

> While Dicketts was living with his parents – highly respectable people – at Leigh-on-Sea, he met and paid attention to Miss Wood, the daughter of Nathanial Farquhar Wood … He made certain statements about his position to her father saying that he was manager to the Gladstone Corporation of New York and was receiving a salary of £1,200 [£66,950 today] a year. He said that he wanted to marry Miss Wood. Mr. Wood thought that his daughter was too young, but eventually he gave his consent.[24]

When Mr Wood changed his mind soon afterwards, the besotted couple eloped. Her horrified parents reacted immediately, calling the police and alerting the media. They begged them to help them find their missing daughter. The public responded to their plight by writing to newspaper editors expressing outrage at Dicketts' actions. That poor girl, and her distraught parents, they emphathised – just imagine if it was our daughter. Others reported sightings of the couple, which turned out to be false.

Every police station in the country was supplied with a poster containing a description and a photograph of Dicketts, and listed some of his twenty-three aliases: 'Age: 30; 5ft 11 inches; dark brown hair and eyes; may be wearing coloured spectacles; has pointed features, receding forehead and a dimple on his chin; well spoken and possessed of charming manners and smile.' [25]

The scandal reached its peak after Mrs Wood's impassioned plea to her daughter to return home was printed in several newspapers. Alma finally responded two days later, and it was revealed that despite all the hoopla, Mr Wood had signed the required consent form giving Alma permission to marry Dicketts. The Registrar from the Marylebone Register Office was interviewed and expressed surprise. 'The girl looked radiantly happy when I performed the ceremony,' he said.[26]

After three weeks of wedded bliss, Alma returned home for what she thought was a fleeting visit. She couldn't understand why police were looking for her husband, and expected to return to him shortly afterwards. For several hours, Alma wrestled with her mother's persuasion about the true nature of her husband, refusing to believe anything negative about Dicketts. As far as Alma was concerned, Dicketts had been the most loving and attentive husband, and she was sure he would turn over a new leaf. When she realized she would never see her husband again, Alma 'pleaded for one last chance to see him' before she went away forever.[27]

Hungry journalists besieged relatives and friends visiting the Woods' home to find out everything they could about Alma. A friend told reporters that now Alma knew the truth about her husband, she wanted nothing more than to help bring him to justice. Her husband invariably adopted an American accent, and 'knew all about New York and American slang, and was never at a loss wherever he was and could enter any drawing room in the country with the greatest of ease'.[28] Dicketts told her he was going to Ireland, and had chosen his next location by closing his eyes and sticking a pin in a map.

Dicketts' trail was picked up by detectives, who discovered how quickly he had moved on from Alma. On 11 September 1929, Walter stayed overnight at Barry's Hotel Cardiff in Wales, where he 'committed adultery' with an unknown woman.[29] A month later, he was in Market Harborough, where he hired a box for the hunting season in the name of Captain Lathom. He spent a night there with an unknown woman at The Briars, East Farndon, then headed for London, spending two nights with a woman called Madge Rowan, who would later be persuaded to give evidence at Alma's divorce proceedings.

He travelled far and wide, moving from one town (and one woman) to the next. At St Martin, on the island of Jersey, he stayed with an unknown woman at the Central Hotel during the night of 17 October. In Austria, he borrowed money from a number of 'hotel proprietors and servants' from the leading hotels, and promptly left town in a hurry without paying them back.[30]

Police caught up with him in Salzburg, and he received a sentence of four months' imprisonment. The Austrian police checked to see if there were any outstanding charges or previous criminal convictions against him, and discovered they had an international criminal on their hands. On 11 November 1929, the *New York Times* reported:

> Walter Charles Dicketts, the Englishman arrested yesterday at Salzburg on suspicion of being an international criminal wanted by the English, Spanish and American police, today confessed to crimes in France, Spain and England. He admitted that he had swindled exhibitors at the Barcelona exhibition out of £25,000 [£1,395,000 today], and acknowledged that he had served prison sentences in France and England, in the latter case for frauds totalling £20,000.

Incredibly, faced with the prospect of police from so many countries lining up to charge him with offences, Dicketts tried to escape. He obtained a file from a fellow prisoner and proceeded to use it on the 'iron bars of his cell'.[31] Prison warders caught him immediately and he was moved into a solitary cell, from which escape was impossible.

On 9 June 1930, seven months after his arrest in Salzburg, the *Daily Mirror* reported 'Scotland Yard Detectives Leave for Austria', asserting that they were 'to bring back Walter Arthur Charles Dicketts, against whom there is an allegation of fraud'.

Having added German to his suite of languages, Dicketts was taken back to England and placed under remand at Brixton Gaol, where he was served with his divorce papers on the grounds of his frequent adultery. He admitted his misdemeanours, and said that his wife was entitled to a divorce and that he 'never ought to have married her with his terrible criminal record'.[32] Alma Dicketts was granted a decree nisi with costs, and they never saw each other again. It is intriguing to speculate whether Phyllis and Dora saw the articles appearing in the media, and what their reactions might have been.

There's no doubt it would have confirmed Phyllis' opinion of her ex-husband, and buried Dora's secret deep inside her.

Dicketts appeared before Marylebone Police Court, described as a company manager of Rue Des Renaudes, Paris, and was charged with three warrants of fraud. The *Daily Express* described him the next day: '[A] well-groomed young man of military build, with glossy black hair and a florid complexion stepped smartly into the dock, carrying a thin paper parcel and light Macintosh.'[33]

Detective Sergeant Smith told the court that after reading Dicketts his rights in Hamburg, he had replied: 'Yes. That is quite right. I want to help you in every possible way and get everything cleared up.'[34] He asked that all outstanding cases should be taken into consideration when he was finally dealt with, saying he had visited the following places and obtained food and lodgings by false pretences: Bournemouth, Blandford, Bristol, Burnley, Brecon, Chester, Cardiff, Church Stretton, Cockermouth, Glasgow, Honiton, Hereford, Hamilton, Manchester, Morecombe, Newcastle, Sheffield and Swansea.

It may be that Dicketts had finally come to his senses. It was a lonely life, dodging police, giving statements, dealing with lawyers, appearing in court and generally living on one's wits, and would only get worse if he continued as he had been. He pleaded guilty to all charges and was sentenced to eighteen months' imprisonment at Hampshire Assizes.[35] It was during this time, with the help of various authorities, that Richard (Dick) Dicketts, as he now called himself, finally decided that crime didn't pay.

Upon his release, he returned to a normal role in society, and began courting his future wife, Vera Fudge, a pretty and petite 20-year-old blonde. People began to trust him and he was able to progress in life. In March 1933, his employer, Sir Wyndham Deedes of The National Council for Social Service, of which the Prince of Wales was a patron, put him forward for a position at the YMCA, saying, 'I am extremely favourably impressed by him. I think his experience of this kind of work is admittedly slight, but he is just the right man for the work.'[36]

Attached to his application is a refreshingly different reference to the ones normally used to describe Dicketts:

> I have known Mr Richard Dicketts for some two years or so, intimately, and can confidently assert that he is a man of superior intelligence, quick and active brain, with an orderly and methodical mind.

I was particularly struck with his quiet influence over those with whom he came into touch, when in charge of a party of men on the land during the past year. He possesses marked organising ability and the attributes of leadership.

[name unreadable], Edensor Lodge, Worthy Road, Winchester.[37]

Dicketts beat five other applicants for the position of Warden and Supervisor of the St James' Square branch of the Unemployed Welfare Association, at a salary of £200 [around £13,030 today] per year, which he accepted. Internal correspondence reveals that there was some reservation in employing him within the committee, as they realized they would be taking a certain amount of risk in employing him. 'However, he starts with a clean sheet as far as I am concerned and we will do everything possible to help him to do something of which he can be proud,' wrote one of the members.[38]

The position was an important one, as over three million people were unemployed in Britain due to the Great Depression at the end of 1931. Although Britain had a relatively advanced welfare system compared to many other industrialized countries, its government-funded unemployment benefit was paid out according to need, but was subject to a strict means test.

Dicketts accepted the position and, aware of the chance they were giving him, wrote to reassure the members that the welfare of the centre would be his one true aim, and he would give his best efforts to that end. He achieved his goal and was proud of it, as indicated by his letter to Air Commodore Archie Boyle requesting a commission within the RAF at the beginning of the Second World War:.

'I have had considerable experience in handling and organising rough labour. I was Warden of Unemployed in Bristol in 1933/1934 with control of 6,800 men.'[39] Dicketts went on to describe that during the time of the unemployed riots in the west, he started with one group of 400 men, and eventually organised a further sixteen groups over a period of fifteen months. He was also responsible for establishing the first Community Land Group at Bedminster, comprised of 300 men.

On 13 January 1934, the *Western Daily Press* published a letter to the editor from Mrs N.B. Taylor of the Unemployed Welfare Association, St James' Square, Bristol:

I am sure a very large number of people in Bristol will regret to learn that Mr. R.A. Dicketts, the very popular Warden of the Unemployed Welfare Association, St James [sic] Square, is leaving us at the end of the month to take up a position as area organiser in land settlement work. The progress of the Association since his advent clearly shows his business capacity and extraordinary organising ability, which, coupled with his kind personality has endeared him to everyone with whom he has come in contact, during the year he has been with us. His must surely be a record of achievements for the benefit of the unemployed, all of which have been tackled with great sincerity. One of his most outstanding qualities has been the really personal and individual interest he has taken in every member who has sought his advice.[40]

Unfortunately, his new-found honesty in the world of employment did not extend to his romantic entanglements. When he married the 22-year-old Vera Nellie Fudge in Bristol on 22 April 1933, he said he was a bachelor and used the name Richard Dicketts instead of his real name.[41] Vera never did discover he had been married twice before and had four children to two different women.

Their son, Richard Anthony, was born on 18 January 1934, while Dicketts was the Area Administrator for the National Allotments Association.[42] The association still exists today as a members' co-operative, founded to protect and preserve allotments for future generations.

In May 1937, he and Vera left their young son behind with a nanny and left for Singapore to look into the business of importing silk. They travelled aboard the Japanese NYK Line vessel the *Haruna Maru*,[43] staying at the Adelphi Hotel in Singapore before travelling throughout Malaya and Ceylon (modern Sri Lanka). Richard has photographs showing his parents relaxing onboard and dressed in fancy dress costumes. Another photograph shows his parents standing in the middle of several Indian businessmen, with the pretty young Vera smiling happily, dwarfed by the men beside her.

The Dicketts family moved to Birmingham after their return from the Far East, where their son attended school for the first time. Tension in Europe was high, and by March 1939, the Nazis had taken over Czechoslovakia, and on 31 August, Britain began evacuating children and the elderly from

London. Dicketts and Vera took their son and returned to Bristol, moving in with her parents. Dicketts intended to offer his services to the war effort, and his wife and child would be taken care of in his absence. When the German bombing raids came to Bristol, they were so frequent that the family spent a great deal of time sheltering under the stairs.

Vera became accustomed to her husband's regular absences, which she believed was due to his business commitments. But in the early part of the war, around 1940, he simply disappeared. There was a rumour going around at that time that a man had jumped off the Suspension Bridge in Clifton, near where they lived, and Vera had become so concerned she went to 'Bridewell Police Station to see if he could be traced'.[44] Poor Vera got more than she bargained for when police told her of her husband's major misdeeds in embezzlement and previous prison sentences. It was the first she had heard of them.

In a repeat scenario of his time with Phyllis and Dora, Dicketts had met another woman and was living with her in London as man and wife. Her name was Kathleen (Kay) Mary Holdcroft, and she would come to play an important part in Dicketts' future activities with MI5. Kay was from Birmingham, where she had been caught shoplifting (a handbag and a purse) in May 1934.[45] It was her first and only offence, and while tempting to believe this was somehow connected to how they met, it took place several years before he and Vera moved there.

Vera discovered the reason for her husband's absence when a woman 'who looked like a model' came to their house and asked her mother if her fiancé Richard Dicketts was at home. The stunned Mrs Fudge told her: 'He can't be your fiancé because he's married to my daughter.'[46]

Chapter 4

A New Kind of Spy

'Oh, what a tangled web we weave ... when first we practise
to deceive.' Sir Walter Scott

With the outbreak of war, Arthur Owens knew his spying days for
Germany were over, and so was his primary source of income.
Indeed, British police had gone to arrest him immediately war
was declared, but Owens wasn't there, as he had moved into a friend's place
and failed to notify them of his change of address. Alarm bells began ringing
at MI5, but a major search was forestalled when Owens got in touch with
Inspector Gagan the following day and offered his services to the British
Government.

Gagan arranged to meet him at Waterloo Station at 4 pm, but as soon as
Owens arrived with Lily, he and two other men from Special Branch stepped
forward to arrest him. Owens told Lily to hurry home and hide the wireless
transmitter, and the pair quickly separated. Gagan asked him where he was
living, but Owens refused to give his address and was taken to Wandsworth
prison, where he was served with his detention order and detained. Once the
reality of his imprisonment finally sunk in, Owens told police where he lived
and said they would find his German radio transmitter in the bathroom.

Meanwhile, Lily had returned home and begged their friend, a 44-year-
old Glaswegian called Myner, to help her hide the transmitter, which they
buried in the corner of his garden. Later that evening, Gagan, in the company
of Owens' boss, Major Tommy Robertson of MI5, and two other officers
arrived and persuaded them to reveal where they had hidden the wireless.
The officers carried out a thorough search of Myner's home and found 'a
two-valve receiving set' built by Owens, hidden in a bathroom cupboard.[1]

Lily was served with her detention order, and she and Myner, a former
costings clerk, were taken in for questioning. Myner told police he was
unemployed and had met Owens in a pub three months earlier, and had

gone with him to Hamburg to meet some of his business contacts with a view to taking up various commercial agencies in England. Myner had only helped Lily hide the radio in the belief that he was helping out Owens with a domestic issue to do with his wife.

On Friday, 8 September, Major Robertson, accompanied by Colonel Yule, a radio expert, visited Owens in his cell and proposed that the wireless set should be brought in and used to re-establish contact with Germany, but this time it would be under MI5's control and direction. Faced with the stark reality of the penalties meted out for spying against your own country, which included execution, Owens agreed to the proposal and the wireless was set up in his cell. MI5 watched carefully as Owens checked over the wireless to ensure it had been set up correctly, but when he pushed a switch on the base, a fuse blew, ending their activities until the following day.

The fuse was repaired, and with Owens keying out the message, closely observed by Yule, the very first MI5 controlled radio transmission was sent out in code: 'all ready have repaired radio send instructions now wait-ing reply.'[2] MI5's radio security section monitoring Owens' transmission reported that the signal strength was very weak, and no reply was received from the Germans. Further attempts to contact the Germans also met with no success, and it was beginning to appear as if Owens was trying to sabo-tage the entire operation. Robertson warned Owens that it was 'in his best interests to cooperate with them',[3] after which Owens appeared to become more co-operative, but MI5 still weren't sure if he was withholding further knowledge.

Their next attempt to establish radio contact also ended in failure, when a prison warden opened the door to Owens' cell and asked Robertson if it was okay for people to use the passage outside. Owens became visibly shaken and begged, 'please don't let them see me – whatever happens don't let them see me.'[4] He relayed how earlier that morning, a fellow-prisoner had taken him into a corner and had quizzed him about what questions the intelligence cops had asked him. Owens knew this prisoner well and was aware that he had just returned from Germany.

There were a number of foreign spies being held and interrogated at Wormwood Scrubs, and MI5's Hinchley-Cooke quickly identified this man as Percy William Rapp, who had offered his services to German intelligence in 1937 and had been arrested by British police on the outset of war.[5] Owens' concern was that his life would be in danger if the Germans discovered he was under the control of the British Secret Service.

Owens was taken to Kingston Police Station, where he was treated as a special prisoner, and then taken flat-hunting by Special Branch. As soon as a suitable top-floor apartment was found in the same area, Lily was released from detention and given some money to furnish it. The couple were moved into the flat, along with a couple of guards, whose role was to keep a close eye on Owens and Lily, and a radio operator. On 12 September 1939, MI5 made their first successful transmission to Germany: 'MUST MEET YOU IN HOLLAND AT ONCE. BRING WEATHER CODE. RADIO TOWN AND HOTEL. WALES READY.'[6] Owens had explained that Ritter wanted to meet him in Holland as soon as possible to pick up a new weather code, which he was to use to provide the Germans with up-to-date weather information about the places they intended to bomb. The reference to Wales meant that Owens was ready to provide Ritter with the name and address of a reliable member of the Welsh Nationalist Party who could be used for sabotage purposes – the Germans intended to smuggle arms to him aboard a submarine that would come up the Bristol Channel. Although the German reply to this message was undecipherable, it was proceeded by the call sign 'OEA',[7] which the Hamburg Abwehr station used to contact Owens.

The establishment of Snow as MI5's first double agent of the Second World War led to the formation of a coordinating body called the Twenty (XX) or Double Cross Committee, who supervised the preparation of information suitable for passing to the enemy. The XX Committee was chaired by Oxford don J.C. Masterman and met for the first time in January 1941. At the end of the war, Masterman was commissioned to write a report of its activities which said:

> There are dramatic moments in the history of most institutions, and this, in the record of double-cross activities, is one of them, for with Snow's first message from Wandsworth Prison, the double-cross system was well and truly launched. Very soon he was receiving a variety of orders and requests for information.[8]

And so began the British double-cross system. Owens' radio was operated by Maurice Burton, a wireless operator who learnt how to mimic Owens'

Morse style, and therefore controlled all his messages to the Abwehr. To a trained ear, the style in which Morse code is tapped out can be as distinctive as a person's handwriting, and therefore the people (Trautmann and his assistant Wein in Hamburg) who had taught Owens how to use his radio, would be able to identify his 'hand' when he tapped out a message. Ritter had no idea his star agent, Johnny, was now under British control.

There was another unexpected and significant bonus. Owens' traffic had been picked up within days by the Radio Security Service (RSS), which worked in tandem with MI5 and provided them with technical expertise in wireless communication. The RSS employed a number of amateur licence-holders, who were volunteers from the Radio Society of Great Britain, to scan the airwaves to detect enemy signals. To their complete surprise, there were almost no clandestine transmissions from German agents from the outbreak of war, except for one in particular - Owens, MI5's first double agent.

Listening in to his transmission, they made an extraordinary discovery. Having learnt to 'recognise the tone'[9] of the Hamburg station and the varying styles of its operators, they noticed Owens' messages were first being routed to another radio, before being re-coded and sent onto Hamburg. By taking bearings from British direction-finding stations, they calculated that Owens' messages were going to an enemy spy ship off the coast of Norway. Within minutes of being received, they were re-encrypted using a cipher generated by an 'Enigma machine'[10] and then relayed to the Abwehr headquarters in Germany.

Since MI5 had drafted Owens' messages in the first place, the RSS could compare his early morning traffic to the subsequent message encrypted on the German Enigma machine. In this way they were able to reverse-engineer the daily settings of the Enigma machine's rotors, to break the Abwehr's most secret communications for the rest of the day, until the settings were changed again at midnight.

By the end of 1940, the hand cipher traffic (encryption methods that are performed with pencil and paper) was being circulated by RSS under the codename ISOS, and the Enigma version as ISK. This remarkable breakthrough encouraged the code-breakers to extend their study of the enemy's Enigma traffic from the Abwehr to the Luftwaffe and others.

Owens was never told, and neither could he ever have guessed how his radio transmissions played a part in cracking the unbreakable Enigma code in the early part of the war. It was left to Major Tommy Robertson and the double-cross team at MI5 to manage the difficult task of keeping Owens in-play for as long as possible.

* * *

Ritter's lateral-thinking British counterpart and Owens' new boss, Major Thomas Argyll Robertson, was 30 years old and at least ten years younger than Ritter. More commonly known to his colleagues as 'Tar' for the way he signed his reports with his initials, Tommy (or Robbie) was a handsome and extremely likeable young man with twinkling blue eyes, who had a natural ability to read people and situations, and was popular with his subordinates.

Tommy Robertson was born in Sumatra in 1909, the son of John, a banker, and Lilian, one of eleven children whose father ran a prosperous grain mill in Tewkesbury.[11] Due to circumstances and the prevailing attitude of the times, which in today's terms would be considered a complete lack of sensitivity towards children's feelings, Tommy suffered a painful childhood. One of his family members believed it lay hidden beneath a genial exterior and a desire 'to be liked'.[12]

Tommy was 4 years old when his father accepted a posting in Kuala Lumpur, Malaysia, and was left behind in England to complete his education. He lived with an aunt who was married to a vicar, and as the First World War raged in France, Tommy attended Sunnydown, a prep-school near Guildford, followed by the historic and beautiful Charterhouse private school in Surrey in 1923. At Charterhouse he became friendly with John Kell, whose father, Vernon Kell, the head of MI5, would later recruit him to the service in 1933.[13]

His family returned in 1923 and settled down in London in the much sought-after Regents Park, where Tommy spent many happy holidays before attending Sandhurst Military Academy. One of his friends at Sandhurst was David Niven, the film star. After graduation, he was recruited into the prestigious Seaforth Highlanders until the cost of paying for his fast cars, tailored suits, wine, women and song exhausted his father's wallet, and Tommy had little choice but to earn his own living.

He resigned his commission in 1930 and became a Bill Broker with one of the discount houses in the financial district of London. A few years later, he left his prestigious career to become a rank-and-file copper with the Birmingham police force. It was an odd choice given his background, and begs the question whether he was unofficially working for Vernon Kell before his official recruitment into MI5 on 31 March 1933.[14]

This was the background of the man who would lead his team of double agents, comprised of an odd collection of crooks, drunkards, gamblers, fantasists and liars, to so completely dupe the German Abwehr that the Chairman of the Double Cross Committee was able to declare with complete certainty that they had 'actively controlled the German espionage system in England during Second World War'.[15]

Tar was an unconventional but inspired counter-espionage professional, who preferred the informality of holding meetings in pubs, often accompanied by his young wife, Joan, who, like him, was an exceptional judge of character. Tar had an extraordinary ability for his secretive profession, and was subtle in his approach: he was an intelligent, natural born leader whose agents respected and relied upon him, but he could also be tough and decisive when necessary. Although only 30 years old at the beginning of the war, Tar had wisdom well beyond his years, but despite all his indubitable skills, he knew he never really got the measure of Arthur Owens.

* * *

At the beginning of the war, Britain's security service was undermanned and under siege, with a flood of reports, enquiries and around 8,200 vetting requests per week that needed to be dealt with. Citizens of Germany, Austria and Italy had to be interviewed to ensure they were friendly aliens, and 64,000 people were interned. Suspected Nazi sympathizers and British fascists like Sir Oswald Mosley were imprisoned and investigated, and among the refugees fleeing the Nazi regime were those whose real identities were German spies.

Towards the end of 1940, Germany attempted to flood Britain with spies – they carried forged paperwork and pretended to be workers, refugees, farm-workers and businessmen. They came by every possible means available; by small boats, seaplanes, U-boats or landed by parachute. A few were Nazi fanatics, and others had been blackmailed to cooperate for fear of reprisals to their families back home in Germany – and incredibly, nearly every one of them was captured.

Owens' pre-war relationship with his German spymaster, Nikolaus Ritter (aka Dr Rantzau), was of vital importance and value to MI5 once war broke out. Ritter notified Owens of the arrival of German agents via his wireless transmitter, unaware that the radio was controlled and operated by MI5. He was betraying his spies without realizing it. They were met by MI5 on arrival and taken into captivity, and their radio sets used to inform the Germans that Owens or one of his sub-agents was taking care of them. When the Enigma cipher was cracked by the brilliant RSS codebreakers at Barnet, and then at Bletchley Park, the British knew everything they needed to know about the arrival of German spies.

Captured spies were immediately taken to Camp 020 at Ham Common, Richmond, where they were interrogated and turned to work for MI5 against their former spymasters. Those who resisted were interned or executed. The chief interrogator at Camp 020 was the terrifying looking Lieutenant Colonel Robin 'Tin Eye' Stephens (so named due to his glass monocle that never moved), who used psychological intimidation as opposed to violence to break enemy agents.

Ever mindful of their dual responsibility of keeping their double-cross activities secret and keeping up the morale of the British public, it was sometimes necessary for MI5 to execute German spies. It would stretch the credulity of the Germans if none of their spies were captured, and news of their execution encouraged the Germans to believe that their surviving spies had not been captured and were working freely, and not under British control. Only a handful resisted being turned, and in the end an unlucky thirteen German agents were executed by Britain during the war.[16]

Each newly turned German spy would be handed over to MI5's double agent section B1(a), run by Major Tommy Robertson. Every controlled enemy agent was assigned a case officer, who, under Robertson's direction, managed the day-to-day operation of that individual. The preferred method of communication between the Abwehr and their agents was via wireless telegraphy, although secret ink, microphotography and, in some cases, direct contact with the agent were also employed. Once Robertson had access to ISOS and ISK[17] intercepts of German secret communications, he could monitor the enemy's reaction to each of his double agents and the information they were passing onto the Germans.

MI5's double-cross system was so successful that by the end of the war, some 120 double agents, including Walter Dicketts, had been employed in counter-espionage, sabotage and deception. It was one of the greatest intelligence coups of the Second World War, as the XX Committee's Chairman, J.C. Masterman, would later reveal: 'For the greater part of the war, we did more than practise a large-scale deception through double agents: by means of the double-agent system we actively ran and controlled the German espionage system in this country.'[18]

The most significant victory for the Double Cross Committee was the D-Day deception campaign, codenamed FORTITUDE, which tricked the Germans into believing that the Pas-de-Calais was the real landing site for the Allied invasion instead of Normandy. It saved the lives of many thousands of Allied soldiers.

The deception by MI5's double agents was so complete that at the end of the war, three agents – Tate, Garbo and Zigzag – received German Iron Crosses in recognition of their espionage activities, yet their entire operation on behalf of MI5 had been financed by funds provided by the Abwehr.

Tar Robertson came to believe that some of his enemy counterparts must have realized their agents had been compromised, but chose to ignore the tell-tale clues. His double-cross team created an experiment to establish this fact by pretending to run a double agent so badly that the Abwehr could not fail to recognize him as a controlled spy. The case had to be abandoned when the Germans accepted SCRUFFY and continued to run him as an authentic spy.

* * *

In late September 1939, MI5 decided to allow their newly doubled spy, Owens, to meet Ritter in Holland to receive a new weather code as planned. It seems an extraordinary step to take, given Owens' previous actions, but MI5 were effectively holding Lily hostage at their apartment in Kingston, where she was closely guarded by two Special Branch detectives. Even if Owens did give the game away, MI5 believed they would still gain benefits from having direct contact with the Germans for deception and misinformation purposes. And before the Enigma code was cracked, it was important to keep Owens' radio traffic going, so the RSS could decode the Abwehr's secret communications for the day.

During his earlier radio transmission on 12 September, Owens had informed Ritter that he had found a suitable Welsh saboteur as requested. Realizing Ritter would expect Owens to provide information about this man, Tar told Owens to say that he had become acquainted with a man who was in touch with the head of the Welsh Nationalist party, whom he thought might be suitable. 'I'll find someone to fit the bill in your absence,' Tar assured Owens.

Owens left Gravesend on 20 September for Rotterdam by sea, where he met with Ritter and gave him the agreed story, which was accepted. Ritter then gave Owens a coin for the Welshman to use as proof of his identity at a meeting to be held in Brussels in two to three weeks' time. Ritter also gave Owens a new call sign, a new weather reporting code and some intelligence requests, which MI5 sifted through on his return.

During his debriefing, Owens told MI5 that the Luftwaffe intended to bomb the new Hawkers plant in Kingston, and that Ritter had assured him he would let him know when the air raids were planned, so Owens could leave town for a few days. Ritter had told Owens to buy a gas mask in London, as they would resort to 'bacteriological warfare' against Britain if all else failed, dropping bombs charged with bacteria into water reservoirs all over the country.[19] Owens believed the Germans were well prepared for this.

While Owens was away, Tar recruited a 50-year-old retired Swansea police chief inspector, Gwilym Williams, who spoke fluent Welsh and was willing to go abroad. He had run away to sea as a young man, and his marine background, together with his skill in languages including French, Spanish and German, made him an ideal choice for his fictitious role as a Welsh Nationalist. Williams was 100 per cent loyal to Britain, and part of his role would be to check up on Owens' true allegiance. Tar considered him to be 'an extremely determined type of individual', and gave him the codename GW.[20]

To enable the two men to become acquainted shortly before their trip to Antwerp, MI5 arranged for GW to travel to London to meet Owens. GW's cover was to pretend he was a retiree who worked as a private enquiry agent investigating road accidents. His job entailed travelling around Wales, where he had seen first-hand the appalling working conditions of his countrymen under English exploitation and had become anti-British in outlook as a result. Owens told him to play up his political convictions, including appearing to be pro-German.

Owens warned GW not to be surprised if the Germans addressed him as 'Colonel', saying that he held this rank in the German Army. GW good-humouredly remarked that it must be rather difficult as he didn't speak any German. Realizing the folly of his statement, Owens quickly replied that what he had meant to say was that 'they *call* him Colonel'.[21]

GW told Tar that Owens had also bragged that 'he knew the approximate position (or perhaps the beat) of every German submarine operating outside Germany!' In brackets after this sentence, Tar wrote in his report, '(Oh Yeah!)'.[22]

After briefing GW on suitable landing spots for U-boats (supplied to him by MI5), Owens took GW back to his flat in Kingston to show him the wireless. They spent some time afterwards with Lily at a pub, and at 9.30 pm returned home, where Owens and Burton, his radio operator, immediately got busy with his nightly transmissions to the Germans. GW was surprised to notice that despite Owens' heavy drinking of both whisky and beer during the evening, he was remarkably clear-headed when it came to his transmission, and believed he possessed 'tremendous will power and an extremely quick mentality'.[23]

He and Owens set sail for Antwerp on 19 October, where Owens introduced GW to Ritter and another man who was in charge of the Welsh sabotage plan, called 'the Commander'.[24] The Commander interviewed GW and taught him how to mix chemicals to create explosions, saying he would soon receive a short-range wireless transmitter and should brush up on his Morse code so he could contact the U-boat when it arrived. When he got back to England, GW was to take up stamp collecting as a hobby because they could conceal miniature photography in microdots under the stamps, and Owens was to get in touch with a man in Manchester who was a Fellow of the Royal Photographic Society in this connection. MI5 were very interested in this information, as microdot technology was relatively new.

Ritter gave GW £50 (around £2,845 today[25]) and Owens £500, which he was to put in a bank account and keep precise records of what money he paid to other agents. In future, Owens would be paid by a woman living near Bournemouth, who would either pass the money to him or place it in his postbox. Coincidently, while Owens was away, MI5 became aware of the existence of this woman when they intercepted two letters sent by her to Owens containing £20 each. They managed to track down Mrs Mathilde Krafft, who was arrested and spent the remainder of the war in Holloway Prison.[26]

German interest in the Welsh sabotage scheme declined over time, and with it their interest in GW. Owens claimed the Germans thought GW was 'too nervous'[27] for the job, but MI5 believed it had more to do with the fact that the insurrection in South Wales was designed to coincide with an invasion of Britain, which never took place in the end. MI5 didn't realize at the time, but this was the beginning of a pattern in which Owens would diminish the stature of any agent MI5 encouraged him to introduce to Ritter. Owens' concerns about another agent blowing his own cover were genuine – it would not be easy to trust another person when your own life was on the line. The problem for MI5 was to determine where Owens' true loyalty lay. In GW's case, Owens told Tar that he was 'a little perturbed at taking GW back with him on their next journey to Germany', as he was rather uneasy about GW and considered that he might make 'one or two slips'.[28]

GW continued to successfully operate independently of Owens until his case was wound up in February 1942, after the arrest of Luis Calvo, the Spanish press attaché and Abwehr spy in London whom GW had cultivated.[29]

MI5's Richman Stopford was sent to Manchester in early December, to interview the photographer whom Ritter had ordered Owens to contact when he got back to England. Stopford 'thoroughly frightened'[30] the photographer, Charles Eschborn, saying he knew all about him, his family and their activities, and if he breathed a word about their conversation at any stage, British intelligence would ensure that he and his brother were 'put inside' and their signed confession sent to the German SS.[31] In fact, Eschborn, who was one of three brothers of German and English parentage, had nothing but English sympathies. He had acquired British nationality at birth and had been forced, along with his brother Erwin, to become German agents by the Abwehr, who threatened reprisals against the third brother, Hans, in Nuremberg if they refused. His job as a German agent was to take illicit photographs and report on shipping movements. He was to convert Owens' reports into photographic microdots, which could be secreted under stamps or within sweet wrappers.

Eschborn immediately agreed to become a double agent under MI5's control and received the codename Charlie. His brother Erwin was also interviewed by MI5, who found him to be a far less trustworthy person and interned him for the remainder of the war. Charlie now had one brother used as a threat against him in Germany and one held for security purposes in England.

MI5 didn't inform Owens that Charlie had been turned, and Owens believed he was an authentic German spy operating under Ritter's instructions. Calling himself Thomas Graham, Owens travelled to Manchester with Lily and checked into their hotel. He sent a telegram to Charlie, asking him to come to their hotel immediately 'as he had a message from his family'.[32] Charlie understood the coded message immediately and made his way to the hotel, where Owens informed him he had come from the Doctor, and passed on Ritter's instructions that Charlie was to take photographs of docks and other strategic sites, which he was to reduce and send to Owens in London. Charlie could have had no doubt of the seriousness of his situation, as shortly after having agreed to work for MI5 he was contacted by a man (Owens) whom he believed to be a genuine German agent.

Charlie reported this meeting to MI5, who admitted that they had a fair idea who Thomas Graham was, but didn't tell Charlie he was operating under their control. MI5's strategy was to test the loyalty of both men and see who reported contact with the other. It was a risky tactic and one MI5 would try again later with another agent, Biscuit, to ill effect.

A few months later, Charlie was ready to show some of the photographs he had taken to Owens, and caught the train to London. Owens was still unaware that Charlie was anything other than an authentic German spy, and the night before his arrival, went to see Tar and reported the meeting. Tar wrote in his report afterwards that he thought Owens could be trusted: 'He is a stupid little man who is given to doing silly things at odd moments, but I am perfectly convinced that he is quite straightforward in the things which he gives me and the answers to my questions.'[33]

Walter Dicketts was waiting in the car outside Tar's home in Queen's Road, Norwood, for Snow to reappear. Dicketts had correctly surmised that this house was where Owens received his instructions, never realizing he would soon meet the occupant of that house, and their relationship would mark a major turning point in his life.

Later, Owens asked Dicketts to go with him to Euston Station the following day, where Dicketts was introduced to Charlie, who was 'obviously a German and appeared to be very scared'.[34] When they arrived at Owens' office in Sackville Street, Dicketts was asked to leave the room for ten minutes, and when he returned the table was piled with photographic enlargements of docks, airports and buildings, and a roll of minute photographic film.

Charlie told Owens he needed a new enlarger, which would cost £68, and Owens took a roll of £1 notes from his pocket and gave him the money. He then told Dicketts to take Charlie to the large photographic shop opposite Chappells Music Store in Bond Street and bring him back by taxi. Charlie became very frightened on the way, and asked Dicketts if they were being followed and whether he knew if his brother had been released from a concentration camp. Dicketts of course had no idea about any of this, but his suspicion about being in a nest of German spies had just been confirmed. 'Don't ask questions,' he told Charlie. 'Just follow the usual procedure.'[35]

When they arrived at the store, Dicketts told Charlie he was going to get a drink and watched as Charlie went inside. Dicketts had decided it was time for him to get help from the British Secret Service, so he crossed the road to Chappells Music Store and asked the manager to let him use his private phone on government business. The manager agreed, and Dicketts called the Air Ministry and asked to see Air Commodore Boyle, the Director of Intelligence, with whom he had served in the last war, but Boyle wasn't in. Dicketts refused to state his business over the phone, and said he would try again the following day.

On his way back to the photographic store, Dicketts spotted a tall man in a Burberry mackintosh, taking photographs of them. He reported this to Owens on his return, along with the information that Charlie had convinced the manager to exchange his old enlarger towards a new one. 'Well, he's got away with an easy £50,'[36] said Owens. Owens subsequently complained to Tar that he shouldn't have to pay for Charlie, as he should be getting the money directly from Germany. In the end, MI5 were forced to intervene, and insisted Charlie was doing dangerous work and Owens must refund him for all the equipment he had bought.

On Wednesday morning, 3 April 1940, Dicketts was ready to report Snow and his entire spy network. He left the office and began walking down Sackville Street, when he noticed a taxi draw out slowly, followed by another one immediately afterwards. Dicketts went into the Yorkshire Grey Hotel in Piccadilly and ordered a drink. After a short while, he came out and jumped into another taxi, telling the driver to take him to St James' Square, where-upon he noticed two taxis following behind them at intervals and asked the driver to stop the cab so he could take a closer look at the occupants. As he pulled over, the taxi driver said, 'You are being "tailed", gov'nor.'[37] Dicketts thanked him for the warning and said he was on government business.

Realizing it was too dangerous to go to the Air Ministry, Dicketts returned to the office and told Owens he had been followed. Owens didn't seem too worried until Dicketts mentioned the two taxis, whereupon Owens tele-phoned someone to report the facts, and asked that a special watch be kept. Dicketts realized Owens' network was larger and more highly organized than he had anticipated, and he would have to be very cautious indeed.

* * *

Tar decided it was time to find out what Owens was up to with Celery. He and Richman Stopford took Owens' business partner, retired MI5 officer William Rolph, to lunch and grilled him closely. It took them a considerable amount of time to extract the information they needed from Rolph, arous-ing their suspicion that Rolph knew a good deal more about Owens' activi-ties than he was willing to say. However, Rolph did provide them with a great deal of information about Celery, including his full name and address, and by the end of their discussion, it was clear Dicketts knew everything about Owens' activities. This presented MI5 with a serious problem: the informa-tion was top secret and could put their entire organisation at risk if it found its way into the wrong hands. They would have to do something to prevent Dicketts from talking about it to anyone.

Later that day, Owens asked Dicketts to drive him to the now familiar Queen's Road address to drop off some expensive aircraft books Owens had purchased earlier in the day. As Dicketts waited in the car, Owens was strongly admon-ished by Tar, who told him he was to 'cut adrift' from Dicketts and his business at Sackville Street as soon as possible.[38] He was to leave Rolph and Dicketts to take care of the business and get on with his proper work of espionage.

When Owens returned to the car, he appeared to be preoccupied and uncharacteristically 'refused to drink' when they got home, which Dicketts put down to concern over his trip to Antwerp the next day.[39] When it was time to go, Owens gave him a cheque for £10 and warned him again of the importance of secrecy.

The following morning, Thursday, 4 April, Dicketts collected Owens at 8 am and took him to Victoria Station to catch the train to Shoreham Aerodrome. Owens carried only a small attaché case and said practically nothing on the way. As the train was about to depart, Owens told Dicketts to go with Kay and stay at his flat to look after Lily, whom he would let know what day he was returning. The last thing he said to Dicketts was: 'If I am successful I shall be able to do anything I like. I'll give you instructions on my return and you will never have anything to worry about.'[40]

As soon as Owens departed, Dicketts went to the Air Ministry to report him as a German spy. He was shown up to the Intelligence Department, but was told by Air Commodore Boyle's assistant that Boyle was in conference and could not be disturbed. Dicketts asked to be put in touch with the British Secret Service, as he believed he was in the heart of the German espionage system in this country, but was interviewed by one of Boyle's officers instead. Dicketts was very frank about his past, saying he had got into trouble about twelve years ago and had gone to jail, and wanted to do something to regain his lost respectability. He had been 'asked to undertake a very peculiar job' by someone who was trading on his past history, and had pretended to fall in with the suggestion as he thought he might be an enemy agent.[41]

Having delivered his report, Dicketts left, and on his way out bumped into an old friend of his, Air Commodore Freddie West VC, and told him of the situation. West said he would let Boyle know what he had said, and would do whatever he could to help him get back to the Service. 'If you bring this off, you will be alright,' said West.[42]

Unfortunately, Boyle remembered Dicketts from his background in the Air Ministry during the First World War and didn't want to see him. It was never going to be easy to overcome his previous dishonesty, particularly in matters of secrecy and during a time of war.

When Tar was informed about Dicketts' visit to the Air Ministry, he immediately ordered Special Branch to find out all they could about Dicketts, along with his criminal record.

* * *

Three months earlier, Ritter had warned Owens to avoid travelling on the Continent during April. The fact that he had gone against his own advice by asking Owens to meet him in Antwerp in April, alerted MI5's suspicions that something was about to take place in Europe. Were the Germans using a more elaborate form of code and procedure as a result, they wondered? Tar and his team came up with a plan for Owens to try to elicit this information from Ritter, which could then be passed onto their codebreakers.

Owens was to appear to be very nervous about using his radio because there had been a number of articles appearing in the British press revealing the large amount of effort the British Government was taking to track down enemy agents operating wireless sets within Britain. He was to make rather a fuss about not receiving the spare parts for his wireless set he had been promised, because a recent breakdown had been very difficult to overcome.

In order to make his life in wartime Britain sound as normal as possible, Owens was to say that he couldn't move around as easily as before because of the new petrol restrictions, and that a number of his agents had been conscripted, leaving him very short-handed.

To build up trust in Owens in the eyes of the Germans, so he could be used as a channel for misinformation, MI5 supplied him with carefully prepared answers to Ritter's latest questionnaire. Some of this was good information (real intelligence) and some was chicken feed – information that was interesting but not significant. MI5's strategy was to entice the Germans to reveal their knowledge, or lack of it, through ever more detailed requests for specific information. This process also worked in reverse. If Owens, as head of a notional network of Welsh Nationalists, asked Ritter for information about the effects of a recent bombing raid, for example, the Germans would immediately treat this as significant. MI5 would later exploit this understanding to misdirect the Germans away from the true British objective. But for this type of strategic deception to work, MI5's double agents would have to be believed by the Germans, and to achieve that, MI5 and the double-cross team had to provide their agents with mostly true information. It was a real case of the needs of the many outweighed the needs of the few, and would ultimately contribute to the success of Operation Fortitude, in which the Allies convinced the Nazis that their D-Day invasion forces would land at Calais instead of Normandy.

Owens' trip to Antwerp to meet Ritter proved to be a productive one, and just as Tar had planned, Owens returned with new operational instructions with regard to his wireless, such as changing his call sign every day. He was also given other secret methods of communication: hiding microdots in the

'&' symbol of a company letterhead, and wrapping a message around a sweet between two pieces of paper, which could be disguised by rewrapping the sweet in its outer wrapper. A tin of sweets could hold several messages, and could be sent quite safely through the normal postal service.[43]

Ritter handed him two small blocks of wood containing detonators and told him that the explosives would be smuggled to him in England inside batteries. He gave him a new list of questions requesting information about specific aerodromes and the Bristol water supply, and paid him £369 in notes. A further £750 was deposited into an account in his name at the Guaranty Trust Company in New York, as Ritter didn't want him spending too much money in England.

Ritter took Owens completely by surprise when he asked him to recruit and train a suitable individual to take over from him, as 'Johnny cannot last forever'.[44] 'If he proves trustworthy, you are to bring him to Germany for training in espionage and particularly in sabotage.' Before Owens could ask 'what about me?', Ritter told Owens he would be offered an espionage job in Germany (which he later assured Tar he didn't want).

While Owens was away, Rainbow, an agent from another network, returned from a meeting with his German handlers and said he had been given a whole new set of contact addresses in Switzerland and Yugoslavia 'for use in an emergency'.[45] It was further confirmation that a major event in Europe was about to take place.

Owens had been home for just two days when, in the early morning of 9 April, Germany invaded Denmark and Norway on the pretext that occupation was necessary to preserve their neutrality. The Danish surrendered within two days, and after scattered resistance, Norway also surrendered on 2 May. The German blitzkrieg was swift and devastating. On 10 May, the Germans attacked Holland, Belgium and Luxemburg across a wide front. Faced with overwhelming forces, Luxembourg surrendered first, followed by the Dutch on the 14th after a devastating bombing attack on Rotterdam, and finally Belgium on the 27th.

Using the combined elements of speed and surprise, the Germans struck at strategic targets in a lightning attack. Stuka dive-bombers streaked out of the sky, sirens wailing, firing on their opponents and blowing up everything that would get in the way of their advancing tanks (communications, for-tifications, artillery, convoys and infantry concentrations, etc.). Before the defending armies even had a chance to recover their senses, German tanks, commanded by elite troops and supported by the infantry, attacked as the planes withdrew. Many of the Wehrmacht's soldiers were high on speed to give them courage and superhuman endurance, and between April and July 1940 'more than 35 million tablets of Pervitin and Isophan were shipped to the German army and air force'.[46]

Having successfully bypassed the heavily fortified Maginot Line along the French-German border, the Germans sped into Northern France and divided the French and British forces into two within just a few weeks. Civilians fleeing the fighting were fired on to create mayhem and hinder the progress of their own forces, and thousands of Allied troops retreated to the French Channel port of Dunkirk.

Across the English Channel, a stunned British military establishment struggled to determine how it was that events had so quickly gone so horribly wrong. The nation was in shock – everyone knew their country would be next. The public mood turned anxious and sombre as they waited for the German invasion to come.

Chapter 5

Loyal Rogue

'War is not only a matter of equipment, artillery, group
troops or air force; it is largely a matter of spirit, or morale.'
Chiang Kai-shek

Owens was still in Antwerp, where he had gone to meet Ritter in early
April 1940, when Special Branch got in touch with Tar and told
him there was an outstanding charge against Dicketts for obtaining
money in Wolverhampton by false pretences the previous year. Tar now had
the perfect excuse to arrest Dicketts and find out how much he knew about
Owens' activities, and what he intended to do with the information.

At 11.14 am on 6 April, MI5 watchers listened into a telephone conversation between Dicketts and Lily making arrangements for her to bring
Kay and meet him at the Buffet Cafe at Richmond Station at 12.05 pm to
go to see a show in Piccadilly.[1] Dicketts was surprised to be met instead
by plain clothes officers from the Criminal Investigation Department
(CID), who arrested him, and to whom he immediately revealed he
had valuable information to give them about a man with whom he had
recently been in touch.

Dicketts was taken to Richmond police station, where he gave his statement, while Tar and a couple of Special Branch detectives went around to
Dicketts' flat in Montague Road and searched it thoroughly. All they found
was a mass of business correspondence, and nothing of relevance to the
Snow case, so Tar decided to go to the police station and interview Dicketts
personally. When Dicketts realized that the pleasant young man in front of
him was none other than Owens' boss, the man Dicketts had been shad-
owing for several weeks, he was very surprised. Far from being a German
agent, Tar was an officer from MI5.

Tar afterwards wrote in his report that he was satisfied Dicketts 'wasn't a
Gestapo agent', and had already tried to report the facts to the Air Ministry:[2]

Although he is a rogue from a financial point of view and in other words a long-term fraud, he is loyal towards this country, his one motive being to try and get some sort of job in the Air Force and in order to do this he saw his chance when he stumbled by luck across Snow and his nest of German Agents.

Things progressed very quickly from there. Tar rang Mr Johnson, the Deputy Chief Constable of Birmingham, where he had served as a policeman in the early part of the 1930s, and told him briefly what had happened. Tar said he was keen to get rid of Dicketts for quite some time if possible, but was particularly anxious to prevent him from saying anything about Owens 'in the witness box' in a plea for leniency.[3]

At 8.00 pm, Dicketts was allowed to call Kay, who was staying at Owens' apartment in Kingston. Unable to tell Kay anything about his meeting with Tar, Dicketts concocted some story about calling from a lawyer's office as he had 'got into rather a business with one of his family' earlier that day.[4] He called her again at 10 pm and said he was finalizing the details 'of this wretched Wolverhampton business', and at midnight he told Kay he had to go up North and wouldn't be back for a few days. This last piece of information was at least true.

When Owens returned from Antwerp the following day, Dicketts wasn't there to meet him at Shoreham Airport as planned. He was in Birmingham, appearing before the magistrate at the Police Court, where he was let off with a £5 fine. Inspector Gagan sent a full report to Tar, saying Dicketts had repeatedly expressed a desire to be allowed to rejoin the Royal Air Force, and attached some notes Dicketts had written giving further information on Owens.[5] This included hand-drawn maps of the premises Owens visited regularly, including Tar's Queen's Road address.

Dicketts' notes contained snippets of information he had collected from his observations and conversations with Owens, which in the wrong hands could have revealed the identity of other British agents and their Secret Service handlers. This was dangerous information for Owens to be bandying about so easily, as it put the lives of these men and their families at risk – particularly at a time when Britain was facing the prospect of a German invasion. Owens had told Dicketts about a 'retired policeman' (GW)[6] who used to work for him, but whose nerve had cracked after a long third-degree interrogation by the Gestapo in Antwerp. Dicketts had also overheard Owens make several phone calls to a number and ask for extension 393, and speak to a man called Robbie (Tar) and one called Bill (possibly Billy Luke, an MI5 case officer). Extension 393 was the War Office number Owens used to contact Tar.

Dicketts' notes also revealed the full extent of Owens' boastful nature. He told Dicketts he was a crack shot with both revolvers and automatic guns, and had been forced to shoot a man in Antwerp 'when he became dangerous'.[7] On another occasion, Owens told Dicketts he could call on two million pounds or more if needed, and suggested if Dicketts were loyal to him, he would be 'on the winning side' and would be 'generously provided for all his life'.

With the court case concluded in Birmingham, Dicketts told Gagan he planned to go around to Owens' apartment and collect his wife. Tar immediately called Owens, and said he would only allow Dicketts to go around on one condition, that Owens wouldn't tell him that he knew Dicketts had reported him to the police. Owens agreed, and said they would only discuss business matters to do with winding up their financial affairs.

Later that evening, Tar received a phone call from one of the MI5 guards living at the Owens' apartment who said the two men had got into a tremendous argument, but had then become great friends again. This was not the objective Tar had in mind, so he immediately phoned the flat and insisted Dicketts 'remove himself at once, and never return there again'.[8] Tar told Dicketts that Inspector Gagan would keep in touch with him, and he would do what he could to influence the Air Ministry to give Dicketts some sort of job.

In his report afterwards Tar wrote:

> Celery fortunately is under the impression that we assisted him considerably in letting him off with a £5 fine in Birmingham. He has also been very strongly warned by Sergeant Gagan that he must not on any account mention that he has this information about Snow in his possession.

* * *

By the end of May 1940, having defeated and occupied Poland, Denmark, Norway, Luxembourg and Holland, Hitler's army burst through neutral

Belgium and stood poised for battle at Sedan on the northern border with France. Within four days, the Germans were victorious and around 400,000 soldiers of the British, French and Allied forces retreated to the beaches of Dunkirk for evacuation before the enemy closed their pincers.

A savage rearguard action was fought to buy their comrades time to organize a proper evacuation, and many sacrificed their lives in the process. Under constant fire from German bombers, the evacuation was a slow and difficult process, as most of the port facilities at Dunkirk had been destroyed. Troops had to be taken off what little harbour facilities remained and with great difficulty from the beach itself. Hundreds of vessels from the Royal Navy and a rag-tag flotilla of over 800 civilian vessels – comprised of yachts, dinghies, fishing boats, pleasure craft, paddle steamers and ferries – sped across the English Channel to rescue as many troops as possible. Under constant attack from Stuka dive bombers and artillery fire, these little ships went heroically back and forth, ferrying troops to the larger Royal Navy and passenger ships waiting offshore.

The RAF and Luftwaffe were engaged in deadly duels in the skies above, and everything seemed to be on fire – cars, buildings, ships and even an oil terminal. Black smoke covered the beach, and as far as the eye could see, abandoned equipment lay scattered on the sand – countless tons of stores and ammunition, thousands of vehicles, motorcycles and guns. The miracle of Dunkirk, as it was later called, rescued 338,226 Allied troops; 68,000 British soldiers were killed, wounded or taken prisoner, the RAF lost 106 aircraft and the Royal Navy 243 ships. [9]

The loss of so many men and their valuable equipment created an enormous shortage in Britain, making it very vulnerable to invasion. The Soviet Union was allied to Germany and neutral America could offer little help in what they considered to be a European war. The international community believed Britain's will to fight would collapse after Dunkirk, but hadn't counted on its determination.

For the tired, dishevelled and weaponless troops who were welcomed as heroes in Dover, many felt humiliated by their defeat. They had been outflanked and outmanoeuvred by a superior German army and cornered in Dunkirk. Fighting against the defeatism and lethargy in his Cabinet and in the country, an upbeat but cautious Winston Churchill – only recently appointed as Prime Minister after Chamberlain's resignation – warned: 'We must be very careful not to assign to this deliverance the attributes of a victory. Wars are not won by evacuations.'[10]

With so many European countries conquered, Hitler stood at the pinnacle of his power. He focused his attention on Britain, certain that they would accept his magnanimous offer to allow them to hang on to their empire throughout the world, provided they publicly acknowledged his right to rule a Nazified Europe without interference. When Britain's Foreign Secretary, Lord Halifax, pushed for a peace treaty, he was defeated in the Cabinet by Winston Churchill, who delivered an impassioned speech. He argued that Hitler would view any discussion of peace as an admission of defeat, and in any event could never be trusted to honour the terms of a negotiated treaty:

> Hitler knows that he will have to break us in this island or lose the war. If we can stand up to him all Europe may be free, and the life of the world may move forward into broad, sunlit uplands; but if we fail, then the whole world will sink into the abyss of a new Dark Age. Let us therefore brace ourselves to our duties and so bear ourselves that, if the British Empire and its Commonwealth last for a thousand years, men will still say: 'This was their finest hour.'[11]

The Cabinet agreed – Britain would fight to the death. Churchill flatly refused to discuss anything with Hitler or his representatives, and told his people:

> We shall defend our island whatever the cost may be. We shall fight on the beaches, we shall fight on the landing grounds, we shall fight in the fields and in the streets, we shall fight in the hills. We shall never surrender.[12]

Furious at such defiance, Hitler assembled his generals on 16 July and ordered them to plan for the conquest of Britain.

* * *

With so many formerly neutral European countries now under Nazi occupation, rendering a visit by Owens impossible, Ritter had come up with an incredible scheme to meet with his number one spy in Britain. He told

Owens to get hold of a fishing trawler and make for a rendezvous point in the middle of the North Sea, where Ritter would arrive by submarine or seaplane. Ritter would deliver sabotage equipment and collect the new agent he asked Owens to find back in October 1939.[13] This agent was to take over Owens' role in England, and Ritter wanted to begin his sabotage training as quickly as possible. Once this new agent was fully operational, Owens would be brought to Germany, where he would be employed in some sort of espionage capacity.

MI5 thoroughly debated the implications of Ritter's plan, and concluded that if he trusted Owens not to set up a trap to capture him, then Ritter may still believe Owens was operating freely and not under British control. Even if Ritter was aware that Owens was controlled and was using him as a vehicle to plant misinformation on the British, it would still be useful to go ahead with the North Sea rendezvous. Tar and his team didn't want to risk losing access to the regular requests for information Ritter asked of Owens, which they compared to information from other sources to try to establish what the enemy was up to. Importantly, Owens' regular radio communications with the Ast. Hamburg section of the Abwehr allowed British codebreakers to gain access to the Abwehr's secret Enigma settings for the day.

Trust was a quality Tar needed in the man who would accompany Owens, and at first sight, the man he selected seemed to be an odd choice for such a vital mission. Sam McCarthy was an ex-drug smuggler, petty criminal and conman who had reformed and become a reliable and honest informer for MI5. His background was ideal to keep an eye on the wily Owens, as McCarthy would not hesitate to report any suspicions he had about his true allegiances. McCarthy was given the codename Biscuit and told to go to the Marlborough pub in Richmond, where Owens was a regular, and become acquainted with him as if their meeting was purely by chance. Owens was a 'tremendous talker', Tar told him, and McCarthy was to say that he was thinking of coming to stay in Richmond.[14] When he got into Owens' confidence, McCarthy was to allow himself to become recruited as a German spy.

McCarthy managed to become acquainted with Owens as instructed, and as anticipated, Owens put him forward to Tar as a potential sabotage agent he could introduce to Ritter. Tar agreed and said he would look into McCarthy's credentials, and after a respectable period of time he reported back to Owens that 'he was most satisfactory in every way'.[15]

Tar found a fishing trawler, the *Barbados*, and a trustworthy and willing crew to man it, whose mission, he told the captain, would be to take two people to a certain rendezvous in the North Sea, where they would meet a German submarine, seaplane or trawler. There would be a short conversation and 'then one or two of our side would not return'.[16]

On Saturday morning, 18 May 1940, Tar got in touch with Owens and asked him if he had made up his mind about taking McCarthy with him. Owens said he wasn't quite sure if McCarthy was the right kind of person, but with time running short, Tar suggested the three of them met in Richmond Park at 4 pm, if Owens decided to go ahead. Owens turned up with McCarthy, and the three of them developed a cover story to tell Ritter about how Owens and McCarthy met and what they discussed, the information they should tell him about McCarthy's real background and his assumed cover, what Owens had already told McCarthy about his history and background with Ritter, and what the Germans would expect of McCarthy.

At a certain point in the meeting, Tar drew Owens to one side and asked him if he was sure McCarthy was a suitable person to take to the rendezvous. Owens said, 'He would fit the bill admirably, and it was just as well that he was a greenhorn at this type of work.'[17] Tar asked Owens to give McCarthy some money to settle his affairs before leaving, but Owens said he had very little cash. Tar wondered why Owens had lied. He had previously seen Owens' wallet, which was bulging with notes about half an inch thick. Tar said nothing about this to Owens, but suggested he give McCarthy a lift in his own car so he could find out more about him. Owens readily agreed, unaware that Tar's real purpose was to get McCarthy on his own so he could give his report.

What McCarthy had to say was worrying. It seemed as if Owens was doing his utmost to convince McCarthy he was a German agent. McCarthy had asked Owens how he should expect to be treated by the Germans and how much he would be paid, and Owens had told him not to worry because 'the Germans were all very fine people and he would be looked after 100%'.[18]

Owens told McCarthy the real reason he had refused Tar's request to give McCarthy some money in the park, was because he didn't want Tar to know he had any. He told McCarthy he was going to try to get as much money out of Tar as possible. 'Why shouldn't he pay, after all?' asked Owens.[19] 'Tar was earning at least £5,000 and pocketing the money he was given by the office to pay him. … He and a good many others in MI5 were for it as soon as the Germans started landing in this country,' Owens told McCarthy.

Owens told McCarthy he intended to introduce him to the Germans as a member of MI5 who was working for Tar Robertson. McCarthy asked Owens if he didn't think that was rather dangerous, but Owens told him not to worry about it – the Germans knew all about his connection with Robertson and exactly what he was doing.

McCarthy was certain Owens didn't realize he was an MI5 plant, he told Tar, but he was convinced Owens was pro-Nazi and working for the Germans.

'It is quite clear that Snow is in earnest and is definitely dangerous,' Tar wrote in his report afterwards.[20] He considered calling off the whole venture, but decided to go ahead after putting several significant changes into effect immediately. Tar called the captain of the *Barbados* and gave him some new instructions. He said Owens was double-crossing them and McCarthy was in their confidence. He was to take the trawler out and fish in the vicinity until the early afternoon of 23 May, whereupon they should head for a point on the western edge of the fishing grounds, leading Owens to believe they were making for the rendezvous at the appointed time. The trawler should pretend to be hanging about for an hour or so after dark, and when nothing turned up, it was to head for home immediately. Owens would think something had gone wrong on the German end and would not be suspicious.

Guy Liddell, head of counter-espionage at MI5, later wrote: 'Meanwhile a submarine would play about in the vicinity of the rendezvous and if another submarine turned up it would be torpedoed, and if it was a trawler it would be captured – hopefully with Ritter on board. Owens would be arrested when he got back and charged with espionage.'[21]

On the due day, Owens and McCarthy travelled by train to the harbour port of Grimsby in Lincolnshire. Owens took copious notes of everything he saw from the carriage window, which he said he was going to hand over to the Germans. Owens continued to run down MI5, saying what a rotten organization it was. The observant McCarthy spotted an unauthorized document among the photographs MI5 had given Owens to show Ritter, and memorized the title. Later that evening, McCarthy managed to evade Owens and phoned Tar to tell him what had taken place during the journey, and about the presence of the document. Tar confirmed that it had not been authorized and was definitely suspicious.

In the early morning of 20 May, the trawler *Barbados* set sail as planned, heading for the cod and herring-rich fishing grounds of a vast and shallow area known as Dogger Bank some 100km off the north-east coast of England. On board, Owens peppered the captain with questions about convoys and what weapons they had on board. Because Owens scanned the skies constantly and oddly asked the mate if he was a German agent, McCarthy became suspicious that Owens expected an early contact to be made. McCarthy's concern seemed to be justified, as a seaplane appeared from nowhere at 5.15 pm, circled the trawler and then flew off again. [22] Unfortunately, the captain wasn't able to identify the markings on the aircraft. He thought they might have been British, except for the fact they were in the wrong place, on the tail instead of the fuselage.

Shortly after midnight on Tuesday, 21 May, the captain of the *Barbados* had just started to lay his nets for a short trawl when the seaplane returned. It circled low, shooting green starlights from port, starboard and rear and giving out calling-up signals on its lamp. As the time and place were different to what had been previously arranged, (Thursday, 23 May), McCarthy was convinced Owens had betrayed them and would soon reveal McCarthy to Ritter as an agent of MI5 to increase his standing with the Germans. Facing torture and execution if captured, McCarthy, with the help of the captain and the mate, locked a protesting and hung-over Owens in his cabin. Once Owens was tied up, they searched him and found the unauthorized document McCarthy had seen on the train. Owens immediately protested his innocence, to which McCarthy responded, 'Heil Hitler, you bastard', and ordered the captain to douse the trawler's lights and head for home. [23]

Owens was taken off the ship on arrival and placed in the Naval Prison on board HMS *Corunia*. He denied knowing McCarthy was working for MI5 and said he had pretended to be a German spy to protect himself. Owens said he was 'never going to allow the meeting to take place' as he thought McCarthy was a German agent who was leading him into a trap. [24]

'I told him quite straight that I considered that he was double-crossing me, which he flatly denied,' Tar wrote afterwards. [25] In fact, Tar was finding it exceedingly difficult to make up his mind one way or another if that really was the case.

'Snow's mind is a very odd affair and it does not work on logical lines, and the arguments which he put up for the things which he had said to Biscuit, were not exactly convincing, but at the same time seemed to me to hold a certain amount of water.'

Despite Tar's misgivings, he wasn't going to give up on capturing Ritter yet. He told Owens he was going straight back to the rendezvous point, but this time there would be a crew of seventeen naval ratings on board, and if there was any sign that he was double-crossing at the time of the rendezvous, he would probably never see this country again. If, on the other hand, he was instrumental in inveigling Ritter on board the ship so they could capture him, he would reconsider his case. In the meantime, Tar said he was perfectly convinced that he was double-crossing MI5, and had already given his name to the Germans.

Although the trawler returned to 'the correct position of the rendezvous on the 23rd which was the actual night for the meeting', there was no sign of any enemy aircraft or submarine.[26] As there was a fog in the area, Owens' radio was used to inform Ritter that they were at the correct place at the correct time, but must have missed him due to the fog.

In his autobiography, written in 1972, Ritter's account was completely different. He said the night was clear and the visibility was good, and there were even some low-hanging clouds they could disappear into if a British aircraft approached. When Ritter's seaplane, a Dornier 18, with its armour-plating removed to save fuel, reached the rendezvous point, they dived down to get a good view of the open sea, but not a single boat could be seen far and wide. The Germans rechecked their measurements but the position was accurate, and after a while they gave up searching and went back to Germany, where they checked their coordinates once more, and came to the conclusion that it wasn't their fault. Meanwhile, Owens had radioed: 'Had to stay under cover. Captain under observation. Report follows.'[27]

Although Ritter's account was drawn from memory, MI5's instructions remain in Owens' security services file for 27 June 1940. Tar gave instructions to Burton, Owens' radio operator, to send a message to Ritter, asking him the reason why he didn't make it to the rendezvous on Thursday, and to send money so Owens' could pay the 'Captain's wages'.[28]

Shortly before publication of his autobiography (written from memory), Ritter was able to get hold of a recently published copy of John Masterman's book *The Double Cross System in the War of 1939 to 1945*. His reaction to

MI5's version of the events was to defend the loyalty of Owens. Ritter said: 'There was no aircraft cruising over the cutter in order to warn it by means of light signals. The captain simply had gotten cold feet.'[29] He believed Biscuit (McCarthy) had deceived the British, and couldn't understand why he would invent such a story.

When the trawler returned empty-handed for the second time, Owens repeatedly denied that he was double-crossing, but was silent when Tar asked him, 'If you really believed McCarthy was a German spy – then why would you be taking a German spy to Germany if he really was one?' Owens had no answer to this, and neither could he explain why he hadn't reported his suspicions beforehand. He implored Tar to give him one more chance, as he was sure they could get Ritter.

After reviewing all the facts, MI5 came to believe that the whole botch-up was due to a genuine misunderstanding between Owens and McCarthy, who both believed the other to be a German spy. Their tactic of keeping both men in the dark about their mutual roles with MI5 had backfired, and without sufficient evidence to bring a case against Owens, he was released the next day.

* * *

After three weeks of anxious waiting, Dicketts wrote to Tar on 29 April asking for his assistance in persuading the Air Ministry to let him back into the service:

> I have built great hopes on the promise you so kindly gave me. I want more than anything to get back in the service, and I feel that my past experience, languages, etc., would surely be of use in the present war. I also believe that you will agree that I have shown my anxiety to make good and to help my country, without thought of myself.[30]

Tar couldn't help but notice that Dicketts had some useful skills, as he continued:

> My French is fluent and colloquial. My German could be polished up in my own time in a month or two. I know Germany and France extremely well, and my work at the end of the last war had to do with the German Islands and Northern Seaboard. I can drive any kind of

car, handle any small boat, sail or motor-craft, and don't mind risk or danger. I hope you will believe that I would not, under any circumstances, let you or the Service down.

Tar wrote to Group Captain F.G. Stammers OBE at the Air Ministry asking to see Dicketts' service record: 'I understand that he had some connection with the Air Ministry Intelligence in the last war.'[31]

When six weeks had passed and nothing appeared to have been done about getting Dicketts a job anywhere, his financial situation had so deteriorated that he wrote to Air Commodore 'Archie' Boyle, Director of Intelligence, whom he had known in the previous war. He outlined his qualifications and asked to be allowed to re-enter the service:

> If it is not possible to place me in the Royal Air Force, I shall be most grateful if you will be kind enough to forward the resume to MI5. I would, however much prefer to come back to the RAF, in any branch whatever its activities, and suggest the motor-boat section on account of my knowledge of motor-craft & Eastern & Southern coasts and Waterways. [32]

Dicketts told Tar he spoke fluent colloquial French, and that one month's refresher course would 'make my German fluent'.[33] But Dicketts' skills were not enough to undo the prejudice against him. As far as his former brothers-in-arms were concerned, once a criminal, always a criminal. Dicketts would not be given a second chance, and his letter to Air Commodore Boyle was forwarded to Tar by Boyle's assistant, Flying Office Baring, with a terse note: 'D of I [Director of Intelligence] can do nothing but consider that MI5 should deal with his application.'[34] Tar wrote back to Baring apologizing for having caused this trouble and said he would warn Dicketts from going anywhere near the Air Ministry in the future.

By 11 June, Dicketts was desperate. He wrote to Tar asking for five minutes of his time:

> I find it very difficult to talk to you naturally on account of your fore knowledge of my life 11 years ago. I owe £2 [around £100 today] for my room, and I have nothing at all for my wife or my small son who

is at Bristol. I have 14 pawn tickets and nothing left to pawn. I am afraid of jeopardising my future by writing in this way, or being a nuisance to you, but the situation is so urgent that I cannot help it.[35]

Dicketts explained that his commercial ventures with Owens had provided him with the opportunity to earn an income, and despite being given a whole set of promises and assurances that something would be done to help him, nothing at all had happened. Together with the unwillingness of the authorities to let him re-enter the Services, it had brought him to a point of financial desperation. Dicketts said he was grateful for everything Tar was doing to help him, but wondered if there was some sort of service fund that could tide him over during his immediate crisis. He added: 'Lastly, will you please believe that I am perfectly honest and sincere, that I am not likely to do anything wrong and would not let you down in any way, in any job. I have several capabilities – I only want to work.'[36]

Tar sent him a brief note enclosing £3 'to tide him over'.[37] A relieved Dicketts wrote to Tar saying he was 'more than grateful I can tell you, and I hope you will let me repay it when I am on my feet again'. It was the first time Tar sent Dicketts money, and it occurred at a point when his faith in Owens was at its lowest, following Rolph's death and the failed trawler incident. It was evident Tar had something in mind for Dicketts as he drip-fed him with cash for the next five months.

Ten days later, Tar wrote to Dicketts saying he had not lost sight of getting him a job somewhere, and enclosed a further £3. Dicketts offered to do something to earn the money, like chauffeuring Tar around, hotting up (boosting the performance) or overhauling his car, translating or copying. Dicketts said he was willing to risk everything, do any journey, any assignment, whatever, on behalf of Tar and his department, and could report within one to two hours' notice.

Despite his appalling financial situation, Dicketts did not return to crime. He knew he had only one chance to redeem himself with Tar, and continued to seek out and offer suggestions about ways in which he could be useful. Having heard in June 1941 that the Emperor Haile Selassie was thinking of returning to Ethiopia with British aid to raise his people up against the Italians, Dicketts offered to help, saying he had met and done business with the emperor in the past.

There were no civilian jobs available and Dicketts needed a valid identity card to apply for government or service positions. Due to the large number of refugees flooding into Britain, the authorities now required persons of authority to validate a person's identity, and Dicketts approached Tar. Unfortunately, Tar wasn't authorized to do this. Without an identity card, Dicketts couldn't obtain a ration card, which meant he couldn't buy meat, butter, sugar, tea, jam, margarine, eggs, cheese, clothing and coal. Dicketts' situation was dire, and the only money he had to live off came from Tar.

* * *

When Owens returned to Grimsby from the North Sea in May 1940, he was imprisoned in HMS *Corunia*, where he was visited by Tar and McCarthy. When McCarthy had finished questioning Owens about various aspects of the voyage and his reasons for suspecting McCarthy was a German agent, Tar asked Owens, 'Why did you take a copy of the IP Club List [Intelligence and Police Staffs of the Army, Navy and Air Force] with you on the trawler?'

'Rolph asked me to sell it to the Germans for £2,000,' Owens replied.[38] 'He's extremely hard up for cash, and already owes me £150.' According to Owens, his business partner William Rolph,[39] a 64-year-old retired First World War MI5 officer, wasn't happy with the way MI5 was being run and had made disparaging remarks about Hinchley-Cooke and Tar in particular. Rolph told Owens that he wasn't being paid enough, and suggested that they should start 'looking after themselves'.[40]

Tar and Richman Stopford immediately went to see Rolph at the office he shared with Owens in Sackville Street, and told him what Owens had said. At this, Rolph became extremely agitated and said he had no idea how Owens could have obtained that document, as he always kept it locked inside his safe.

Tar called his bluff and said he would have Owens brought over so Rolph could confront him face-to-face. As they waited for Owens to arrive, Rolph appeared to be searching for something in his desk and Stopford saw him tear something up and conceal it in his hand. Rolph stood up and went out of the office, shouting instructions to his cleaning boy, with Stopford hot on his heels and seeing Rolph throw something into a dustbin in the hallway.

Owens arrived shortly afterwards and was asked to repeat what he had told Tar. 'I did nothing of the sort,' said Rolph. 'You must have stolen it from my safe when my back was turned.' Owens reminded Rolph that they had 'also arranged a code together',[41] at which point Stopford calmly walked over to the bin and collected the evidence, which turned out to be the code just mentioned, and confronted Rolph with it. After many lies and excuses, Rolph eventually confessed and said he had been recruited into the Abwehr by Owens and had asked him to sell the IP List to the Germans.

Shamed and disgraced, and facing charges of espionage, Rolph went back to his house in Dover Street and gassed himself by placing his head inside the oven. MI5 realized that if the Abwehr found out Rolph had committed suicide, they would assume his cover had been blown, and by association Owens' entire network – currently comprised of GW, Biscuit, Summer, Tate and Charlie – would also be blown. Bentley Purchase, the local coroner, was asked to falsify Rolph's death certificate, saying he had died of a rupture of the aorta, and disaster was averted.[42] Coincidence or not, Bentley Purchase also signed Dicketts' death certificate.

Tar and Stopford realized they had insufficient evidence to bring a case against Owens, and he was allowed to go home to his apartment. However, it was virtually house arrest as Owens wasn't 'allowed out without instructions' from Tar,[43] and he was closely guarded by MI5's Mr Williams and his radio operator, Maurice Burton. Tar had Owens' phone disconnected and a microphone was installed in his apartment so MI5 could listen into his conversations with Lily.

Tar went around to Owens' apartment and gave him a severe dressing down. Tar said he had been persuaded against his better judgement to allow McCarthy to go ahead with upcoming plans to meet Ritter in Portugal in late July, and was concerned about McCarthy's safety. He said he wasn't sure if Owens had already double-crossed McCarthy or would do so at his next meeting with Ritter. Tar added:

> I'm not at all satisfied with your conduct, and from now on, I shall have nothing to do with you personally. … McCarthy is my agent and he is 100 per cent honest, loyal and patriotic and if you wish to communicate with me in future, you shall have to do so through him.[44]

Tar said he had received a signed confession from William Rolph, and just as he was leaving the room told Owens that Rolph was dead. Before Owens could ask any questions or register any surprise, Tar had gone.

* * *

While the debacle with Owens was progressing, Tar not only continued to drip-feed Dicketts with cash, but mysteriously appears to have employed him in some unknown task. In his letter to Tar on 29 June, Dicketts was upset he hadn't heard anything further from him:

> Gagan told me himself, and also passed on a message from you, to the effect that I had done a really good service to the country. I had also honestly thought that I was doing good work and had hoped to carry it on further and complete the job up North and in the provinces.[45] Will you therefore, be kind enough to give me a letter of recommendation to the effect - without of course, specifying the nature of the services rendered. With an official letter of this kind I could apply for one of the following: Sergeant Pilot in the Air Force; Pioneer Corps – with reasonable chance of quick promotion; civil or military coastal defence work or Coastal Motor Boat Service RAF.
>
> I'm sorry for being such a darned nuisance, but I am still living on the edge of worry and hope combined, and reliant on your generosity. I am neither lazy nor dishonest – and am still willing and anxious to do anything, go anywhere and risk everything. If you can only give me an opening, I will make something of it. With my thanks for your patience.[46]

A week later, Dicketts hadn't heard anything and wrote to Tar to ask for the letter of recommendation to show to Lord Beaverbrook, the energetic media baron and friend of Churchill, in charge of aircraft production at the time. A friend of his had suggested he might be able to get Dicketts an interview with Beaverbrook. 'As he is a cabinet minister, may I tell him of the events of the last four months?' asked Dicketts. 'I shall do nothing without your permission, but shall be very glad if you will let me have a reply by Monday as I am afraid I shall have to leave my room on Tuesday.'[47]

This time, the response was immediate: Tar said he would much rather Dicketts 'did not disclose any of the past circumstances to Lord Beaverbrook, as the less said to anyone the better … I'm still doing all I can to get you some sort of job, but unfortunately these things are terribly slow.'[48]

What Tar didn't say, was that he had written to Colonel [redacted] at SIS, asking if Dicketts could be of any use to him. He said that although Dicketts had a criminal record for fraud, 'he had been on the level for the last nine or ten years'.[49] He was a man who would be prepared to do anything, and as far as Tar could see, had fairly reasonable qualifications and spoke one or two languages. His opinion of Dicketts was that 'he was absolutely loyal to this country, and as long as he wasn't given large sums of money to play with, he should be perfectly satisfactory'. Tar would even go so far as to say that 'Dicketts is a man who is capable of keeping his mouth shut as he happened to bump into a double cross agent of his, and as far as he knew, had not mentioned a word about it to anyone.'[50]

Unfortunately, the intended recipient of Tar's letter never received it. The letter arrived in the general post and was read by Valentine Vivian, the vice-chief of SIS, who showed it to CSS (Chief of the Secret Service), who in turn asked Vivian to send it to Tar's boss, Guy Liddell, so he could have a word with him about the 'rather doubtful propriety' in asking them to consider someone with a criminal record for employment.[51] Ironically, Vivian was sharply criticized in later life for fostering the career of the Secret Service's worst communist and traitor, Kim Philby, after he joined SIS in 1940. Vivian wrote:

> CSS [Sir Stewart Menzies] is most anxious that you should not think he is being rigid or censorious. But you know yourself what troubles there have been over some of D's people, and CSS would rather that any chance of D employing another crook should be made as difficult as possible.

'D' was the assignation of the imaginative and enthusiastic Colonel Laurence Grand, who signed all his communication as such. Grand established SIS's Section D in 1938 to carry out sabotage, subversion and propaganda to undermine Germany's economy and war potential. His modus operandi was very different to the 'old guard', and there was a great deal of tension and mistrust between the two. In the summer of 1940, as Tar was putting Dicketts' case forward, Section D merged with two other SIS departments to form the SOE (Special Operations Executive). Churchill had directed SOE to 'set Europe ablaze' through sabotage and disruption, creating mayhem and confusion, and ultimately revolt, behind enemy lines.

There were qualities in people with criminal backgrounds that made them suitable for their roles as agents, and Tar already had one ex-con on his payroll, Sam McCarthy (Biscuit). He would soon employ Eddie Chapman (Zigzag), a professional criminal and blackmailer - and member of the Jelly Gang ,whose specialty was in blowing up safes - who became one of MI5's most successful agents. Chapman's activities under MI5's control so impressed the Germans that he was awarded an Iron Cross, their highest award for bravery.

There was a lot going on behind the scenes that Tar couldn't explain to Dicketts when he wrote to him in August:

> I am terribly sorry that I have not been able to do anything in con-
> nection with obtaining a job for you, but I trust the enclosed [£5]
> will assist you. ... I hope however, you will continue to keep in touch
> with me and let me know how you progress. If there is anything I can
> do in connection with helping you in any specific case where I can
> get in touch with an individual, I should be only too ready to do so.[52]

It was an agonizingly slow financial death, but Dicketts still hung on in hope. But if the day came when Tar stopped sending him cash, even that would be lost.

Chapter 6

Parachutes and Dinghies

'It is essential to seek out enemy agents who have come to conduct espionage against you and to bribe them to serve you. Give them instructions and care for them. Thus doubled agents are recruited and used.' Sun Tzu, The Art of War

By the summer of 1940, Hitler stood at the height of his power. Worshipped by his people and feared by his enemies, the victorious megalomaniac turned his attention to his one and only remaining foe – the island kingdom of Great Britain. Convinced the British would accept his magnanimous offer to allow them to retain their empire around the world, provided they publicly acknowledged his right to lead a Nazi-ruled Europe, Hitler was profoundly shocked when Winston Churchill flatly refused to talk to him or his Nazi representatives.

On 3 July, still smarting from Dunkirk and stung by the Vichy French collaboration with the Nazis, Churchill ordered British warships to attack and sink the French fleet at the port of Mers-el-Kebir in Algeria to prevent the Germans gaining control of them. It was a desperate time that called for desperate measures. Facing an imminent invasion, with its European allies defeated, Britain's act of self-preservation signalled to the world, and particularly to the USA, that the war would not be over within months, and that the British would fight to the death.

Furious at such blatant and unprecedented defiance, Hitler assembled the Wehrmacht High Command and ordered them to plan for the conquest of Britain. His generals were not convinced: they knew the British Royal Navy vastly outnumbered their own Kriegsmarine, and a seaborne invasion would be blasted out of the water before it even reached the shore unless the Germans dominated the skies above it. Reichsmarschall Herman Göring, Chief of the Luftwaffe, seized the moment to curry favour in the eye of his beloved Führer, boasting that his warplanes alone could force Churchill to his knees.

What became known as the Battle of Britain began on 10 July, when the first Luftwaffe bombers began attacking British convoys in the English Channel and Royal Navy forces around the coast of Britain. Churchill's rallying BBC broadcast to the British people in response to German invasion plans was clearly intended for the ears of Hitler, as well as those of his fellow countrymen:

> Should the invader come to Britain, there will be no placid lying down of the people in submission before him, as we have seen, alas, in other countries. We shall defend every village, every town, and every city. The vast mass of London itself, fought street by street, could easily devour an entire hostile army; and we would rather see London laid in ruins and ashes than that it should be tamely and abjectly enslaved.[1]

On 16 July, Hitler gave his backing to an invasion, codenamed Operation SEALION (*Seelöwe*), which would take place on 15 September (provided the Luftwaffe controlled the skies). Admiral Wilhelm Canaris, head of the Abwehr, was given just over two months to establish a brand-new spy network in England, codenamed LENA, to prepare the way for the invasion. The man he appointed to head Operation LENA was none other than Owens' spymaster, Captain Nikolaus Ritter.

It was a lucky break for the British double-cross team, and made the Snow network more valuable than ever. Ritter was responsible for recruiting and training spies to enter Britain as pre-invasion scouts. They were given radios to report back on the location of landmines, troops, frequency of patrols, the best beaches to land on, places where gliders and parachutists could land and any other defensive preparations.

On 24 July, McCarthy travelled alone to meet Ritter in neutral Portugal. Since Tar didn't trust Owens, he left it to the last minute to send a message to Ritter, saying Owens 'had been taken off the boat due to illness'.[2] He had thoroughly briefed McCarthy beforehand on what to tell Ritter about the work he did in Britain, and that done by Owens.

Tar said that despite McCarthy's personal feelings, he must be convincing in his defence of Owens. Sure enough, Ritter tried to elicit information from McCarthy about Owens, saying he thought Owens was becoming rather slack. McCarthy gave Ritter a glowing account of Owens' activities, saying Owens wasn't able to get about as much as before because he had to be on the radio every night, and was concerned about leaving his pregnant girlfriend Lily alone. Tar's strategy was to encourage Ritter to send someone to help Owens. The more agents Owens controlled, the higher his stature with the Abwehr, which MI5 would then exploit to gain further insights into what the Germans were up to, and to control what information they sent to the Abwehr.

Exactly as Tar had anticipated, Ritter brought up the trawler incident. McCarthy told him that he and Owens had shown up in the trawler, but the weather was very foggy and no-one had appeared. In contradiction to what he would later say in his 1972 memoirs, Ritter said they were there on Thursday night (the night Owens told MI5 the meeting was arranged) and it was his plane that had circled the trawler on the previous Monday night.[3]

Ritter asked McCarthy a number of detailed questions about British defensive measures and seemed very pleased with his information, despite the fact it had been exaggerated to give the impression they were very strong. 'When you get back, I want you to find out as much as you can about British aircraft, and to find a suitable place in Wales where sabotage equipment could be dropped by parachute,' said Ritter.

In the summer of 1940, Ritter suddenly started sending Owens advance warning of the arrival of the first LENA invasion spies. Although MI5 attributed this to Ritter's belief in Owens, there was another factor. Ritter's section was the only one in the entire Abwehr Air Intelligence division that had a secret transmitter in England – and his star agent, Johnny, was their 'single direct contact with England'.[4] If Ritter had any doubts about Owens' loyalty, this was not the time to raise it. Admiral Canaris' Abwehr was in competition with Reinhardt Heydrich's Sicherheitsdienst (SD), who wanted to take over control of all intelligence-gathering operations.

Ritter was very busy trying to find and select volunteers who were ready to parachute into England or arrive via fishing boat from Belgium, and on 22 August asked Owens to establish a 'secret residence in Swansea' for three German spies who were due to arrive shortly.[5] MI5 found a suitable house and instructed Owens' radio operator to tell Ritter they had done so, and his agents should contact GW (Gwilym Williams, the MI5 double agent) on arrival.

Next, Ritter contacted Charlie – MI5's double agent Charles Eschborn – and asked if he would be willing to have a German radio expert stay with him. This was a tricky situation for MI5, as Charlie was now under their control, so they made up an excuse and Charlie found an alternative residence instead. In the end, Ritter never used either house, and MI5 gave the houses up.

Meanwhile, Ritter was flying by the seat of his pants. He later recalled: 'There were no models we could use for guidance. Everything had to be created from scratch, and no time was to be lost.'[6] In September 1940, his first four spies were ready. They were split into two pairs and travelled aboard fishing trawlers which were towed by German minesweepers until they were within a mile of the British coastline. From there, they were released into rubber dinghies and rowed quietly ashore.

The first pair, Carl Meier and Charles Van Den Kieboom, landed on the Kent coast at Dymchurch, and the other pair, Carl Waldeberg and Sjoerd Pons, around 6 miles further south at Lydd-on-Sea. Due to the alertness of an Air Raid Warden, the first pair were captured the next day, and the other two almost immediately by two British officers who thought their behaviour was suspicious and alerted the police. All four spies were sent for interrogation to MI5's secret Camp 020, the British interrogation centre located inside a gloomy Victorian mansion in Ham Common, a village outside London, where details of their training soon emerged. Ritter's agents had received a crash course in wireless communication, Morse and other codes, and were trained to identify the uniforms and rank of British service personnel, and the make and model of British vehicles and armaments - which they would use to report back location and other intelligence data to Germany. All but one of these spies were executed; Dutchman Sjord Pons escaped death after convincing the British that he had been forced into service by the Germans.

Ritter's next two volunteers were of German extraction, and spoke fairly good English. Wulf Schmidt was a Dane and Gösta Caroli a Finn, and they were both good-looking young men. According to Ritter, Schmidt was about 24 years old, quite tall, slim and with dark-blond hair and energetic facial features, whilst Caroli was older and taller, with clear blue eyes that inspired Ritter's confidence.[7] Ritter liked both of them, and felt badly deep inside as he thought about the dangers they would be facing. He told Schmidt and Caroli what their mission was, and said their training would begin the next day.

'You can rely on us, as we must rely on you,' said Schmidt simply. Caroli nodded in agreement.[8]

On 5 September, the 27-year-old Caroli made his very first parachute jump from 5,000ft over England into an unknown darkness. When his rip cord was pulled automatically from the aeroplane, he felt like he was being jerked upwards for several feet as his parachute suddenly opened. He landed blindly in 'field near Oxford'[9] and was knocked unconscious by his radio equipment. He was still groggy when he woke up five hours later, and after dragging all his equipment into a nearby ditch, promptly fell asleep again. A farm worker thought he was seeing things when he noticed a pair of shoes protruding from a fence, and reported this strange incident to police.

Caroli was arrested and taken to Camp 020. He was interrogated by the monocle-wearing and terrifying-looking commandant of the camp, Lieutenant Colonel Robin 'Tin-Eye' Stephens. Despite opposing violence as a means of getting a spy to confess, Stephens applied every form of psychological pressure available, often interrogating his prisoners for hours beyond their physical endurance. Stephens spoke seven languages fluently, including German, and had been an officer with the Gurkhas before being seconded to MI5 in mid-1940. Caroli was expertly turned by Stephens and given the codename Summer.

MI5 were aware that the Germans would have expected to have heard from their agent by now, so Caroli was ordered to send a message (closely observed by a British radio operator) to Ritter, saying he had injured himself on landing and was experiencing considerable difficulties. Later, he sent a second message saying he had gone into hiding near Oxford and was going to seek shelter by posing as a refugee. 'Desperately', he asked Ritter for help.[10]

Although Caroli and Schmidt knew Ritter 'had Johnny in England', Ritter had told them repeatedly that they had to get through on their own.[11] Now, with Caroli hurt, Ritter knew there was nothing else he could do – he had to risk putting his agents in contact with one another by asking Owens for assistance. MI5 used Owens' radio to say he had sent McCarthy to collect Caroli and would take care of him at his home until he recovered.

During interrogation, Caroli had let it slip that his training partner, Schmidt, would arrive on 20 September, and they had arranged to meet at the Black Boy Inn in Nottingham.[12] Schmidt's parachute jump over the Cambridgeshire countryside was no less eventful than Caroli's, as he got tangled up in some telegraph wires. As soon as he freed himself, he dropped heavily to the ground and twisted his ankle. In some pain, Schmidt hid his equipment, changed into his smart blue suit and limped into the nearby quintessentially English village of Willingham, where he bought *The Times* and ate breakfast in a cafe. He was arrested after a local civilian became suspicious and asked him for his identity card.

MI5 had been expecting him, so Schmidt was immediately sent to Camp 020 and interrogated by Stephens, who told him Caroli had given him away:

> Now I've got no sentiment at all. You are a spy and you've been fairly caught as a spy. If I'd done the same thing as you had the guts to do in Germany, I'd be shot, and that is your proper reward – you should be shot, but there are certain mitigating circumstances in this case and we've looked at it because we've tried to be just, but at the same time we intend to be practical because that's stark business in war – you're following me?[13]

Schmidt answered: 'I am following correct, yes.'

Stephens continued: 'There is no sentiment whatever about this – you have forfeited your life but there's one way of saving your life.' After offering Schmidt the opportunity to work for Britain against his former German spymasters, Stephens warned him that he would always check up on him, and if he ever found out that he was double-crossing him, 'it wouldn't take long for him to finish him off'. 'Excuse, I must answer now?' asked Schmidt. 'I think it is a good thing to answer now,' said Stephens.

'Yes, I'll do so,' Schmidt said.

Schmidt was given the codename Tate and provided with a house and full-time guard at Radlett in North-West London. Tate proved to be totally reliable in his work for MI5 and received a small allowance of £1 [around £45 today] a week, which was invested in National Savings Certificates for him to use when the war ended.[14] He became a British citizen after the war, and continued to go by his Abwehr alias, Harry Williamson. 'Nobody ever asked me why I changed my mind, but the reason was really very straightforward. It was simply a matter of survival. Self-preservation must be the strongest instinct in man,' 'Harry' later remarked.[15]

Ritter was so pleased with Schmidt's reports about airfields, aircraft and other matters, that he had him nominated for an Iron Cross,[16] never realizing that his valuable contributions all came through MI5. Tate, as a double agent, played an important part in deceiving the Germans that minefields had been laid in certain areas where they hadn't; U-boats avoided these areas and Allied convoys were able to pass through the final leg of their journey without being attacked.[17] As a result, vital supplies reached Britain safely and many lives were saved.

At a certain point, MI5 realized that if Tate were a genuine German spy, he would have started to run out of money, so a story was developed to get Ritter to send him some money urgently. Ritter was so convinced by Tate's story of having to hide in barns and almost starving to death, that he implored him to hold out for a couple of more days. Tate radioed back: 'I sh… upon the shitty German Intelligence Service.'[18] This message was so typical of Schmidt that Ritter had no doubt that it really was him, and it 'really calmed him down'.

Caroli was sent back to Camp 020 –MI5 discovered he had not been telling the truth about his pre-war spying activities for Germany – where he tried to commit suicide by slitting his wrists with a razor. Caroli was sent to an MI5 safe house to recover, but tried to escape by strangling Poulton, his guard, apologizing in the process, saying 'he had to do it, even though he knew he could be hung for it he could not go on'.[19] Caroli tied up the semi-conscious Poulson before escaping on a motor-cycle, carrying a 12ft canvas canoe, which he intended to use to make the sea-crossing to Europe. It would have made a funny sight if only it wasn't so serious. Several hours later, the motor-cycle broke down and Caroli was recaptured at Ely.

XX Committee Chairman John Masterman would later write that it was a very valuable lesson for the double-cross team:

> A double agent is a tricky customer, and needs the most careful supervision, not only on the material but also on the psychological side. His every mood has to be watched, and his every reaction to succeeding events studied. For this reason, we always afterwards insisted that a case officer should be personally responsible for each agent, with his hand as it were on the pulse of his patient from morning until night, and with an eye on every turn and twist of his patient's mind. For double agents are not as ordinary men are.[20]

Owens' radio was used to inform Ritter that Caroli was under suspicion by the police and had decided to use his seaman's papers and make a run for it. He said Caroli had left his wireless set at Cambridge station, and Owens had sent McCarthy to collect it.

* * *

At 3.30 pm on Thursday, 16 August 1940, the Luftwaffe launched an all-out aerial attack against Britain using three-quarters of its bombers and half of its fighters. Some 1,120 aircraft headed across the Channel, intending to entice large numbers of RAF fighters into the air. Göring's plan was to wipe out the RAF's aircraft on the ground and in the air, but although British runways were littered with craters and communication posts were destroyed, Britain's radar and early detection systems had ensured the RAF was prepared: they lost thirty-four planes to Germany's seventy-five.

At Fighter Command HQ, Churchill, Air Chief Marshal Sir Hugh Dowding, Churchill's chief of staff Lord Ismay and Lord Beaverbrook 'stood in silence as they watched the tangled mess of the huge map board below them unravel. They watched the wall as squadron after squadron came in to land, refuel and rearm then take off again.' When the Germans headed back across the Channel, an emotional Winston Churchill said 'he had never before been so moved. Never, never in the field of human conflict, was so much owed by so many to so few.'[21]

Meanwhile, MI5 were feeding the Abwehr with intelligence, mostly chicken feed and real information (approved by the XX Committee), through the German radio transmitters of Snow, Biscuit, Summer and Tate. MI5's strategy was to encourage the Abwehr to ask ever-more-revealing questions about what they needed to know by building up the status of their agents in the eyes of their German controllers. In this period of intense aerial warfare, MI5 were able to deduce a great deal about German strategy by the frequency and type of questions they asked.

The course of the war changed forever on the evening of 24 August, when German pilots targeting London's docklands perhaps mistakenly dropped bombs on the city's financial heart and Oxford Street in the West End, contravening Hitler's explicit orders to avoid bombing London or its suburbs. The incident escalated when Winston Churchill gave orders for Bomber

Command to fly a retaliatory raid against Berlin the following day, and for the first time in aviation history, civilians now became a target.[22]

Hitler was furious at this attack on his homeland and promised to raze British cities to the ground. From the winter of 1940 through to the spring of 1941, over 30,000 British citizens lost their lives in terrifying bombing raids, and Dicketts was one of the many injured. 'Please excuse the sprawl as I am in plaster from waist to shoulders, and writing is rather difficult,' he wrote to Tar on 12 September.[23] 'I have three broken ribs, a dislocated left thumb, and cut and bruised knee-caps, and will be ready to work again within two to three days.'

Dicketts wrote that he was becoming very depressed about money, and not having an identity card or a ration book. He said that due to Tar and Inspector Gagan's assurance that a job would be forthcoming, he had been unable to seek further employment in the meantime. 'You know that I am the reverse of ungrateful or grasping, but I am unable to earn anything or get a job and I have had £10 from you during the last 5 weeks,' he wrote. 'This has caused me to get a little bit more in debt each week.'[24] Dicketts attached a series of dated receipts for Tar to check and proposed that instead of continuing to send him small amounts, Tar could lend him £55 [around £2,500 today] to clear his debts and get a few minor things out of pawn. 'I should be able to start in the job within two or three days, and also start to repay everything at a minimum instalment of £3 a month.'[25] He continued:

'I have plenty of energy and I want to be earning money and doing a job. The day that I can cease to be a nuisance and a liability to you, will be the greatest relief to me.'

When Tar replied, his tone was noticeably different – there was something in the wind for Dicketts. Tar said he was sorry to hear about his unfortunate accident, and enclosed another £5, which he hoped would help Dicketts, adding: 'I am considering the possibility of advancing you £50 to put you on your feet. With regard to your registration card, I am confident I shall be able to let you know something about this in the very near future.'[26]

Dicketts was quick to pick up on this more positive note, saying the money was a godsend and that he was really at desperation point trying to live on £2 7s. a week, particularly as he sent some money away for his young son in Bristol. 'I have come across another matter that looks suspicious. I don't want to waste your time, so I will report it on Tuesday when I have confirmed the facts.'[27] Dicketts' security services file does not reveal what type of work he was doing for Tar during this period, but it is clear from this statement that he was doing something to earn his money.

Behind the scenes, changes were taking place within British intelligence that would provide opportunities for men like Dicketts, which before the war would have been impossible. The demands of running an increasing number of double agents and providing them with facts and misinformation was burdening the senior members of British intelligence who were authorized to make decisions about what information could be given to agents. The risk was that the longer it took MI5 to provide their agents with carefully crafted answers, the greater the chance that the Germans would suspect their spies had been captured and turned. MI5 would have to find a quicker way.

Finally, Dicketts got the news he was waiting for. 'I should like to see you at the War Office, Room 055 at 12.30 pm. Tomorrow October 3rd Saturday,' wrote Tar.[28]

Dicketts' sigh of relief is almost audible over the seventy-five years that have passed. Buoyed with the prospect of finally getting a chance to be useful and prove his worth, he replied to Tar's letter, saying it was the best news that he had had for a very long time, and he was very keen to begin work:

> I am perhaps, over-anxious at the moment, but I will soon get over this nervy state (caused by my accident and the past seven months of waiting and suspense), and shall be quite capable of carrying out the job in a calm and ordinary way … I thank you most sincerely for your friendship and your trust and will do my utmost to prove to you that it is not misplaced.[29]

Dicketts enclosed a list of his debts as requested, confirmed that he had begun taking up the matters he and Tar had discussed the day before, and expected to be proficient in a few weeks. Although what these 'matters' were is unknown, the chances are that it was brushing up on his Morse code skills learned initially as a pilot and Air Intelligence officer during the First World War.

As head of MI5's section B1(a), Tar Robertson was responsible for the day-to-day administration and management of their double agents. All the daily needs of their agents were taken care of, such as housing and food, and they were provided with housekeepers, guards and radio operators. To maintain the integrity of the notional life the Germans believed their spy to be living, each agent was assigned a case officer who knew his every move and thought, and was responsible for ensuring that the information sent to the Germans matched their agent's brief and personality traits.[30] The devil was in the detail, as even the smallest slip could mean the end of many months or even years of building up an agent's cover, and if that agent was in contact with another agent, then the whole network was blown.

As the number of double agents grew, the complexity in handling the different personalities increased, and towards the end of 1940, cracks began to appear in the Snow network. Concerned that Owens' radio could be destroyed during the London Blitz, MI5 moved the entire Snow ménage, including his radio operator Maurice Burton and guards Mr Price and Mr Williams, to Addlestone in Surrey. Once the wireless was set up, it continued to be operated by Burton, who responded to nightly requests from Hamburg for detailed weather reports and information about aircraft movements.

In early September, McCarthy (Biscuit) turned up at the house, very drunk, and threatened to murder Owens, Lily and all their connections unless Owens gave him some money. It was never easy to get money out of Owens, and although McCarthy was successful in obtaining a cheque for £200, Mr Price, Owens' guard, let Tar know that McCarthy 'was verging on the D.T.s' and was quite serious about bumping Owens off.[31] Price said McCarthy was also becoming too well-known at the local pub, where 'he gets very tight on double whiskies and shows off in a most disgusting manner'.

It was obvious that any future cooperation between the two agents was unlikely to be successful. Owens had also managed to upset Charlie, who had a low opinion of Owens personally and thought little of his ability as an agent. What MI5 needed was someone who could work with Owens and keep a close eye on him at the same time. Tar immediately thought of Dicketts, who had been friends with Owens until Tar had insisted they terminate their personal and professional relationship. Perhaps they could work together again, if MI5 planned and executed Dicketts' re-entry with great care. Owens was bound to be suspicious, and even angry, that his former friend and employee was now back on the scene, revealed as an agent of MI5, and yet he was expected to pick up exactly where they had left off as if nothing had happened.

Tar's idea was that Dicketts would play the part of being an agent of MI5 whose role it had been to hang around public houses and report back any gossip. Dicketts was to tell Owens that he had been paid minimally for this task, and to appear to be 'slightly disgruntled'.[32] Given that MI5's tactics were always to stick to the truth as close as possible, it is highly likely Dicketts had genuinely been carrying out this role, in return for the regular amount of cash he received from Tar. In his letters to Tar over the previous seven months, Dicketts had referred to work he carried out for Tar 'up North and in the provinces',[33] and two weeks previously had reported another matter he thought was suspicious.[34]

As far as Owens was concerned, Tar had brought Dicketts in to assist him, but in reality, Dicketts was there to spy on him, as Owens himself actually suspected.[35] In Owens' eyes, MI5 had tried this tactic one too many times.

'You are to appear as if you only take instructions from Owens, and have no other contact with MI5, other than through Owens or with Owens' consent,' Tar told Dicketts.[36] He was to take his lead from Owens - 'if Owens becomes pro-German, then you are to become pro-German'.

The two men were reacquainted in this manner in early December. During their initial conversations, Owens gave Dicketts the distinct impression that he knew a great deal about his criminal past, not just in England but also in the USA and Europe. Dicketts raised this matter with Tar, who thought Owens must have obtained his information from an inspector at Special Branch whom he knew very well.

Dicketts managed to overcome Owens' initial hostility and to regain some of his trust, and he and Kay were moved into the house in Surrey. After a short while, Dicketts reported that the general atmosphere was improving, and he was once again being accepted into the bosom of the family. However friendly they may have appeared to be, Dicketts was spying on Owens and Owens was spying on him. 'Owens is an inveterate liar, and even lies to his wife about everything,' Tar said he was informed by Dicketts.[37] 'He is bone idle and terrified of air raids and was forever trying to lay traps to find out why Dicketts had been put in touch with him.'

Owens questioned Dicketts very closely about money matters and debts, and said he had been told to give Dicketts as much money as he wanted. Playing his role as he had been instructed, Dicketts told Owens he was dissatisfied with how little money he had been paid, and showed Owens some of the letters he had received from Tar in proof. 'I would never have believed it, unless I had seen it with my own eyes,' Owens responded.

Dicketts' financial situation had improved enormously since then. He received a weekly salary of £10, and was so eager to justify Tar's investment in him, that he barely let Owens out of his sight. He told Tar that Owens was buying Lily a fur coat costing £1,500 [around £68,170 today] for Christmas and was drinking very heavily – bottles of whisky were disappearing like magic, and he had even caught him drinking at half past seven in the morning. Owens and Burton (Owens' radio operator) had private conversations every day and were always going out drinking together at the local pub. Despite Burton having told Dicketts that he didn't like Owens, he behaved as if he did. Tar had to reassure Dicketts that Burton was perfectly alright and should be regarded as such for the meantime.

The checking up was going both ways, however, and when Dicketts returned from an intelligence-gathering visit to Bristol, Owens asked him for a full report on the names of the people he had met and the pubs where he had met them.[38] It became clear that with Owens breathing down his neck, Dicketts would not be able to write up his reports in the house, so Tar gave him money to hire a hotel room for this purpose.

Celery, like all MI5 double agents, was sent on intelligence-gathering missions and left entirely to his own devices. MI5's rationale behind this was that a spy had to actually live the life of being a spy. Unlike normal people, genuine spies obtained their information at great risk, facing capture, interrogation and even death if caught. For this reason, information obtained directly was more likely to appear convincing if an agent had genuinely visited a particular factory and travelled there by train from Station A to Station B, than if they had never been there. For agents who met up for *treffs* with their German controllers in neutral countries, this was particularly important, as they may have to stand up to cross-examination. It was the sort of attention to detail that Ritter's LENA spies had evidently lacked.

Believing that his spies were operating freely, Ritter's requests for information increased exponentially during the summer of 1940, and all of his answers came from MI5. He asked what were the results of the Luftwaffe bombing raids, the morale and general state of the RAF, the Army and British citizens; what obstacles and defences were in place around airfields, and their locations; and what plans existed for the evacuation of citizens?

He also asked what the British ate, and even what their bread tasted like? Tate's response to this last question was typical of his character: 'Have you nothing more important to ask about? It tastes good.'[39]

MI5 sent their agents into the field to obtain the information and report back what they found. The data would then be discussed by the double-cross team and members of the XX Committee, who decided what information could be sent to the Germans, and in what form. Was there an opportunity to use the information in such a way as to deceive the enemy? Was the information too sensitive, and if so, what creditable excuse could they give the Germans as to why their agent had been unable to obtain it? The double-cross team had to be very careful that the questions posed to one agent were answered by that agent, and that the information they provided didn't conflict with information they had previously given the Germans, or with information they had given to other agents.

On 11 November, Dicketts was sent to the 'British Manufacture and Research Company in Grantham' to obtain production information about aircraft cannons for Summer.[40] He was to achieve this objective without being discovered. Dicketts inspected the aerodrome from three sides, counting the number of hangars, buildings and number of aircraft on the ground, and then spent an hour in the local pub listening to and joining conversations.

Using his powers of persuasion and charm, Dicketts struck up a conversation with a Miss Nickerson, who had recently left the company and was still owed money by them. Dicketts offered to take it up for her, and purchased her badge so he could obtain admission to the factory. The next day, Dicketts entered the factory without being questioned, and inspected the general layout for about an hour. 'I could very easily have destroyed part of the factory if I had had two Mills bombs in my pocket,'[41] Dicketts told Tar, who immediately wrote to MI5's Major Ronnie Haylor, based in Nottingham, and asked him to look into it. He said he was concerned by the ease with which a real German spy could enter the factory by simply purchasing a badge.

Although Dicketts' role was intelligence-gathering, his next visit revealed how easy it was for a genuine German spy to obtain secret information, simply by offering cash. At the Nottingham Aircraft Factory, Dicketts made the acquaintance of a Mr Fryer and offered to pay him £10 for production figures and future plans. When Fryer agreed and asked to meet Dicketts again later that evening, Dicketts immediately got in touch with Tar and asked him what he should do.

The situation placed Tar in a dilemma about whether Dicketts should go ahead and pay the bribe. MI5 was always anxious to avoid any knowledge of their activities finding their way to the enemy, and those in the know were kept as few as humanly possible. He wrote to Major Haylor again, saying Fryer should be taught 'a very severe lesson, and a great deal of publicity should be given to the case so that others may learn from his mistake'.[42]

'Incidentally,' replied Haylor, 'can you spare Dicketts for a short while? I have a number of small inquiries in which a man of his type would be extremely useful.'[43] Tar agreed, and Haylor asked Dicketts to look into the circumstances of the managing director of an iron works who was having an affair with the German-born wife of a Nottinghamshire county cricketer, and to investigate the security of several factories, including the 'Rolls Royce works at Derby'.[44]

Dicketts spent a lot of time in public houses, and in late November 1940 learned about discontent at Boulton & Paul's aircraft factory in Birmingham. He travelled there and spent three hours in various licensed premises, and incredibly managed to obtain a great deal of information about the production and fitting of Britain's super-secret infra-red equipment. In the guise of carrying out a secret inspection, Dicketts established that 6,000 employees worked in the factory in three shifts, and the staff from the night shifts were escorted in and out of the factory by the Home Guard. Despite the security, a list of six production steps was pinned on a blackboard in full view of passers-by, and the blueprints were kept in the stores and left lying about.

Between fourteen and twenty Defiants – two-seater fighter aircraft – were manufactured at the factory each week, and both they and old Defiants were 'fitted with secret infra-red radio detectors for night raider interception'.[45] Dicketts also discovered that the Defiants were easy game for the Messerschmidt BF 109 fighters as their maximum speed of 300mph was too slow. Apparently, twelve young pilots of 141 Squadron were dived on by Messerschmidts and five of them were immediately shot down, without any loss to the Germans. If Dicketts had been a genuine spy, this information would have been highly prized in Germany. Indeed, much of what Dicketts was later instructed to tell the Abwehr was accurate, although production figures were altered to appear less than they really were. A limited number of Abwehr records have survived the war, and a few contain details of the information provided by Dicketts during his trip to Germany in early 1941. By comparing Dicketts' original investigative reports, to what he was eventually instructed to tell the Germans, it is clear MI5 strongly intended Dicketts to be accepted as a valuable source of information by the Abwehr.

As Ritter had instructed Owens to recruit agents and saboteurs from the Communist Party or the Irish Republican Army, Dicketts was sent to uncover sympathizers working in the factories. In Coventry, Dicketts learned that several Irishmen had been arrested for reputed sky signalling, and there was considerable local unrest about the great number of Irishmen working there and manning the anti-aircraft guns for the city. In Surrey and the west of England, Dicketts discovered Communist propaganda material was readily available in the factories, but most of the men were very patriotic and thought it was stupid for the government or local authorities to allow propaganda of this type to be distributed to them freely and without comment. This was precisely the sort of useful but not important information (chicken feed) which MI5 could pass on to increase Owens' reputation with the Germans.

In early October 1940, when summer became autumn and the weather in Britain began to deteriorate, Germany came to the conclusion that the RAF could not be defeated, and the Battle of Britain gradually came to an end – although the bombing would continue for many years to come.

Ever mindful of Ritter's instructions to Owens to find his own replacement, MI5 came up with a plan to introduce Dicketts to Ritter. His reports on British factories were carefully prepared to enable Dicketts to use this information to build up his value to the Germans. Remarkably, almost seventy years later, I was able to compare Dicketts' British reports to what he told the Abwehr in early 1941.[46] British strategy at the time was to appear as if they were building fewer planes than they actually were to encourage the Germans to slow down their own production, or to assume the British were close to defeat, when they weren't. This stratagem is best described by the ancient military leader, Sun Tzu, in *The Art of War*: 'Appear weak when you are strong, and strong when you are weak.'

Chapter 7

Penetrate the Abwehr

'Every man has a right to risk his own life for the preservation of
it.' Jean-Jacques Rousseau

Did the Germans trust Owens? If they did, the information Ritter
asked Owens to provide was probably genuine, the intelligence
he gave Owens about sabotage and invasion plans was likely to
be true, and Ritter was more likely to believe that his other spies in contact with Owens were still operating freely and not under MI5 control.
The reverse was true if they didn't trust Owens or suspected he was
under control. If that was the case, then the information they were giving
Owens was bogus and he was being used to plant misinformation on the
British.

MI5 considered it to be of the highest priority to establish exactly how
Owens was being perceived by the Germans, and Tar asked Dicketts if he
would be willing to try to get himself recruited as a German spy to find
out. The idea was that Owens and he would travel to Lisbon, where Owens
would introduce him to Ritter on the basis that Dicketts could provide
information on the RAF and Air Ministry in Britain. MI5 would make certain that Dicketts was provided with good intelligence to build him up in the
eyes of the Abwehr. If they were successful, Dicketts could then be used as
a separate channel to Owens.

It was an enormously risky venture, as Dicketts' life would depend upon a
man he didn't trust as far as he could throw him, and if Owens betrayed him,
it would be a suicide mission. Despite his reservations, Dicketts agreed. He
wanted to wipe the slate clean and regain his lost respectability, and Tar's
offer gave him a chance to achieve that. Even though Tar didn't make any
promises, Dicketts knew the success of his mission would open doors previously closed to him, and what he wanted more than anything was a role in
the RAF or British intelligence.

Dicketts also believed in Tar, who had honoured his word and found Dicketts a job. Although it was dangerous work, Dicketts was grateful. He had been through months of living hand to mouth, totally dependent upon Tar's charity and good word, and now finally he had a chance to prove himself. Dicketts had no illusions over the risk of this venture, having faced the enemy before as a teenage soldier in the First World War. But his desire to prove that he was a responsible, resourceful and better man than most people perceived him to be, was stronger than self-preservation. And he was willing to risk his life to achieve it.

Once Tar had spoken to Owens, his radio was used to tell Ritter he had a new sidekick he thought he might be interested in meeting. Ritter understood the meaning of the message immediately and suggested they meet in neutral Lisbon. Hoping to lure Ritter to Ireland, where he would be captured, Tar suggested Eire as an alternate meeting place as the waiting lists for visas to Lisbon were so long. However, Ritter refused to go to Ireland and suggested they might be able to obtain a transit visa to Lisbon if they were en route to Canada.

Although it would have been easy for MI5 to obtain Dicketts' and Owens' visas, they knew the Germans would question the ease by which they had obtained them. There was also the risk that if either of them slipped up when questioned about it, the Germans would know they worked for British intelligence. Since Dicketts was being introduced to them as Owens' sidekick, they would expect him to do the work for both of them, so Dicketts visited the London Chamber of Commerce to obtain letters of introduction for various business agencies in neutral Portugal.

Dicketts visited Tar at his club on 28 December and was handed his new passport. 'I had a conversation with "the little man" last night, who made various negative comments about the way MI5 was running things,' Dicketts told him.[1] This had increased his doubts about Owens' loyalty, whom he suspected had other means of communication with the Germans. Owens had said he knew there was going to be an air raid the other night, and said he was worried about his son Robert.

A few days later, the three of them had a long conversation about how Owens could persuade Ritter to take Dicketts into Germany for training. The agreed plan they came up with was that Owens would introduce Dicketts to Ritter as an ex-RAF officer who had worked in Air Intelligence during the First World War, and who held a grievance against the British for what he perceived to be his unfair treatment and inability to gain a commission during the current war. In typical MI5 fashion, Dicketts' cover was as close to the truth as possible so he would be less likely to slip up under interrogation.

By 17 January, there was still no sign of the Portuguese visas coming through, but Dicketts' business cover, which he obtained himself through his contact Mr Lindley from the Federation of British Industries in Lisbon, was approved by Tar. Tar gave Dicketts a plain language code to memorize so he could communicate with them while he was away, after which Dicketts expressed concern about what might happen to his wife and child if he were killed. He asked Tar for a written agreement that they would be taken care of if that event were to occur.

MI5 weren't sure what to do about Dicketts' request; one suggestion was that they would pay his wife 'a sum of £3.10 a week for life, or the equivalent which would amount to approximately £6,000 [around £272,700 today]'.[2] Brigadier Jasper Harker, MI5's Director General, agreed to stand him up to £2,000, and Felix Cowgill, head of SIS's counter-intelligence unit Section V, thought they should be able come up with the same amount. In the end, Tar managed to persuade Dicketts that if anything happened to him while he was away, 'our obligation would be honoured as far as his wife and child were concerned'.[3]

Dicketts met with Felix Cowgill, who gave him a questionnaire to memorize. The information was similar to what the Germans wanted their agents to acquire in Britain: what were the reactions of the German workers and citizens to the RAF's air raids, the blackouts and the food rations; how was their morale and did they continue working in the dockyards and factories after blackout; And did they carry gas masks and so on?[4]

If possible, Dicketts was to try to obtain details of the markings on unexploded bombs (very risky if he was observed doing so), and how long the Germans left them and timed bombs before they considered them duds? Could he see any preparations for invasion such as concentrations of troops, barges or ships, and what they were loaded with? If he saw any warships, he was to memorize the date he saw them, and where, and was to try to find out their names or identifying numbers. Could he see any factories or ships being built, and if so, what was their size and location?

The risks of spying on the enemy in the middle of war were significant, and to try to obtain information from right under the Nazis' noses, sometimes in direct view of others, was very dangerous work. If Dicketts was detected, MI5's entire operation was at risk, as was his life. Compounding the problem was the fact that Dicketts was working for two different masters, MI5 and SIS, whose aims were different and would judge the information he obtained at great risk from two very different perspectives. Although Dicketts' intelligence-gathering experience in British airfields and factories had been profoundly useful, this time the risks of discovery were almost certainly fatal: he would undergo a slow and painful interrogation before being executed as a spy.

To survive, Dicketts would have to use all his powers of observation, quick-wittedness and memory. First, he would have to convince Ritter of his value as a potential German agent by providing him with strong bona fides, and significant intelligence sufficient to whet his appetite for more. He needed to convince the Germans of the potential of the future information he could provide, and should expect to be questioned closely on how he planned to obtain it. There was only so much MI5 could do for him; the rest was up to Dicketts himself. His biggest preparation was mental. It would take all his inner strength and faith in his own ability to willingly enter an aggressive enemy country in the middle of war and spy on it.

As the time for his departure drew near, Dicketts' mistress, Kay, showed her willingness to support him by secretly obtaining a large amount of details about Owens' bank accounts. Kay thought she might also be able to obtain the names of the people Owens had given Lily to contact in the event of an invasion. The risk to both women was very real if the Gestapo discovered their husbands were British agents, as they would be used to apply pressure and extract information about their husbands and who they were in contact with.

Fearing a German invasion would occur in their absence, Owens told Dicketts to withdraw all the money he had been given by Tar, and use it to purchase some portable property for Kay which she could use in an emergency. He said he was buying diamonds with his money, as he didn't want to leave anything in England because of the risk of invasion.

At his final meeting with Tar, on 28 January 1941, Dicketts said he was convinced that Owens was 'both mad and double-crossing us'.[5] Owens, on the other hand, seemed to be quite happy about the trip, and believed he 'could get away with most things with the Doctor',[6] (Dr Rantzau, the German codename for Ritter).

The Portuguese consulate eventually said their visas would be available in two weeks. It was a close call – Dicketts was already in Liverpool on 4 February when a last-minute delivery of his stamped passport arrived shortly before his ship, the SS *Cressado*, departed at 1 pm. For extra precaution, he and Owens travelled by two separate routes, Dicketts by sea and Owens by air from Whitchurch Airfield, Bristol, on 14 February.

In Hamburg, exercising the same caution as the two British spies they were going to meet, Major Ritter and his assistant, Georg Sessler, travelled separately to Lisbon. Sessler's orders were to 'shadow Owens and Dicketts unobtrusively before and after their meeting with Ritter'.[7]

The *Cressado* joined Convoy No OG.52,[8] made up of twenty-nine merchant vessels carrying coal, tin and other general items, and their escort of eleven naval vessels, and set sail from Liverpool, bound for Gibraltar and Lisbon. To avoid being detected by U-boats, the convoy ploughed its way across the North Atlantic in a zig-zag course which alternated frequently.

Dicketts spent most of the voyage playing cribbage with the chief steward, who considered him to be a first-class card player. He gave no indication that he was on any sort of special business, and when people asked him why he was travelling to Lisbon in the middle of the war, Dicketts said that he was a trader in 'corks, wine and spirits'.[9] To add further credence to his story, he discussed problems with imports, exports and shipping.

Owens arrived safely in Lisbon as planned, and went to the agreed cafe at 11.00 am to rendezvous with local German Agent, Henri Dobler (alias H Duarte). Owens' instructions were to order a large glass of lemon juice and read *The Times* newspaper, but he ordered orange juice instead. After an hour of sitting and waiting, both men gave up and returned the next day at the same time, to repeat the same procedure as instructed. Once again, Owens ordered orange juice. This was too much for Dobler, who was becoming rather hot under the collar. 'Excuse me,' he said. 'It's not really my business. But why do you always order orange juice and why do you not drink it then?'[10]

Owens stared at him without comprehension, until finally he got it and burst out smiling. 'Waiter, take this thing away and bring me lemon juice,' he said. They laughed about it later, but at the time Ritter was waiting at Dobler's apartment so he and Owens could meet without being seen.

Meanwhile, Dicketts' voyage had turned into a nightmare, when a violent storm in the North Atlantic headed eastwards towards them and remained in place until the 15th. As severe winds and massive waves assailed the vessel from every direction, conditions on board the SS *Cressado* were horrendous, and the convoy was delayed for days.

After almost a week of waiting for his arrival, Ritter was becoming increasingly anxious as he had to return to Berlin. Facing the prospect that their whole trip might come to nothing, Owens sent an urgent telegram to Lily saying, 'Dick not arrived. Worried. Can you help?'[11] Tar immediately contacted Commander Ewen Montagu at the Admiralty and asked him if he knew where the *Cressado* was.

When Kay, who was living in the MI5 safe house with Lily, discovered that Dicketts hadn't arrived, she made arrangements to meet Tar at the Grosvenor House Hotel, where she plied him with questions. 'Is he definitely going into Germany?' she pressed.

'In all honesty, all I can tell you is that I am not entirely sure, as this decision is up to Owens and Dr Rantzau,' said Tar.[12] 'Mind you if he did go into Germany, I'm sure he won't take any unnecessary risks.' What else could he say?

Montagu's reply when it came later that day was an enormous relief. The *Cressado* had not been sunk, and to the best of his knowledge would be putting into Gibraltar later that day. It should arrive in Lisbon in two to three days' time.

In Lisbon, a frustrated Ritter was making his own inquiries. SIS heard via their local agent that Kuno Weltzien, an important Abwehr agent, had given strict instructions that the *Cressado* should not be attacked. Weltzien was extremely annoyed that it might have been sunk, as he had a reliable agent on board, who at one time had served with the RAF and was a valuable medium 'for planting false information on the British'.[13]

It was with considerable relief all round that the *Cressado* finally put into Lisbon at 6 pm on Friday 21st in a rather weather-beaten condition. A German spy working at the docks immediately reported its arrival, and Ritter knew many hours before Owens that the boat had arrived.

Aware that he was several days late, Dicketts made a big song and dance that he must get ashore, and managed to persuade the captain to lend him £10. He was allowed to leave the docks in the company of the chief steward to see if any messages had been left for him at the Metropole Hotel, and was very surprised to discover that there was nothing there for him at all. They returned to the ship, stopping at the English bar for a couple of drinks on their way back, and by midday the following morning Dicketts was back at the hotel.

Having been told to stay in separate hotels, Dicketts was rather surprised when Owens came rushing over after recognizing his voice as he filled out the registration forms. It was purely by chance that both men had been in the same vicinity at the same time, and Owens was so pleased to see him 'that he very nearly fainted'.

'We had given you up for lost,' exclaimed an excited Owens. 'I must tell the Doctor immediately, as he is leaving for Berlin.'

They went up to Owens' room to wait for Dobler to call back with instructions. 'You wouldn't be alive, if you had arrived before me, Dick,'[14] he said. Dicketts couldn't tell if Owens was telling the truth or just boosting his self-importance, so he played along with it as a means to elicit further information.

'You promised to tell me certain things when we got here, Arthur. What have you told the Doctor, and what am I supposed to do if I go into Germany?' Dicketts asked.

'All I can tell you, Dick, is that you will be safe and I give you my word on that. I am not like these people in England who send you out here blindfolded and to your death if I had not been here before you.'

Dicketts tried to stir him up a bit, saying he thought it was scandalous that he had been sent out without any instructions, totally reliant upon Owens and his influence with the Germans. However, Owens had spotted the German tail and said he wouldn't talk in the room as there was a man in the next room he didn't trust. Owens walked over to his cupboard and pulled out a wad of notes amounting to £5,000 from under a pile of dirty washing, and waved it in front of Dicketts. 'Look what they think of me and how they feed me,' he said. 'They don't even think about expenses at all.'

It's worth pausing for a moment and reflecting on why Owens did this. Was he showing off, to prove how important he was to the Germans? MI5 certainly didn't pay him that much, and most of what the Germans gave him was used to fund his double-cross network in Britain. Was Owens inferring that if the Germans thought this well of him, then Dicketts was safe? Or was he warning Dicketts not to let him down, as the Germans trusted him so much they were willing to pay him such a great deal of money? On the other hand, if Owens was working for the Germans, and believed Dicketts would do anything for money, then this demonstration would prove to Dicketts that there was plenty of money about. Had Ritter ordered him to do this and Owens feared being found out if he didn't?

Dicketts' only comment was to say he thought it was rather unwise to hide his money like that, and suggested he put it in the safe. Just then the telephone rang, and Dicketts listened as Owens made arrangements to meet someone at the arches at 1.15 pm. 'It's good news,' Owens told him. 'The Doctor is going to postpone his departure by a day so he can meet you.'

With an hour to spare, they went down to the bar and had a few tumblers of Scotch and soda before walking down to the arches together. Owens was exhausted and partially drunk, as he had been up all night with the Doctor, who was meant to leave for Berlin the following day. Dicketts' arrival had changed all that, and now he and Owens were collected by Dobler in a grey Opel saloon and driven to his nearby apartment, where he was introduced to the Doctor. Ritter was very friendly towards him, and after pouring Dicketts and Owens half a tumbler of whisky each, he asked Dicketts for his opinion of the war and his attitude towards England. Dicketts told him the agreed story and the Doctor appeared to accept it.

Ritter didn't disclose that he had already heard the story from Owens, who said Dicketts had been thrown out of a technical branch of the Air Ministry, where he had been working on radar and secret devices. He had been summoned by a very senior officer and told that he must resign from the RAF at once. No explanation was given, but Dicketts had felt sure it was because of his political views. 'I think he's a communist, but I'm not sure,' Owens had told Ritter.[15] 'He needs money desperately, and he's willing to tell you everything if you pay him enough.'

Dicketts had been told to take his 'first staff appointment'[16] with him to Lisbon as proof that he had worked for British intelligence during the last war. It would make him more valuable to the Germans if he was able to overcome their suspicions, and prove he had access to information they wanted.

Ritter didn't believe the British would throw out a senior technical man at this stage of the war, but wondered if perhaps he was being too suspicious. Perhaps Dicketts really was a communist, and if he was, there was no doubt the British would push him out at high speed.

At the time of their meeting, Nazi Germany and the communist Soviet Union were still allies. On 23 August 1939, both nations had shocked the world by signing a non-aggression pact agreeing not to attack each other for the next ten years, and to divide up the spoils of a conquered Europe between them. In reality, both Hitler and Soviet leader Stalin despised each other and were playing for time. Stalin knew he could not trust the communist-hating Hitler, and saw the treaty as a means of keeping his nation on peaceful terms with Nazi Germany until he could build up his military. For Hitler, it was an opportunity for his armies to invade Poland virtually unopposed and to deal with the forces of Britain and France without also having to fight the Soviets on a second front.

* * *

We may never really know the truth about the events that took place in Lisbon and Germany during February and March 1941, involving Ritter and Sessler from the Abwehr and Owens and Dicketts from MI5. The intellectually impressive members of MI5's double-cross team sifted through hours and hours of Dicketts' and Owens' interrogations, developed hypotheses, compared notes, observed their reactions and recorded private conversations. Their decision made in the middle of war, against their invisible opponents in Germany, is still debated today.

In the account that follows, I have interwoven MI5's version of events with German testimonies that have recently come to light, as well as others written at the end of the war.[17] It demonstrates the complexity of handling these two double agents from both sides of the conflict, and reveals information previously unknown.

* * *

'There was unmistakable tension in the room,' wrote Ritter of his first meeting with Dicketts in Lisbon on 22 February 1941.[18]

'How do you do?' Jack Brown (Dicketts' Abwehr codename) said when they were introduced. Ritter noticed that compared to his soft voice and pleasant facial expression, Brown's eyes 'had a hint of Graves' disease' (slightly bulg-ing). In fact, Dicketts' eyes were a perfectly normal size, as his photographs reveal. By the time Ritter wrote his memoris, many years had passed since he last saw Dicketts and he must have confused his appearance with someone else.

'Johnny has told us your story,' said Ritter. 'Do you think you can bring us anything?'

'I believe you are looking for an expert with aviation training. That's what I am. And with my contacts, I can certainly answer many of your questions.'

'And your compensation?' asked Ritter.

Brown said he wanted £200 [around £9,090 today] a month, as he had debts and needed money. 'If you are worth it,' Ritter replied. He was disappointed, as this was the usual ruse, and thought it would have sounded more credible if Dicketts had stuck to the story of his discharge as Owens had told it to him.

Just to ensure Brown understood the game he was playing, Ritter told him he could easily have him arrested there in Portugal.

'My God, Doctor,' shouted Johnny (Owens) as he sprang up. 'You would not do that. I told Jack that he can rely on you.'

Dicketts had expected something like this, but Ritter wasn't the type of person he had been lead to believe he was. Dicketts had been told to expect a heavy drinker who liked 'dirty stories',[19] but the man in front of him appeared to be a very shrewd American Mid-West businessman. Ritter's English was fluent, with a strong American accent, and he was used to commanding the respect of others.

Ritter continued: 'I've asked Johnny many questions about matters I wanted to discuss, but all he would say was we had to wait for Jack to arrive, as he would be able to answer them.'

'What matters were those?' asked Brown.

'About Beaufighters and Infra-Red Detectors etc.,' said Ritter.[20]

Dicketts said he was sorry to disappoint him, but he could not help him with this information as 'the little man' hadn't given him any instruction as to what was required. He understood the reason for this was that Owens, quite natu-rally, would not be willing to expose his hand to him until he was sure of him.

Ritter appeared to accept this explanation and suggested they continue the interview at his villa in Estoril, about 25km west of Lisbon. Owens fell asleep in Dobler's car on the way there, and had sobered up by the time they arrived. More whisky was produced on arrival, and although Owens remained throughout the interview, he soon became inebriated again. Dicketts showed Ritter a cutting from *The Times*, which Tar thought would add credence to his dislike of the conditions in England and support his claim that he was a disgruntled man who was willing to work for Germany. Ritter appeared very pleased with it, and told him that he knew everything about his past history and thought he had been treated very badly.

Owens did not take part in the actual conversation, and 'was almost in a stage of collapse with excitement and alcohol'.[21] His hair was in disarray and he had nothing to say except: 'Good old Dick, let's have another drink. We will look after you. The Doctor is a good friend of ours.' Dicketts realized he couldn't rely on much help from Owens' quarter.

Ritter noticed Johnny was getting a little impatient and kept trying to cut into their conversation. He wondered if he was afraid that Jack might say something that didn't fit in with what he had told him earlier. It seemed to Ritter that Brown did not care much for Johnny, and Johnny was afraid of him. As if reading his thoughts, Johnny said, 'You aren't going deceive me, are you Jack?'[22]

'Naturally not,' said Brown, completely detached. With this exchange, Ritter began to see through the smokescreen. He thought Johnny had really tried to remain honest with him, but had fallen into a trap laid for him by Brown. He felt sad that he could no longer expect anything from Johnny and would have to drop him. He wondered if they could still get something out of Brown if they took him back to Germany and interrogated him.

'Why don't you come with me to Germany?' he said. 'We need all sorts of time for our work, but I'm not technically inclined, and besides I do not have the time to stay in Lisbon. Come with me to Germany and I will assure you have a safe return.'

Johnny was excited: 'That's wonderful, Doctor. Let's go with him, Jack.'

Forcing himself to be tough, Ritter waved him off: 'I'm sorry Johnny, but I can't take you both.'

Johnny looked at him without understanding, so Ritter turned to Jack and said,

'So, how about it, Mr Brown?'

Ritter knew he had given Dicketts a dangerous test, and that he would have to accept it if he wanted to continue playing his role. He later wrote: 'If he was a real representative of the Intelligence Service, this would be a chance for him like none other – to travel to enemy territory in the midst of war. But that took courage.'[23]

Ritter was embarrassed when a sad-looking Johnny came to his aid. 'Go along, Jack,' he said. 'When the Doctor promises something, he keeps his promise.'

'If you promise that I can soon get out of Germany safely then I will come along,' Brown said, and extended his hand. Without really wanting to, Ritter shook it. Owens made another attempt to go along, but Ritter's decision was firm - there was no place for sentiment.

Years later, Georg Sessler, the Abwehr officer who escorted Dicketts into Germany and back, told Austrian journalist Günter Peis that,

> Dicketts was well aware that his life depended on the outcome of this impending game of questions and answers. The fact that he nevertheless placed his neck in the German noose, fully aware of the dangers of his action, and dared to enter the lion's den as a British agent, must surely rank this as one of the bravest deeds ever enacted during World War Two.[24]

With Ritter on his way back to Germany, Dobler took Dicketts to meet von Kramer (Major Kremer von Auenrode, alias Ludovico von Kartsthoff), the head of the Abwehr at the embassy. His photograph was taken for a *Fremdenpass* (alien's passport) in the name of 'Walter Anton Denker', a merchant who had the same age and birthday as his own.[25] The speed by which his exit and entry visas were arranged during the same day, and his fake passport handed to him on Monday, was indicative that the Portuguese police were in German pay. When Dicketts mentioned this to Ritter later, he said the Portuguese police were 'not in our pay, they are with us'.

Owens had no choice but to remain in Lisbon, and whether he realized it or not he was effectively a hostage. Ritter had warned Dicketts in front of Owens that 'he could easily have him arrested' in Lisbon, and Owens knew only too well what that would entail if Dicketts messed up in Germany. Owens may have been confident he could rely on Ritter, but what about his colleagues in the Abwehr or the Gestapo?

Owens sent a telegram to Lily, which she would pass on to Tar. 'Have found Dick. Everything is going well. (Am not going into Germany.)'[26]

An hour later, Dicketts sent a telegram to Kay: 'Just arrived darling. Very bad trip. All my love sweetheart. (Things are not going well.)' Dicketts had been given a plain language code to communicate with Tar in his absence, so the meaning of his telegram is probably in code.

With their husbands away and their country under threat of an imminent German invasion, Kay and Lily would have been horrified to discover the plans MI5 had made for them. From MI5's perspective, the women had information which could expose their top-secret double-cross system if they were captured by the Germans – the identities of several MI5 officers including Tar, addresses, phone numbers, operational procedures and the existence of other double agents like Biscuit, GW, Charlie, Tate and Summer. But by far the most important information they possessed was the knowledge that Owens' radio was being operated by Maurice Burton and that the Abwehr had been talking directly to MI5. If the Germans discovered any of this, their husbands would immediately be arrested, interrogated and executed in Lisbon and Germany.

Ronnie Reed and another MI5 officer were given 'Burn after Reading' instructions and told that the moment they heard an invasion was taking place, they were to take two cars and go to Owens' house in Surrey. When they arrived, they were to burn any incriminating documents and take Owens' radio apart and stow it in the back of Reed's car, along with any other wireless apparatus.

Mrs Owens and the baby were to be placed in one car, and Mrs Dicketts and Owens' son Robert in the other. They were to head immediately for North Wales along a specific route, without losing sight of the other car, and report to the Regional Security Liaison Officer when they arrived. Mrs Owens and the rest of the party must not be captured by the Germans, and Reed and the other MI5 officer had to be prepared 'to take any step necessary, including "liquidation"[27] to prevent this from occurring'. To this end, they were provided with a revolver, two pairs of handcuffs, a car pass, petrol coupons and £10 in cash.[28]

* * *

On Sunday, 23 February 1941, far from the wintery cold and besieged atmosphere of London during the Blitz, Dicketts and Owens were taken on a tour of the beautiful coastal district of Setúbal, about 50km south of Lisbon. The contrast between a darkened and bomb-shattered Britain and this sunny coastline, with people going calmly about their usual business without fear of bombs or imminent invasion, was vast. Despite the balmy atmosphere and beautiful scenery, Dicketts was unable to relax as he knew he would soon be entering Germany, with only Ritter's word that he would be allowed to return.

Sensing his unease, the local German Secret Service agent, Henri Dobler, took him to a cafe while his girlfriend, Alicia, took Owens for a stroll along the beach and gave him some advice. Dobler was around 40 years old, born in Hamburg and had lived in Argentina for many years. He had only returned to Germany six months after the outbreak of war, and spoke fluent Spanish, German and French, but his English wasn't very good. Dobler wore horn-rimmed glasses and looked like a scholar. He had a long thin face and a nervous disposition, with trembling hands.[29] He told Dicketts 'he used to fear the Nazis in the beginning, but found out later that if you treat them squarely, you get well rewarded. You are going to have a great experience … Take care of yourself and tell the truth. I hope you will be advised by me.'

Dobler didn't tell Dicketts what he had told McCarthy (Biscuit) during his visit to Lisbon the previous year, or he would have felt a lot less confident about the credibility of Ritter's word. Dobler and McCarthy had spent a lot of time together and got along well, and Dobler had said that he didn't understand how Ritter 'had risen to the position he was in' and that 'he was always lying'.[30]

That evening, Dicketts invited Captain Stafford of the SS *Cressado* for drinks at the Avenida Palace with Dobler, whom he introduced as Senor Duarte, an Argentine business associate of his. Dicketts' plan was to set up a secure way of communicating with Dobler when he went back to England. 'I'd like to obtain certain delicacies from England which I would be willing to pay for,' Dobler told Stafford, who agreed to bring them with him on his next trip. Although the journey would take an average of three months, Dicketts and Dobler now had a means of sending sensitive information to each other inside these packages. In case something should happen to Stafford, Dicketts later made the same arrangements with Bert, the steward from the *Cressado*.

The rest of the week dragged slowly until Dobler finally told him all the arrangements had been made and he would be leaving from Estoril station at 6 am on Thursday. An embassy car would collect him, and he would be driven to Madrid by a very pleasant man who had lived in America. 'Just treat him normally,' said Dobler.

As the day for his departure loomed, Owens told him on several occasions not to go unless he wanted to. 'I will look after you,' he said. The night before his departure, Dicketts joined Owens and two German girls at the Arcadia nightclub, and left shortly before midnight. Owens remained behind to watch the cabaret show and returned to the hotel around 5 am, where he found Dicketts getting dressed in his room. They went downstairs together and a taxi pulled up with the two German girls who had come to say good-bye. Dicketts shook hands with one of the girls and kissed the other, and after they had gone, Owens shook his hand and said, 'You are a very brave man. They have sent you over blindfolded and if it weren't for me your life would be worth nothing. If you want to change your mind now you can do so.'[31]

'No Arthur, I am trusting you in this matter and I am going,' said Dicketts.

'Please don't let me down,' replied Owens. Dicketts said it was really up to him to ask that, as after all it was he who was going into Germany while Owens remained behind in Lisbon.

At Estoril station, Dicketts got into a dark Ford V-8 driven by Dr Hans Ruser, who worked as a diplomatic courier for the German Embassy in Lisbon. The night before Ruser was due to leave for Berlin, taking a diplomatic bag with him, Cramer (Abwehr lll's Lieutenant Fritz Kramer) from the embassy came to see him and asked him to take an Englishman with him. Ruser said he needed to get permission first, but Cramer told him it was very important as Canaris was interested in this man.[32]

Admiral Wilhelm Canaris was a small, softy-spoken, highly intelligent and cultured spymaster who had eyes and ears everywhere. He played an incredibly dangerous 'double-game' as head of the Abwehr German Secret Service whilst also maintaining close links with the German resistance to Hitler.[33] He had a staunch sense of honour and loyalty, and knew who to trust, giving them positions of responsibility with the Abwehr. Canaris passed intelligence onto the Allies and 'almost certainly exaggerated' Britain's preparation for invasion in 1940 by overestimating the size of British forces.[34] Although he took no part in the failed July 1944 plot on Hitler's life, Canaris was later arrested and endured an agonizingly slow death by hanging at the Flossenbürg concentration camp in the last few days of the war. Erwin Lahousen, head of the Abwehr's Section II, later said of Canaris: 'He hated Hitler, his system and his methods. He hated war. He was a human being.'

Ruser coached Dicketts on how to behave at the Spanish–Portuguese frontier, saying the car and bags would not be searched because he was travelling as an embassy courier. Dicketts was to allow him to do all the talking and to say nothing other than '*Ja* or *Nein*'. Ruser's English was fluent, as he had grown up in the United States. He said he did many favours for the Secret Service, but would probably lose his job if the German minister found out.

He behaved very coolly towards Dicketts, telling him bluntly that he did not like travelling with a traitor. Dicketts replied:

> In my opinion, I'm not a traitor. I have great admiration for the German system of government and intense disagreement with my own. I believe Germany will win the war and I am willing, also on account of my Irish mother to go to any lengths to try and stop this war.[35]

At this, Ruser changed his attitude entirely and said he hoped for the same thing. He was very pro–British and had relations in England, but although he was violently anti-Nazi he still considered Hitler to be the saviour of Germany. Ruser seemed to believe Dicketts was going into Germany on the auspices of the German Secret Service to put out peace-feelers.

By the time he and Ruser reached the Portuguese border, they had become very friendly. The guards knew Ruser well and simply bowed him through the checkpoint, and the same thing happened on the Spanish side at Badajoz.

They arrived in Madrid at 6.30 pm on 28 February, where Walter Denker (Dicketts) had a reservation at the Palace Hotel, one of the city's grandest hotels. Because the desk staff spoke fluent German, Ruser did all the talking and filled out the paperwork. He asked Dicketts not to leave his hotel room under any circumstances as it was too risky, and he would collect him for meals. As an extra precaution, they never ate in the hotel once during their four-night stay.

Later that evening, they went to the German Embassy, where Dicketts was introduced as a repatriated German-American. After a cocktail with Lieutenant Meyerduner, the Air Attaché, they returned to their rooms, and two days later returned to the embassy to collect Dicketts' exit permit, signed by Colonel Kramer, the Military Attaché. At the end of the war, Kramer came under suspicion for helping to hide paintings stolen by Hermann Göring from the extensive Jacques Goudstikker collection of 1,200 Old Master and nineteenth-century paintings.

In the early morning of 4 March, Dicketts and Ruser boarded a Junkers 52 and flew to Barcelona, checking into the Ritz. Once again, they went to the German Embassy, where Dicketts was introduced to the Chancellor, Dr Fisher, who was going to accompany him to Berlin the following morning with his wife, the Baroness von Elten.

That night, Dicketts faced the reality of going into Germany the next day, wondering if he would ever return. He wrote a short letter to his wife, enclosing the last of his English money – which amounted to £11 – and another letter to his mother and father. By this stage, Ruser had become close with Dicketts and feared for his safety in Germany. He refused to censor Dicketts' letters for secret codes or hidden messages, and promised to post them as soon as he got back to Lisbon – they arrived in England two weeks later.

Dr Fischer collected Dicketts at 6.30 am and drove to Barcelona airport, where they boarded a four-engined Heinkel. When they landed in Lyon to refuel, Dicketts left the airport and had a drink by himself at a French cafe. German troops completely controlled the airport, and there were ten German fighter aircraft on the ground and around a hundred French fighters stacked nose to wing-tip in the south-west corner, left out in all weather conditions. Dicketts asked a German officer about the French planes, and was told: 'The Luftwaffe don't need them and they will all be destroyed if we are forced to leave.'

They arrived in Stuttgart just after lunch, where Dr Fischer saw Dicketts safely through passport control and then left – leaving Dicketts to continue alone to Berlin. He arrived at 4.30 pm and was just about to call the telephone number he had been given, in case no-one showed up to meet him, when a good-looking young American with 'a four-inch scar across his left cheek' approached him and introduced himself as George Sinclair.[36]

Sinclair showed Dicketts his red Gestapo card and said they were going to leave immediately for Hamburg. There was only one taxi, which four people were in the process of getting into, so Sinclair showed them his Gestapo card, said 'excuse me', and the people immediately gave him the taxi.

They caught the 6.12 pm train to Hamburg, and over a bottle of wine in their private compartment became rather friendly. George was 24 years old and had learned to speak excellent English when he was stationed in New York as an employee of the Hamburg Nord-Amerika Shipping Line. He used to play football for the German Youth Movement, and had toured America, South Africa, Malaya and around Europe. His real name was Georg Sessler, and he had been in the German Secret Service for two years.

Sessler's Abwehr colleagues had arranged for a female agent to hopefully share Dicketts' bed and his secrets, and it was Sessler's job to prepare him. He told Dicketts about all the great things to do in Hamburg, including the attractive girls in the Reeperbahn, the city's red-light district. When he thought he had Dicketts' keen attention, Sessler told him he knew 'a cracking girl with long slender legs, and full bosom who had a romantic disposition'.[37] Little did Sessler realize that 'Anna' would soon fall prey to Dicketts' charms, and want to protect him.

It was 11 pm when they arrived in Hamburg and went straight to the luxurious Hotel Vier Jahreszeiten, where a small suite, No. 344, had been reserved for Dicketts. Sessler said they would call for him at 8 am the following morning and left.

Sessler told journalist Günter Peis in 1973 that Dicketts was about to face a horde of 'intelligence-hungry, army, navy and airforce experts'.[38] Potent drugs had been placed in a safe in case they had to render Dicketts rapidly unconscious, but the greatest risk to Dicketts was the Gestapo, who had installed themselves in the room next door with special microphones, handcuffs, pistols and chloroform.

After Sessler left, Dicketts went downstairs for a drink at the American Bar and immediately discovered the presence of his Abwehr watchers. As he opened his door, one man followed him downstairs and another took over in the lounge and watched him enter the bar. The sequence was repeated when he went back to his room.

Ritter had arranged for technical experts to present him with a long list of questions that had been especially prepared for him in Berlin, and the next morning Sessler arrived with two men, who greeted Dicketts very warmly. The more senior of the two was introduced to him as Dr Schwarz, who reminded Dicketts of the prominent British comedian Arthur Askey. He wore heavy horn-rimmed spectacles, with his hair shaven three-quarters of the way across the scalp, and spoke perfect English with the pure intonation of a typical country clergyman. His second-in-command, who was introduced to Dicketts as Dr Powell, was tall and dark, with hair going slightly grey, a strong, straight nose and grey-blue eyes.[39] Sessler later told Dicketts they were from Abteilung II, the Abwehr division responsible for sabotage and exploitation in foreign countries.

The four men sat down in Dicketts' room and the interrogations began, continuing relentlessly for five long days. Sessler took notes, while the others asked Dicketts to describe in very great detail how he and Owens had met. Dicketts told them the same story he gave Ritter in Lisbon, except in much more detail, saying he had been kept apart from Owens' other activities.

Trying to throw him off-guard, his German interrogators interjected constantly. What were the actual dates he and Owens had met, and what contact had he had with Owens? What had he done in between the period he and Owens parted to when they picked up their relationship again? How had he been living and what had he been earning? It was a very ruthless interrogation, and there was no doubt they were very suspicious. The first part of his interview lasted until 12.30 pm, when they took him out to lunch.

By 2 pm, they were back in his room asking for full details of his First World War service career, complete with dates and ranks, his intelligence work at the end of the war, and what friends and contacts he possessed in Germany. What countries had he been to, and what he had been doing since 1930? The Abwehr were trying to establish if he had a network in Germany, or whether Dicketts was operating alone. Since Dicketts had offered to become a German spy, their next questions were about his personal faculties, in particular his memory.

Their questioning was never-ending; they broke for dinner at 6 pm and returned to his room at 8 pm, after which they asked him questions that were totally out of context. Dicketts suspected his testimony was also being recorded by a shorthand-typist in the adjoining suite, and knew everything he said on his first day would be compared to each subsequent day, so there was never a moment when he could let his guard down. Finally, at 10.15 pm, they concluded the interview and left.

Day two was a repeat of day one. The Abwehr wanted to know in great detail what Dicketts had been doing during the last year, where he had been living, how much he had earned and which firms he had worked for? They asked him to repeat the circumstances of his meeting with Owens, and whether he had any contact with the British Intelligence Service. As Dicketts had no idea what Owens had already told them, he gave vague answers to their questions about people he had met through Owens. He said he had heard the name Mac, and had met a man named Williams (GW) for about ten minutes. He was asked to describe GW, which he did, keeping as close to the truth as possible, as he had been briefed.

During their break for lunch, they took Dicketts to a cheap restaurant so he could see how the rationing system varied in different standards of hotels and cafes. Sessler told Peis in 1973 that every one of these restaurants had been carefully selected beforehand so Dicketts could report back how well everyone ate in Hamburg.

Back in his room once more, Dicketts was asked to repeat his war history and his record since 1930. In an effort to throw him off-balance, they interrupted him constantly and asked him questions that were totally out of context. Then, after an hour's break for dinner, they questioned Dicketts for two hours as to why he wanted to work for Germany, what his feelings were about England and the government, and how much he expected to make in the way of money and so on. Just as they were leaving, they handed Dicketts some foolscap paper and a pencil, and asked him to write down everything they had discussed in great detail.

Dr Powell was left behind to supervise Dicketts, and finally, at 10.00 pm, an exhausted Dicketts handed him his notes, which were referred to constantly over the next three days of questioning. No word was left unexamined – Dicketts' German interrogators went through every single detail on these pages, checking and double-checking the information. It was like being a bug under a microscope.

On day three, they brought along another man, whom they didn't introduce to Dicketts by name. He had receding mouse-coloured hair, a hooked nose and many gold teeth, apologized in fluent English that he had not been there before and asked Dicketts if he could repeat the whole story all over again. Dicketts never saw this man again, and thought he might have come from the Gestapo or Propaganda Department. After lunch at the hotel, Dicketts, accompanied by his four Abwehr inquisitors, returned to his room, where his cross-examination continued until 7 pm.

Sessler would later describe how people came from all over Germany to obtain information from the alleged RAF deserter, but few of them realized that 'he could be a sticky customer when he wanted to'.[40] During his long interrogation, Dicketts was threatened and sometimes contradicted. He was asked, over and over again, how they were to know that his information was correct and that he was sincere. Dicketts blandly and disarmingly replied: 'Do you really believe for one moment that I would have come to Germany voluntarily as a spy, to be caught out and possibly hanged? Surely all you have to do is to have my statements checked by your agents in England.'[41]

On the fourth day, Ritter finally appeared with Dr Schwartz and Dr Powell, apologized for the necessity of the interrogation and asked Dicketts if he would be kind enough to go over the whole story again, as he had not been present. Their interview continued until 5 pm, with a small interval for lunch. Dicketts took the opportunity to thank Ritter for the great accommodation and hospitality he had been shown, and Ritter rather transparently tried to boost Dicketts' ego by saying that as soon as he met him, he realized Dicketts was a very different type of man to Owens. They wanted to show him the best kind of treatment, as they thought he could be of great value to them. Dicketts knew what Ritter was up to; he was trying to impress Dicketts by showing him how much money was available to him if Dicketts decided to work loyally for Germany.

That evening, after Ritter had left, the remaining three Germans – Schwartz, Powell and Sessler – gleefully announced that they had decided to treat Dicketts to lobster as he seemed rather tired. No doubt they were also looking forward to a slap-up meal at a very expensive restaurant called Schumann's, where they had reserved a private room. It was a wonderful meal, but the constant questioning meant Dicketts could never relax. Even on the way to and from the restaurant, they tested Dicketts on his memory. As they had done on all their previous outings, the Germans pointed out a particular building and then drove past it several times, asking Dicketts to recall various details like how many windows it had, the colour of its brickwork etc. Dicketts had an exceptionally good memory, almost photographic, but his ability could be perceived in two different ways. If Dicketts was accepted as a German agent who worked loyally for them, his memory could be very useful, but the reverse was true if Dicketts was a British penetration agent, as some of Ritter's colleagues in the Abwehr believed.

On Monday, 10 March, Dicketts faced his fifth day of interrogation, the toughest one yet. He was about to face the classic interrogation technique of 'good cop, bad cop'. The new man who arrived with Ritter, Schwartz and Powell was violently anti-English and showed great hostility towards Dicketts. He was introduced to Dicketts as Dr Decker, who was about 5ft 6in tall, with an intensely pale face, protruding teeth and thick, ash-coloured hair, whom Sessler later said was an air expert from Abteilung II. Decker began a cross-examination on Dicketts' story to date, which was a very lengthy process as Decker didn't speak English very well. He questioned Dicketts on his knowledge of the RAF, checked up on his war service and asked him what contacts or knowledge he had acquired lately.

MI5 was well aware that Dicketts would be questioned on these matters, and suitable answers had been prepared for him - but MI5's real goal was to get the Germans to reveal what they didn't know and what they wanted to know. MI5 hoped Dicketts would be accepted by the Germans, so their strategy was to build up German confidence in Dicketts, his knowledge and his connections. Dicketts was to appear to be entirely capable of procuring information, but needed proper instruction about what they wanted him to obtain. If Dicketts succeeded, and the Germans began asking for genuine information, he was to memorize everything they said, which would be analyzed in great detail on Dicketts' return, to establish the Germans' preferences and priorities.

Dicketts was told to be alert to the possibility that they would try to plant misinformation on him by feigning ignorance, when in fact they already knew the answers. Dicketts was to achieve all this under the pressure of numerous interrogators, some of whom were extremely aggressive, in the full knowledge that if he slipped up, he would never make it out alive.

After lunch, Decker produced a detailed questionnaire, which had been carefully prepared beforehand, and showed complete disbelief when Dicketts said he had not received any briefing from Owens about what was required, and therefore had very little information. It was a reasonable response which MI5 hoped would elicit further questions, either through frustration, lack of caution or during casual conversation. The dangerous side of this tactic was that Dicketts had been sold to the Germans as someone who could provide them with a great deal of information, so some of what he gave the Abwehr was good information, and the rest was chicken feed. As instructed, Dicketts memorized the questions Decker asked him so he could report back to MI5, some of which were:[42]

1. What are the exact strengths of the 3rd, 4th, 5th and 6th Bomber Commands?
2. How many planes to a Wing?
3. What is the personnel strength of the [Bomber] Command, and does it work in conjunction with the military?
5. Give details of the Beaufighter (a multi-role, heavy fighter aircraft). Where is it made? What is the output? What is its armament?
6. Are they using the new cannon? Is the cannon the Coventry cannon (Dicketts visited several factories in Coventry) or Hispano-Suiza? Obtain the exact location of cannon factories and the number of men employed.
7. Is the Avro-Anson (a 2-engine multi-role aircraft used to train aircrew) still in use?
8. Is the S.29 (Short Stirling 4-engine bomber) in active service? What is the production of the S.29 and what are the chief factories making this plane?
9. How are the new American planes being delivered, and how are the spare parts being delivered?
10. Are the new Flying Fortresses (a Boeing USA 4-engine bomber) already in use? State how many if possible.
11. Give the fullest details of the aerodromes from which night bombers take off.

Dicketts apologized to Decker and said for the reasons he had just stated, he couldn't answer any of the questions, except he believed the Avro-Anson was still in use. Decker was exasperated at his apparent ignorance, but Ritter told Dicketts not to worry, as he understood he had received insufficient instruction. For the next hour, Dicketts was taken back over various points in his story, particularly those in connection with Owens and what knowledge he had of his links with British intelligence. Dicketts explained that he had been kept apart from Owens' other activities, as Owens thought he would be useful to him in another sphere, and the less he knew, the less dangerous it would be for him.

'Do you know any of the people who Arthur is in contact with in England? First of all, the people who are working for him?'[43] asked Ritter. Dicketts stuck to the agreed story, and said that he had heard of a man called Biscuit and had seen GW for ten minutes.

Do you know 'anyone in the British Secret Service?'[44] they asked. This was a dangerous moment: Dicketts had no idea what Owens had already told them, and neither did he have any proof that Owens was a genuine German spy. 'I had to be very careful,' Dicketts told MI5 later. 'I had to try and escape around the question.'[45] Dicketts told the Germans he had met some people with Owens but didn't know who they were.

'Have you met Major Robertson?' asked the Germans.

Dicketts felt sure if he had answered 'no' at once, and Owens had previously told Ritter that Dicketts was in contact with Major Robertson, then he was in a very bad spot. 'As a matter of fact I was finished. My use to them was finished. So I thought the best thing to do was to hedge,' Dicketts told MI5.[46]

'Have you met people who were apparently in the Services, people who might look like him [Major Robertson]?' asked the Germans.[47]

Dicketts said he had met someone with an 'army look', and when asked to describe him said, 'he was around 6ft 2, with fair hair',[48] and suggested they ask Owens, as he would know better. According to Ritter's memoirs, Dicketts worked hard and filled in sheet after sheet of information, and his work was checked by experts over and over again.

'It was found that he was indeed a pilot and an expert, as he had maintained. Some of his answers were new and good. That gave me some satisfaction. In other words, the mission had not been in vain,' Ritter wrote in his autobiography.[49]

To Dicketts' considerable relief, the following morning, Dr Schwarz and Dr Powell came in and shook him by the hand, and said he had passed the test. 'You are all right,' they said, 'now go and relax and enjoy yourself. You are at complete liberty to go anywhere you want, but don't do anything foolish.'

To complete the illusion that Dicketts was free to go wherever he wanted, they gave him the telephone number of their headquarters, in case he got into any difficulties. Dicketts already knew the number, as he had watched them dial 221693 from his room and had committed it to memory.

Although Dicketts didn't say anything in his report to MI5 about being followed, he knew it was inevitable, and had acted accordingly. According to Ritter, Dicketts was tailed discreetly by a man from the secret police, and during his entire stay he never tried to get into contact with anyone: 'That proved that he never really planned to stay in Germany.'[50]

Far from being able to relax during his first interrogation-free day, the Germans had planned a sightseeing trip for Dicketts in meticulous detail. Appearing as if he was going out of his way to be hospitable, Ritter offered him his personal car, the latest model Wanderer in black, and suggested Sessler take him on a tour around Hamburg to see the air-raid damage. The route had been prepared in advance and was to form part of his 'psychological preparations', Sessler told Peis in 1973.[51]

The air-raid damage Sessler showed Dicketts was minimal, limited to two streets of houses and a hospital. Sessler had been told to take a note of everything Dicketts said, no matter how trivial. The only comment Dicketts made during the tour was to say that British pilots were told that the Germans disguised their munitions factories with a Red Cross. 'How are they to know the difference?' he asked.

Suspecting the Germans had planned to demonstrate to him how poorly aimed British bombs were, Dicketts later came back to the docks alone on several occasions looking for evidence to the contrary. During the First World War, Dicketts had flown bombing missions on German ports, and he was disappointed to see how little damage the RAF had inflicted twenty-five years later. Dicketts wasn't to know that up until November 1940, Bomber Command had been targeting oil refineries, and the first bombs directed at Hamburg were to its oil refineries in late May 1940. By October, Bomber Command's strategy shifted to concentrated attacks on industrial targets, and heavy damage was inflicted on the 'Blohm & Voss shipyard in Hamburg with over sixty fires started' on 15 November.[52] They were unable to inflict any serious damage, as bomber crews had difficulty identifying individual targets in the darkness of the blackout.

That same day, Dicketts and Sessler had stopped for a drink at a cafe located on the high ground just above the Hohelbrucken ferry, when Dicketts noticed three grey ships of about 12,000 tons, which appeared to be in the process of being supplied by the smaller vessels alongside them. There was a large body of troops, who appeared to be ordinary infantrymen, going off on a tender, who carried one Tommy gun to every twenty or thirty men. Dicketts noted there was nothing special about their equipment, such as special winter clothing etc.

The next stop on Dicketts' tour was the storehouses next to the Altona Bridge, where Sessler proudly informed him that the whole of last year's harvest had been untouched, and that school buildings, drill halls and churches all over the country had been commandeered to store the harvest. If Dicketts was a penetration agent, as they suspected, he would report back that the Germans had plenty of food to feed their people for a very long time. German strategy at the time was to starve Britain into submission by sending U-boats into the Atlantic to sink merchant vessels bringing it vital supplies.

That evening, Sessler took him on a comprehensive tour of the dance-halls and nightclubs of Hamburg. If ever there was a time for Sessler to introduce Dicketts to the Abwehr's honey-trap, 'Anna', this was probably it. To Dicketts' surprise, these places were almost full with hostesses and men in uniform, despite the fact it was not a recognized day for dancing, which was only permitted on Wednesdays, Thursdays and Saturdays. Prices were clearly marked and any attempt at extortion was severely punished.

'On account of my personal liking for you,'[53] said Sessler, 'Dr Schwartz is trying to prevent you leaving Germany as he doesn't trust you, and thinks you are double-crossing.' Dr Decker had agreed with him, and there had been an argument with Ritter. Sessler said he detested Dr Schwarz, who had been in the bureau for far less time than he had, but had managed to somehow rise to a higher rank. This was worrying news, and Dicketts knew he would have to be very careful.

At 4.45 am on 12 March, when Dicketts and Sessler had been out drinking all night at various Hamburg nightclubs, Sessler left to take a girl home. Shortly afterwards, nearly 'seventy RAF bombers'[54] appeared, focusing their attack on the Blohm & Voss shipyards. Police ordered Dicketts and others to go to the air-raid shelter deep under the Hauptbahnhof railway station, where he struck up a conversation with three German staff officers and a junior officer, who spoke to him in German, and then in English after he told them he was a repatriated German-American.

'Do you think America will enter the war?' they asked. Dicketts remained purposefully vague, letting them do most of the talking. The officers thought that even if America did enter the war, it would just prolong it, as Germany's hold on Europe was so strong, and wouldn't make any difference to their ultimate victory. Unless the US conveyed food and materials to England, they thought the war would be over by the end of the year. When the all-clear sounded at 7.20 am, Dicketts only just got back to his hotel before his German investigators arrived.

This was the first time the Germans brought anything with them. Decker handed Dicketts a detailed book of the airfields of England. Each photograph had a separate page attached to it, containing an index of the buildings and personnel stationed there, and Dicketts was asked to go through it and see if he could supply any additional information. After what Sessler had just told him about Decker's suspicions of him, Dicketts knew he had to be very careful, and was concerned that he had to keep saying the same excuse – that he hadn't been given any instructions by Owens about what sort of information was required.

Two hours later, Ritter appeared to be convinced that Dicketts had no additional information to offer and asked him to memorize certain factors which Dicketts should try to obtain when he returned to England. Decker, however, made it quite plain that he didn't like or trust Dicketts, and he and Ritter started to argue. Ritter told Decker to mind his own business and to leave the room.

'Don't worry about this at all,' Ritter told Dicketts afterwards.[55] 'I am looking after you and I am only responsible to Hermann Göring. These people will do as I tell them.'

After Decker left, Dicketts was alone with Ritter for the first time. Ritter invited Dicketts to join him and his wife to see a show at the Hansa Theatre that evening, which Dicketts accepted and said he would enjoy very much. 'I'm a very good judge of character,' said Ritter. 'I have trusted Owens, and now I am prepared to trust you.' Dicketts had seen Ritter display genuine affection for Owens in Lisbon, but still had no firm proof of Owens' true status within the Abwehr. Dicketts made his first attempt to find out, but during this and subsequent conversations, Ritter's comments were always along the same lines: 'Arthur is a fool in many ways, he drinks too much and he lives on his nerves but I am prepared to go on trusting him because I have known him for more than four years and he has never, to my knowledge, let me down.'[56]

'He must have been giving you some very good information,' said Dicketts. Ritter replied:

'No, Arthur hasn't given me very much but I think he is going to be very useful to us in other ways.'

'What ways are those?' asked Dicketts casually.

Ritter told him not to ask too many questions, then said, 'Arthur is a very clever chemist. In fact, in some ways he is brilliant. He is a goddam lazy son of a bitch, who wouldn't get going unless someone gave him a good kick in the pants.'

'Arthur spends a hell of a lot of money,' Ritter continued, 'but we don't mind as we have plenty of it here.' Sometimes, Ritter's strategies were so transparent to Dicketts that it is a wonder he managed to keep a straight face.

By the end of his trip, Dicketts concluded that Ritter regarded the information he received from Owens as 'innocuous, but reasonably accurate and only of use in a confirmatory sense'. Dicketts thought the real reason Ritter was keeping Owens in play was to use him as a valuable contact point in England during the invasion.

According to Sessler, Admiral Canaris feared Dicketts was 'one of the toughest agents of the British Secret Service',[57] but his subordinate, Ritter, believed Dicketts was 'a traitor in need of money' and had gone all out to impress upon him how wonderful everything was in Germany. Ritter had accommodated him in the best hotels, and wined and dined him at the best restaurants, and finally it was time to get down to business.

Ritter told Dicketts he wanted him and Owens to operate separately. They were not to send or receive messages through each other:

> I can see you are the type of man who could go around and get information without suspicion. I want you to memorize certain factors, which I want you to try and find out when you go back to England. Owens has told me about your boat, and I wondered if it would be possible for you to deliver your reports personally by sea-going launch from the south coast of England to a rendezvous point off the coast of the Channel Islands?

Dicketts said the journey would take around twelve to fourteen hours from a small Devon village where he was well known, where it would be simple for him to obtain a boat. Provided there were no patrols, it should be easy for him to slip out and head for the Channel Islands, which were currently occupied by the Germans.

'I told Arthur I would give you what you wanted for your personal spending. How much do you require when you get back in England to secure yourself against any eventualities?' asked Ritter.

Dicketts replied: 'Very little, as I'm not here to sell information. I'm anxious to help end the war and from what I have seen the German government is excellent and Germany has every chance of winning.'

Ritter agreed and asked how much he would need to buy the boat and have some extra money on hand. 'Would £300 or £400 be enough?'

Dicketts agreed, and with instructions and money matters out of the way, Ritter asked him what his contacts in England thought about the prospect of peace? Ritter said that despite the propaganda in the British and American newspapers, Hitler was sincere about making peace with England but was willing to go to any lengths to prove that the new Germany had the right to become a major player in European political and economic matters.

'I am informed you have a number of friends in England in influential positions,' said Ritter. 'Germany sincerely desires peace, and if you can come back accredited in some way, I will take you to see Herman Göring who would probably take you to see Hitler.'

'How could I possibly come back accredited, and in any case what could a small man like myself do in a situation of such tremendous and worldwide significance?' said Dicketts.

'You never know, you may have been selected by some kind of fate to help in this matter,' said Ritter, who suggested Dicketts spoke to some of his trusted friends and asked their opinion.

'Do you know why Sir Wyndham Deedes returned from the Near East?' asked Ritter.

Dicketts wondered where the conversation was going. He used to work for Deedes at the National Council of Social Services before the war, and Deedes had been sent to Palestine as the Chief Secretary to the British High Commissioner on the outbreak of war. Dicketts wondered if Ritter was going to ask him to try to obtain the names of members of the Pacifists' Party in England, and what positions they held.

'Out of the matters we have just discussed, which issue is more important – to obtain the information you asked for or to tackle the peace question?' asked Dicketts.

Ritter told him he should try to do both, but he was not to take any risk in obtaining information unless it was something of great importance. 'Take the rest of the afternoon off,' he said. 'My chauffeur will collect you at 6.20 pm and take you to the theatre.'

Dicketts reported this conversation to MI5 when he returned, and was asked for his opinion of Ritter and his peace overtures. Dicketts said that in his opinion, Ritter 'was a high pressure salesman of the American type – a clever man and an extremely lucid and convincing talker, but I am inclined to believe that he has a really genuine desire of peace (favourable of course to Germany) – and would welcome a move from our side'.[58]

When he and Ritter parted, Dicketts took a taxi to the poorer suburbs in St Pauli on the south side of the docks, where some of the streets had been hit during the recent air raid while he was sheltering under the Hauptbahnhof railway station. Dicketts couldn't understand why RAF bombs had been dropped there, as there was no important factory or industry, just low-class nightclubs and government housing. Dicketts wasn't aware that, as of 9 March, Bomber Command was no longer restricting its attacks to military targets only, and was selecting congested areas where the greatest impact on the population's morale would result. The Luftwaffe was doing the same thing in Britain.

Dicketts noticed two new submarines with high fore-peaks cruising down the river, and went into a cafe overlooking the river so that he could observe the ships without drawing attention to himself. When the waiter, who spoke reasonably good English, came over to serve him, Dicketts pointed to the submarines and made a comment in American-accented English. 'Yes,' said the waiter proudly. 'They have just been completed, and are now going out to sink English ships. We are sending down two a week like this.'

That evening, Dicketts was collected by Ritter's chauffeur as planned and taken to the Ritz, where he met Ritter and his wife at the bar. Irmgard von Klitzing was a thin, well-dressed woman in her mid-20s, who spoke very good English with a Bavarian accent. She came from a prominent background with lineage to one of the German Kaisers, and told Dicketts she hated the war and claimed to be pro-British; she was actually 'a member of the Nazi party and politically influential within the Abwehr'.[59]

Irmgard had been Ritter's secretary when he was still married to his American wife, Aurora, at a time when Hitler was actively discouraging his officers from forming close personal relationships with foreigners. With Irmgard's encouragement, their relationship soon became more than platonic, and Ritter was completely torn between 'his political ambitions and his emotional ties and affection for his wife and child'. Aurora made the choice for him, filing for divorce, and he had married Irmgard soon after the divorce became final. Dicketts could see Ritter was completely devoted to her.

He spent a very pleasant evening with the Ritters and Dr Powell in their private box at the Hansa Theatre, followed by supper at Hamburg's most famous cafe, the Alster Pavilion. As they were making their way to their reserved niche, Mrs Ritter whispered to her husband, 'Did you see his big ring? It's made for opening. Shall I ask him?'[60]

Ritter agreed, but was annoyed with himself for not having noticed this before. Commonly referred to as poison, locket or box rings, these large rings have a secret compartment inside them which can be opened to reveal a photograph or a locket of hair etc. They can also be used to carry poison – to kill someone or avoid capture or torture.

Mrs Ritter inquired after Dicketts' wife and suggested he should bring her with him on his next trip to Germany so she would be safe from reprisals in England if he were found out, or if the invasion suddenly took place. Ritter later wrote:[61]

> The meal was good; the wine was also good. Brown enjoyed it. As he raised his glass, I heard my wife say: 'My, what a beautiful ring you have there!' That was the first time I saw the man look baffled. 'Look out,' I thought. Brown smiled and showed my wife the ring but did not take it off. Then she asked him quite harmlessly: 'It looks as if one could open it.'
>
> Brown was prepared. 'You are a good observer, Madam,' he said politely and opened the ring.
>
> 'A pretty girl,' said my wife and looked at the tiny photo. 'Your wife?'
>
> 'Not yet,' Brown smiled and closed the ring again.
>
> 'Interesting,' I said and acted as if I was no longer interested in the ring. After a couple of minutes, I excused myself. From the phone booth in the restaurant, I called the duty officer at our duty

station and gave him some instructions. The waiter brought the after-dinner drink. We urged Brown to keep drinking. After the meal, I had my wife driven home. The gentlemen left for a nearby bar. Brown protested: 'I am not accustomed to drinking so much. I would rather like to go back to the hotel,' he said.

'But you wanted to take a good look around,' I said and insisted that he come along.

When Ritter's party arrived at the bar, they were greeted with special politeness by the business manager and led to a table. There was only one other person in the bar, a harmless-looking gentleman whom they greeted briefly and then sat down. After ordering three large cognacs, Ritter excused himself and went to the bathroom, returning just as Dicketts and Powell were toasting each other, '*Prosit* ...' Suddenly, Dicketts stopped in the middle of a sentence. He had fallen asleep.

The stranger said: 'Everything is in order, Herr Doktor.'

'How long?' Ritter asked.

'At least two hours,' he replied.

The stranger pulled the ring off Dicketts' finger and took the picture out, checking there was nothing else behind it. He placed it carefully into an envelope and pushed the ring back onto Dicketts' finger, and returned an hour and a half later and reversed the procedure. 'Everything is in order,' he told Ritter.

Ritter wanted to know if he should wake Dicketts up, but the gentleman said it wasn't necessary as he would wake up by himself. There would be no after-effects and Dicketts wouldn't notice anything. Sure enough, Dicketts woke up about half an hour later, and looked around annoyed until he recognized them.

'Did you sleep well?' Ritter asked.

'I am sorry,' Dicketts apologized. 'I am not accustomed to so much alcohol.'

'That's all right,' said Ritter. 'Now we will have a little snack, and then we'll go to sleep.'

The next morning, Ritter received an enlarged copy of the back of the photograph, which displayed a meaningless series of letters and numbers which seemed to be in code. Unfortunately, the code would take several weeks to be broken in Berlin, and by that time Dicketts would have left.

'Now I'm really curious,' thought Ritter. 'We cannot possibly let him go before we have an answer.'

At 9.30 am the following day, an increasingly suspicious Ritter, accompanied by Schwartz and Sessler, visited Dicketts at his hotel. Determined to find out what they believed to be the contact information for an accomplice, hidden in code at the back of Dicketts' wife's photograph, they began interrogating Dicketts about his contacts in Berlin, Hamburg and Lisbon.

Despite all his precautions, Dicketts realized he had been followed in Lisbon after Ritter challenged him about his visit to 'Mr [redacted]', whom the Germans were aware was doing Secret Service work for the British Government. Dicketts said his conversations with him had been purely commercial, relating to the 'export from Portugal of sardines, cork, fruit and wolfram'.[62] They had met twice to discuss the export trade, the difficulties of shipping, and the possibilities of obtaining tin from England, since most of the sardine factories in Portugal were closed.

'Would it be difficult for you to return to Lisbon?' Dicketts was asked. He replied:

> I went over there with quite good credentials in the first place. And I now have letters and inquiries for tin, food and other exports which are of vital importance to Britain. If I was to take those letters and apply for another export permit and a visa for Portugal it shouldn't be difficult. In my opinion, if you hadn't already known the true reason for my visit, you wouldn't have had any reason to question my business activities.[63]

Realizing there was nothing more they could get out of Dicketts, Ritter took him to lunch and told him to take the rest of the afternoon off. Dicketts walked around Hamburg's inner lake, the Binnen Alster, examining the method of camouflage, which they had been working on day and night since he had been there. Hamburg's most important bridge divided the outer lake and the smaller inner lake, which had been covered completely with 'plaited wickerwork mounted on 20 or 30 foot poles projecting about eight feet from the water'. The plan was to blot out all sign of water from the air, so the RAF couldn't identify and bomb the bridge. British reconnaissance images taken five months later showed how successful this camouflage was from the air.

(*Right*) Petty Officer Walter Dicketts
RNAS, 1915.

(*Below*) British Mark 1 (Male)
tank, 1916.

A "Splatter Mask" worn by tank crews in the
Their faces from the thick lead n...
flying across th...

(*Above left*) First World War tank crew splatter mask.

(*Above right*) Dicketts (left) as a trainee RNAS pilot in 1917, with a Maurice Farman Shorthorn aircraft.

(*Left*) Phyllis Hobson, Dicketts' first wife, whom he married on 13 May 1918.

Captain Walter 'Dick' Dicketts (first left), Dept. A1., Air Ministry (Intelligence) 1919.

Dora Viva Guerrier, (top row, second left left) Dicketts' first mistress appearing with the Helena Stars, Gaumont Palace, Paris, 1924.

(*Above left*) My grandmother, Dora Viva Guerrier, Dicketts' first mistress, 1919–22.

(*Above right*) Dicketts' mistress Dora, with his daughter Effie (centre) and Dora's mother, Euphemia Smith, (right). Effie was lied to that Euphemia was her mother and Dora was her sister.

(*Left*) My mother, Effie Dicketts, born on 20 September 1920. Effie changed her name to Tonie Witt in 1940.

(*right*) Dicketts' second son, Rodney, to first
wife Phyllis, born on 13 October 1921. Rodney's
surname was changed to Adair by deed poll.

(*below*) Dicketts' son, Eric, ('Dick' to his first
mistress, Dora) was born on 18 February 1922.
With his wife Mary and daughters Susan and
Geraldine in the late 1950s. Dick and his sister
Sofie would never meet.

Above left: Kathleen Mary Holdcroft, Dicketts' second mistress, who played a role in h[...]
spying activities for MI5 during the Second World War.

Above right: Vera Nellie Fudge, Dicketts' third wife whom he married on 22 April 1933, with [...]
son Richard, born on 18 January 1934. Richard's surname was changed to Tudhope by deed po[...]

Miss Alma Farquhar Wood, aged sixteen, who has been missing since April 30 from her home at Leigh-on-Sea.

Mr. Walter Dicketts, to whom, it is stated, Miss Wood was to have been married in London shortly. He has also been missing since April 30.

Alma Farquhar Wood, Dicketts' 16-year old second wife with whom he eloped and marrie[...]
on 16 April 1929.

rthur Owens, MI5
ouble agent Snow.

olonel Thomas Argyll
ar' Robertson, in charge
MI5's double agents.

John Cecil Masterman, Chairman of the Double Cross Committee.

Members of the Double Cross Committee during the Second World War. Chairman John Masterman (centre), with Tar Robertson to his right, and Guy Liddell, Director of B Division (counter-espionage) behind him.

Lieutenant Colonel Robin 'Tin-Eye' Stephens, Camp 020 Commander.

German agent Gösta Caroli in 1938 – he became MI5 double agent Summer.

REPÚBLICA DOS ESTADOS UNIDOS DO BRASIL

MODÊLO S.C. 139

FICHA CONSULAR DE QUALIFICAÇÃO

Esta ficha, expedida em duas vias, será entregue à Polícia Marítima e à Imigração no pôrto de destino

Nome por extenso SESSLER Georg

Admitido em território nacional em caráter TURISTA
(temporário ou permanente)

Nos termos do art. 7 letra A do dec. n. 7967, de 1945

Lugar e data de nascimento RUSTRINGER (Alemanha), 14/6/1917.

Nacionalidade Alemã Estado civil Casado

Filiação (nome do Pai e da Mãe) Georg SESSLER e de Cécilia Schneider Profissão Capitão

Residência no país de origem Sessler Marie-Françoise, 13 Rue Beaumont. Marselha. (B.du Rh.)

NOME IDADE SEXO

FILHOS MENORES DE 18 ANOS

Passaporte n. 163/52 expedido pelas autoridades de Clnsulado Geral de Alemanha, Marselha na data de 26/2/1952.

visado sob n. 81.

Consulado do Brasil
em Marselha

ASSINATURA DO PORTADOR:

NOTA—Esta ficha deve ser preenchida à máquina pela autoridade consular, sendo as duas vias em original

DAVID LINS
CONSUL

O CÔNSUL: David Luis

de abril de 1952

George Sessler, Dicketts' Abwehr bodyguard and escort from Lisbon to Hamburg and Berlin in 1941.

Admiral Wilhelm Canaris, Chief of the Abwehr in the Second World War.

(*above left*) Nikolaus Ritter, Chief of Air Intelligence for the Abwehr in the Second World War.

(*above right*) John Bull magazine, 1957, article showing Dicketts being drugged in Hamburg.

(*below*) Ritter and wife Irmgard von Klitzing. Irmgard was involved in Dicketts being drugged in Hamburg in 1941.

Alfred Naujocks, a major in the SS, was sent to kidnap Dicketts in Hamburg in 1941.

Reinhard Heydrich, head of the Sicherheitsdienst (SD), one of the main architects of the Holocaust.

(*above left*) Dicketts' Brazilian visa on behalf of MI5 in 1941. The strain of war is etched upon ~~s~~ features.

(*above right*) Dicketts on his boat around 1947.

(*below*) Dicketts' prosperous period after the Second World War. With his fourth wife Judith ~~·~~lman, whom he married on 8 September 1943, and their son, Robert, who was born on ~~·~~ August 1944.

(*Left*) Dicketts on Dartmoor, 1956.

(*Below*) Mike Adair, grandson of Dicketts' first wife, Phyllis, and Carolinda Witt, granddaughter of his mistress, Dora Guerrier. Dicketts was with both their grandmothers at the same time.

:ketts' two children to Dora Guerrier: my mother Tonie Witt, who died on 27 June 2007, her brother, Eric 'Dick' Dicketts. Dick was awarded a Distinguished Flying Cross during Second World War. They never met in real life.

orge 'Robin' Graeme
:ketts Adair, Dicketts'
t son to Phyllis – he
ved with T-Force in the
:ond World War and
d on 6 June 2006.

(*Left*) Dicketts' son, Robert, to fourth wife, Judith Rose Kelman, born on 31 August 194 (*Right*) Dicketts' son, Richard 'Dick' Anthony, to third wife Vera Nellie Fudge, born on 18 January 1934. Dick's surnam was changed to Tudhope by deed poll.

Dicketts' grandson, Corporal Oliver Simon Dicketts, of the Special Reconnaissance Unit, d in Afghanistan in 2006. He was the only child of Robert and Priscilla.

The whole of the Binnen Alster Basin appeared to have been covered with streets (which were in fact floating barges, made to look like buildings) and a completely false bridge appeared to have been constructed north of the real one.

That evening, Dicketts and Sessler went to the Trichter dance hall, followed by the Young Nazi Political Club, where they remained drinking and singing until 5.30 am. By that stage, the entire club was in a state of drunkenness and some of the men took great exception to him, saying he was an American and trying to pick a fight. Dicketts suggested they fight their way out, but Sessler refused and produced his police permit. He called the ringleaders together and gave them a warning about concentration camps, and told them that they were the worst kind of German. One man then called him a few filthy names, so Sessler, who was a first-class boxer, hit him twice and knocked him out. They left the club in silence and went home.

After very little sleep, Dicketts was collected by Dr Schwarz and taken to meet 'Dr Goebbels' assistant'[64] at the Ministry of Propaganda. Dicketts wasn't introduced by name to this boisterous older man with grey hair and many gold teeth. He was extremely deaf and his eyes were hidden behind very thick glasses. He told Dicketts he was going to give him some books to read, and some gramophone records to listen to, which were just for amusement as they were parodies on popular British songs such as *We're Going to Hang out Our Washing on the Siegfried Line*, etc.

Goebbels' assistant said he was sure that the people in England were being fed completely false information, but there must be thinking people there who disbelieved the government's statements and wanted to end the war. 'I am informed you have some influential friends,' he said, and suggested Dicketts took these books with him and circulated them privately to people of importance. Dicketts could get them reprinted if necessary. These books were *The German Foreign Office Documentary of the Polish Atrocities*, *The Reminiscences of a British Staff Officer* and various other pamphlets which he claimed Germany was sending to every country in the world.

Schwartz said it was too dangerous, and besides 'Brown' had more important work to do. Undeterred, Dr Goebbels' assistant gave Dicketts two pamphlets which he wanted him to present personally or post to Winston Churchill. He also insisted Dicketts went to collect some other pamphlets and books from another section at 2 pm.

By the time Dicketts had collected these materials, the effects of the alcohol and lack of sleep from the night before had caught up with him. He told Schwartz he didn't feel well and spent the rest of the afternoon and evening in his hotel room.

During his final days in Hamburg, Ritter arranged for him to have dinner with Air Kapitan Kommandant Turner, who was pitched to Dicketts as an old brother pilot of the last war. Turner was aged about 48-50 and very English-looking. He was of average height with a slight build, receding brown hair and rather large unsightly teeth. According to Ritter, Turner was second-in-command of a section of the Luftwaffe involved in invasion plans.

Dicketts knew exactly what the Germans were trying to achieve. They hoped Turner - aka Kapitänleutnant Tornow - would engage him in an argument about the various merits of both air forces and their planes, so Dicketts would let slip some information they hadn't been able to get out of him during his five-day cross-examination.

After a friendly chat about their mutual air forces and personal experiences during the first war, Tornow tried to put Dicketts on the defensive by saying he was very disappointed with the RAF at the moment, because of their poor targeting in Hamburg and Berlin. Dicketts didn't rise to the bait, despite having been injured during a German bombing raid on London on 12 September 1940 at the height of the Blitz.

Tornow boasted their new Messerschmitt could beat any scout the British had, except perhaps for the Beaufighter, which they had little information about. He said they had 3,400 of their newest fighter jets based at Liège in Belgium and 4,500 bombers which were well camouflaged and would be used for the specific purpose of the invasion.

'What about troop-carrying gliders?' asked Dicketts.

Tornow replied: 'Although we have one or two thousand of them, they could easily be shot down provided the British had sufficient fighters to repel the invasion.'

It was a game of cat and mouse, which got rather heated at times as both men pretended to outdo the other, with the specific aim of eliciting information from the other.

'You do not understand the strength of the British Air Force and Navy,' said Dicketts.

'Our plan will render the Navy of no use,' Tornow said.

'That is ridiculous,' Dicketts continued. 'How can you as a clever man possibly make such an absurd statement?'

Although Tornow was most friendly and plied Dicketts with different drinks from about 7-11.30 pm, Tornow rapidly became quite drunk and was more anxious to talk to Dicketts about the merits of the Luftwaffe than to ask him questions about the RAF. The only essential question he asked Dicketts was if he knew the top cruising speed, weight and armament of the new Beaufighter.

The day before he left Hamburg, Dicketts met two staff officers with Ritter at a bar. They were very keen to learn what preparations had been made in England to repel their invasion and to counter-attack. Hitler had actually already postponed the invasion after the RAF's convincing defeat of the Luftwaffe during the Battle of Britain, and had turned his attention towards an invasion of the Soviet Union in June 1941.

Winston Churchill knew of Hitler's decision to postpone the invasion via top-secret German radio intercepts (ISOS), but decided to keep Britain on high alert. If he did otherwise, the Germans might realize the British had cracked their 'unbreakable' Enigma cipher.

While Germany prepared in secret for Operation BARBAROSSA, the invasion of the Soviet Union, Hitler developed a deception plan codenamed ALBION, to convince the British and the Soviets that an invasion of Britain was still about to take place. The first component of this plan, codenamed *HAIFISCH* (shark), was scheduled for the coastline in France during April 1941, shortly after Dicketts returned to England. It may have accounted for the troop concentrations Dicketts saw at the docks on 12 March.

Dicketts continued to field questions from the German staff officers in the bar. Was it true the British had electronically controlled mines in layers of one to three miles on the Essex, Suffolk, Yorkshire, Kent and Sussex coasts? Ritter interjected and said that the most important information he needed from Dicketts when he got back to England was to tour the neighbourhoods of Hornchurch, Maplesham, Friston, Scarborough and Hornsea aerodromes, and collect every piece of information he could on the dispositions and numbers of troops, ammunition dumps and how the railways were guarded.

Ritter suggested Dicketts took his Air Ministry friends out to lunch or dinner and spent money on them – Ritter would make sure funds were available for Dicketts to do this. Dicketts was to find out where his friends were stationed, and ask them if he could look over the aeroplanes. Once inside the aircraft, he was to try to obtain the latest manuals and other top-secret information they carried aboard the bombers and fighters.

'If you can obtain a copy of the latest War Office Manual that would be of vital importance,' said Ritter. It would be worth any risk to obtain this information, and if Dicketts was successful, he should purchase a motor boat and proceed without delay to the Channel Islands, where they would have a daily patrol waiting for him between 7-15 April. If Dicketts had to buy or steal something that would be found out within forty-eight hours, he was to pack everything up and leave England, bringing Owens, Lily and Kay with him.

At their last meeting, Ritter told Dicketts they had no intention of using gas, as Germany had a new secret weapon which would blast any defence Britain had. He couldn't tell Dicketts what it was, but said he should stay away from the coast and meet them at an agreed spot when the invasion occurred. Ritter said:

'We hope very much that you will be able to get back within fourteen days and bring us as much of this information as possible. You will be rewarded by anything that you like to ask and we will look after you and your family for life.'[65]

Chapter 8

Escape From Germany

'Today's enemies can be your friends tomorrow. And today's
friends can be tomorrow's enemies.' Suzy Kassem

It had been nineteen harrowing days since Dicketts left Lisbon, and he was still in Hamburg awaiting the Abwehr's decision as to whether his offer to become a German spy had been accepted – or whether his luxury suite at the beautiful Vier Jahreszeiten Hotel was about to be replaced with the cold, impenetrable walls of a Gestapo prison cell.

On Monday, 17 March, Dicketts had his last meeting with Ritter, who told him he had been 'passed as their agent'[1] and would be leaving for Berlin that day. Dicketts' photograph was taken for his *Reisepass* (German passport), which arrived while he and Ritter were still talking. Ritter gave Dicketts £400 (mostly bank notes plundered from France)[2] and said if he needed any further money for entertainment of any kind, or for bribing officials, he should ask Owens.

'Don't hesitate to spend money,' said Ritter, 'Arthur has more than he needs and will be instructed to give you whatever you require.'[3]

Sessler came into the room and had a private talk with Ritter, then asked Dicketts for his *Reisepass* and said, 'we have to go and get another photograph'. By the time Dicketts returned to his hotel suite, Ritter had gone. Sessler arrived a few hours later and said he was very anxious to leave Hamburg, but because it would take too long to obtain a Portuguese visa on Dicketts' ordinary *Reisepass*, Sessler had taken upon himself to obtain a *Dienstpass* (diplomatic passport) No. 135,[4] nominating Dicketts as Walter Anton Denker, an embassy courier. Sessler was very nervous about having done this, and swore Dicketts to secrecy. He said he had obtained it without the knowledge of the German Foreign Office and 'would be for it' if anyone found out.

As an Abwehr courier, Sessler travelled everywhere on a legitimate *Dienstpass* with a sealed bag, and had obtained one for Dicketts as his assistant –

'Syndikus [Consul], Assistant of German Minister of State, travelling with and as Assistant Courier'.[5] If Dicketts was caught with a false diplomatic passport, there is no doubt what would happen to him, let alone Sessler.

Dicketts sent a plain code message by cable to his mistress, Kay, saying he expected to be back in around three weeks' time and would make his own arrangements. Tar would interpret this as 'I am not fleeing the country under duress and will not be needing assistance.'

On the same day, Owens cabled Lily from Lisbon, saying he was ill and asking her to bring the baby to Lisbon to take care of him. 'Even if that were possible we should certainly not agree to it,' wrote Guy Liddell in his diary on 15 March.[6] It was a curious request, given the difficulty Owens and Dicketts had in obtaining their Portuguese visas. Besides, with Lily and the baby safely out of Britain, Owens himself may not have returned.

Sessler told Peis in June 1973 that he and Dicketts had to leave Germany very quickly because Reinhard Heydrich, the feared chief of the Nazi's intelligence and security agency, the Sicherheitsdienst (SD), had discovered that he and Dicketts 'were getting ready' to leave Hamburg for an unknown destination.[7] Fortunately, Sessler had a friend in the SD who showed him a confidential telex which had just arrived from Berlin, saying that the Englishman in the care of the Abwehr was to be arrested 'on some suitable pretext' and brought to the Reich Security Agency headquarters in Berlin.[8] Heydrich was showing a personal interest in what was going on with Dicketts, and if necessary wanted to take control of the matter himself.

The man Heydrich sent to capture Dicketts was SS Sturmbannfuhrer Alfred Naujocks, who had lured two British SIS officers – Sigismund Best and Richard Stevens – into a trap at the Dutch border town of Venlo in November 1939. Best and Stevens thought they were meeting a German general who was supposed to be the leader of the resistance movement in Nazi Germany, but were captured instead. Heydrich set up the trap after suspecting the British had some involvement in the failed assassination attempt of Hitler at the Munich beer hall earlier that month, and wanted to capture these agents to obtain the names of their German conspirators. To Canaris, it was powerful proof that the SD had designs on the Abwehr. 'This *schweinerei* is Heydrich's doing!'[9] Canaris shouted when he heard about it.

If there was anyone you didn't want after you, it was Naujocks. He was 'a callous murderer' who liquidated opponents of the Nazi regime under

Heydrich's command, and was suspected of 'war crimes, particularly in Denmark'.[10] Günter Peis interviewed Naujocks in 1968 at the Hamburg nightclub where he was acting as a bouncer. Naujocks said he had been given orders in early 1941 to capture the Englishman 'whom the Abwehr were handling like a raw egg', and take him to the Prinz Albrecht Palace in Berlin for a confrontation with Best and Stevens.[11]

Sessler knew he had 'to act quickly and on his own initiative or both he and Dicketts would land up on the gallows'.[12] He told Dicketts he would collect him at his hotel later in the evening so they could slip out of Hamburg under cover of darkness, but when he arrived, there was a complication – 'Anna', the prostitute, had fallen in love with Dicketts and refused to let him go without her. It was easier and less of a security risk for Sessler to take 'Anna' with them, so they fled the hotel behind the backs of two men from the SD and went into hiding at the Hotel Timmendorferstrand on the Baltic coast, about an hour's drive north-west of Hamburg.[13]

Sessler spotted the two SD men in brown leather jackets in the lobby of the hotel two days later, and quickly led Dicketts and Anna out of the back door and hid them in a lodging house in the suburb of Hamburg-Hochkamp. He told them not to leave the house until he returned, and caught the train to Berlin to get Canaris' approval. He came upon Canaris purely by chance in the corridor of the Abwehr headquarters, and told him what was going on. Canaris seemed to know already about the activities of the SD, and ordered Sessler to 'get that man back to where he came from. Do you understand?'[14]

Sessler understood perfectly, and returned as quickly as he could to where he had hidden Dicketts, expecting the Gestapo to arrest him at any moment. He arrived at around 2–3 am and found Dicketts sitting on the bed, dressed and ready to leave. He kissed his German lover for the last time, said, 'Goodbye Anna, God bless you,' and for the first time in the years he had known her, Sessler saw 'Anna' cry.

Dicketts didn't say anything to MI5 about his flight from the hands of the SD in Germany, and Sessler could easily have justified his actions to Dicketts by blaming the risks associated with discovery of the false *Dienstpass*. As far as Dicketts' reports are concerned, the whole event never took place, although there is one interesting connection. When Dicketts arrived in England, a complete inventory of the contents of his clothing and personal items were itemized on a list, which included two packets of matches from Timmendorferstrand – their hideout on the Baltic.[15] One packet was from the 'Bar al Sibarita' and the other was from the Kurhotel Denker – Denker was Dicketts' bogus surname in his *Dienstpass*. It wasn't a coincidence, as Sessler had invented the name Walter Anton Denker at the German Embassy when he spontaneously thought of his 'old friend, Werner Denker', the former owner of the Hotel Denker in Timmendorferstrand.[16]

The war had been over for almost thirty years when Sessler told this story to Gunter Peis in 1973, and begs the question why Sessler would have invented such a tale had it not transpired at all. The fact that the Abwehr and the SD were acting independently and in competition with each other would have been of significant interest to MI5. And for Dicketts, who had undergone this dangerous mission to regain his lost respectability, intelligence of this calibre would have gone a long way towards helping him achieve his goal. Yet all he had to say was how nervous Sessler was about using the *Dienstpass*. It is entirely feasible that Sessler never told Dicketts as his concern about his own fate was real, and if the SD captured Dicketts, the less he knew the better.

The issue of the *Dienstpass* also caused credibility issues with MI5 when Dicketts returned to England. As with any double agent who had recently been in contact with the enemy, MI5 needed to establish if the information Dicketts brought back was real or planted on him. More ominously, MI5 needed to establish if Dicketts had been turned by the enemy, and it was left to Dick White, the future head of both MI5 and SIS, to find out.

'Do you think the German Embassies and Foreign Office don't know that this goes on all the time?' White asked when interrogating Dicketts upon his return.[17]

'I am sure the Minister did not know,' replied Dicketts.

'You come back on a diplomatic pass and no official knows. Are they leading you up the garden path?' White continued.

'No, I am quite certain they were not. … I would request that no action is taken on this, otherwise it would destroy all means of communication,' said Dicketts.[18] 'As far as I am aware this is the first time that this has been done with a foreign agent ostensibly working for Germany and without the knowledge of the German Foreign Office.'

* * *

In the early morning of Monday, 17 March 1941, Dicketts and Sessler boarded their first-class carriage on the train taking them from Hamburg to

Berlin. Dicketts purchased some food from the Mitropa dining car and put the receipt in his pocket to show MI5 when he returned to England.

They arrived in Berlin in the afternoon and checked into their double suite at the legendary Adlon Hotel, located on the Unter den Linden (main boulevard) opposite the Brandenburg Gate. The hotel was situated in the heart of the Reich's capital and cultural centre, where Nazi symbolism abounded. Numerous red and white flags with huge black swastikas fluttered from flagpoles and from banners draped in front of buildings. Statues of imperial eagles atop swastikas loomed from giant columns above streets filled with people in military uniforms of grey and brown. Here and there strode the feared SS (Schutzstaffel), Hitler's personal bodyguards, in their jackboots and all black uniforms. The overall effect was to portray the invincibility and might of the German Reich, and contrasted greatly to the bruised and battered appearance of London following the Blitz.

Sessler and Dicketts spent until dusk touring Berlin's factory quarters, the Templehof district and the major railway stations. Ritter had suggested they take a picture of Dicketts in front of each station to prove how little air-raid damage there was, but someone must have quashed his idea before it could take place. However, it was true that there was very little damage from the RAF bombing raids, as Berlin had only been bombed a few times, the first raid having taken place on 23 August 1940 in retaliation to German bombs being dropped on London. An American journalist, William Shirer, was staying at the Adlon at the time, and recorded the Berliners' reaction in his diary:

> The Berliners are stunned. They did not think it could happen. When this war began, Goering assured them it couldn't. He boasted that no enemy planes could ever break through the outer and inner rings of the capital's anti-aircraft defence. The Berliners are a naive and simple people. They believed him. Their disillusionment today is therefore all the greater. You have to see their faces to measure it.[19]

As night fell in Berlin on 17 March 1941, Dicketts noticed that the blackout was not as well done as it was in London. Sessler took him to meet three officials at a club who wanted to see Dicketts and gauge his attitude towards Germany and England. They showed great interest in the 'working man's attitude towards the war' and the morale of the British people. [20] Such was their pronounced interest in the Welsh coal valleys, that Dicketts suggested to MI5 on his return that anyone living in Wales who was free with their money, but without a lucrative or permanent business, should be watched or interrogated.

After a long night of drinking, which concluded at 5 am, Sessler and Dicketts had just one hour to board their Heinkel aircraft, which stopped at Stuttgart for a passport and customs inspection. Sessler appeared to Dicketts to be very nervous, and admitted he was worried about being questioned too closely over his *Dienstpass*. 'My green Abwehr pass had never been more important to me than during that journey', and it was only through it and sheer luck that no mishap occurred, Sessler told Peis in 1973. [21]

They stopped at Lyons, followed by Barcelona, where Sessler called the local Abwehr official. 'Where are you?' the official answered, with fear in his voice. Sessler instantly realized that the SD had already 'stretched their tentacles to Spain', [22] so he and Dicketts went to ground until it was time for their flight to Madrid.

Having spent so much time together, Sessler and Dicketts had become quite good friends. Sessler told him 'he was at loggerheads with everyone in his department' except Ritter, of whom he was very fond. [23] He would like to get out of Germany and go to England, as he was very pro-British and American.

Sessler was stressed when they arrived in Madrid and found Ritter's instructions had gone astray, and there were no seats booked for them on the flight to Lisbon. Sessler booked them into the Palace Hotel and then called the local Abwehr officer, who said he would like to meet him in the lobby straight away. Fearing a trap, Sessler suggested they should meet at a crossroads where he could observe the area better.

Sessler knew that before he left he would have to confide in Dicketts, as he realized 'the most important Allied secret agent we had ever had in our grasp could quite easily escape from me here in [neutral] Spain'. [24] Sessler told Dicketts what he was going to do, and said he had honoured his word and got Dicketts safely out of Germany; now it was Dicketts' turn to give him his word that he would wait for his return. 'If you don't, I will go to the wall,' said Sessler.

The Abwehr official gave Sessler a small, sealed attaché case to smuggle across the border to Portugal as diplomatic luggage, and warned Sessler not to let it out of his sight. When his Abwehr colleague left, Sessler held the case up to his ear to check if anything was ticking inside, 'as it would have been just like the SD to send them into the next world with their own bomb'.[25]

Sessler was quite surprised and very relieved to see Dicketts waiting for him in the cafe as agreed. According to Ritter's autobiography, Dicketts escaped Sessler in Madrid: 'The fact that he did not go to Lisbon or return directly to England confirms my suspicion that he was a communist.'[26] But Ritter's assistant, Major Julius Boeckel, told his British interrogators at CSDIC (Combined Services Detailed Interrogation Centre) at the end of the war that Dicketts 'was escorted back to Lisbon by Uffz Georg Sessler'.[27]

Dicketts told MI5 that there was nothing to do in Madrid as everything was closed for the festival of San Jose. He went for a stroll in the afternoon and went out drinking with Sessler to the 'Casablanca and the Rex' in the evening.[28] The following morning, they took their luggage to the German Embassy, where it was corded and sealed, and then caught the 11 am train to Lisbon. They conversed in German because Dicketts was travelling on a German passport, and later in English with American accents when they discovered that the extremely good-looking woman sharing their first-class compartment was English. Sessler was very taken with Mrs Marcelle Quenall, who was being repatriated to England from Marseilles. He offered her a gin fizz from his large bottle of Gordon's gin, but she refused, saying 'she wouldn't drink with a German'.[29]

When passport officials entered their compartment, they checked their diplomatic passports and embassy bags and passed them without any difficulty. As this was happening, Dicketts glanced at Mrs Quenall and caught her studying him intently.

It was 8 am by the time they arrived in Valencia on the east coast of Spain, where Dobler was waiting to exchange Dicketts' German passport for his British passport, which had the Portuguese visa stamped inside it. Dobler removed the diplomatic seals from Dicketts' luggage and they set off for Lisbon. After a long and uncomfortable drive across Spain, they arrived in Lisbon at 8 pm, and for security left Dicketts on the outskirts to make his own way to the Metropole Hotel.

As Dicketts waited in the bar for Owens to show up, he discovered that the little Welshman had become embroiled with a cast of characters who seemed to know rather too much about his activities as a British spy than they ought. A Frenchman called Regnault joined him at the bar and said Owens had been ill and 'constantly drunk and very worried since you left on your tour abroad'.

'I'm afraid you've made a mistake,' said Dicketts. 'I've been in Portugal on a business trip, travelling to Setúbal, Badajoz and Oporto.' Regnault said Owens had helped him out with some money after he had been thrown out of his hotel for not paying his bills, but Owens had since dumped him in favour of an Englishman, Patrick Nolan, and his wife.

'Who is this man [Owens]?' Regnault asked Dicketts. [30] 'He told me he worked for the British Secret Service and could give me lucrative employment immediately.'

'I've never heard so much nonsense in my life,' said Dicketts, laughing.[31] 'I can only imagine that as a result of his having been extremely ill, combined with heavy drinking and Lisbon fever that he must have gone temporarily out of his mind.' Dicketts later told MI5 that by the end their discussion, he had managed to convince Regnault that this Secret Service story was a load of rubbish.

Neutral Lisbon was full of people like Regnault. In the shadows of that city of light, refugees scrambled desperately for visas and repatriation to the United States, South America or anywhere to escape the advancing Nazis. Fleeing Jews and anti-Nazis brushed up against German agents and the feared Gestapo, and in the avenues, hotels, cafes and bars, businessmen and spies from every country swapped information and received payment.

Dicketts received a message from Owens asking him to come to the Arcadia nightclub, where he found him in the company of the Nolans and two girls who were German agents masquerading as dancers. They moved to a separate table, where Dicketts told Owens about his trip. He stuck to the truth as closely as possible and provided Owens with very little detail. Sticking to his role, Dicketts said he had been deeply impressed with the Germans' organization, food situation and the lack of air raid damage.

'I brought you back,' said Owens. 'Nobody else could have done it.'[32]

Dicketts brought up the subject of Regnault and warned Owens of the great danger of discussing his connection to British intelligence. Owens cut him off: 'Pay his bills for a further two days. I'll have him got rid of as he is dangerous.'

'Don't be stupid, Arthur, you don't want yourself mixed up in any troubles in Portugal,' Dicketts replied.

Unknown to Dicketts, Dobler had suggested to Owens that he loaned Regnault some money, so that they could recruit him to work for Germany. However, after checking into Regnault's record they had decided not to use him.[33]

Dicketts and Owens finished their conversation and rejoined the girls, and Lotti, who had become acquainted with Dicketts before he left for Hamburg, immediately latched onto him until 5 am. She said she worried about him during his absence and that she was being recalled to Berlin for a while. If Dicketts ever came back, she asked him to look her up and wrote her name and address on a piece of paper, and gave him a photograph of herself. These items remain in Dicketts' Security Service file today.[34]

Aware that German spies were operating throughout Lisbon, Dicketts and Owens went by separate routes to the British Embassy the following morning. They met with two men, one of whom was the SIS man operating under the cover of Passport Control Officer. Dicketts said he must get back to England as quickly as possible as a result of certain information he had obtained. When asked where he had been and what the information was about, Dicketts replied, 'I'm sorry but I have nothing to say.'

It was clear Dicketts wasn't going to tell them anything, and they finally agreed to do whatever they could to get he and Owens back on the first available plane. Dicketts said he had some information he wanted to go in the embassy bag, and was told to come back on Monday so the items could be sealed and placed in the bag in front of him.

Dicketts' telegram to Tar Robertson saying they would be back within a week arrived the same day as a letter from Ralph Jarvis, head of SIS's Section V (counter-intelligence) station in Lisbon. Jarvis said he had 'some disquieting news' about Owens, who had come in to see him on 12 March.[35] Owens told Jarvis that Ritter had confronted him at their first meeting, saying he knew Owens' messages had been 'faked' for the last few months, and Owens hadn't denied it. Owens told Ritter he had been discovered by the British and forced to continue sending messages. Ritter accepted Owens' explanation and gave him £10,000, along with instructions for further work in England.

Owens thought Ritter may have come to suspect him by the ease with which he had been allowed to leave England, or by the poor quality of his recent information. 'Perhaps McCarthy [Biscuit] had said something.' He wasn't sure.

This was very bad news for the fledgling double-cross team, who were forced to confront the possibility that the entire 'party', including Snow, Celery, GW, Biscuit, Summer, Charlie and possibly Tate, were blown.[36] They would also have to assume that Rainbow, an agent from another network, was also compromised, as Tate had been given his address by the Germans. This left MI5 with just four agents – the soon to be very important double agent Tricycle and three others, Giraffe, Stork and Lewis.

Not only would MI5 lose their only direct contact with Ritter and Ast. Hamburg via Owens' wireless transmitter, it meant they would no longer be able to obtain advance warning of the arrival of the pre-invasion spies, and all their efforts in building up their double agents would be lost.

* * *

Meanwhile, in Lisbon, Dicketts and Owens were still waiting for a flight to take them back to England.

Owens wasn't well, and was being taken care of by a Portuguese girl called Madame Elisabeth Fernanda, who stayed with him in his hotel room and looked after him extremely well. Dicketts was certain there was no relationship between them, because he had come into Owens' room on many occasions and found her sitting fully dressed on the edge of his bed giving him cold towels and medicine, and holding his hand while he was asleep. In return, Owens treated her lavishly and bought new furniture for her parents. Owens trusted her implicitly to cut down and pay all his bills for him, for which she accounted for every escudo. Owens later told MI5 that he had hired her to help him out, as no one spoke English in Lisbon, and he had a temperature of 104 and felt like hell.[37]

Owens told Dicketts he only wished he could be in Canada, as his stomach was so bad and he had so many worries. Dicketts completely disregarded the whole conversation, as it took place at 6 am when Owens was 'three parts tight and taking Veronal [sleeping pills]', which could be purchased anywhere.[38] Owens was drinking heavily, but on the whole was very friendly towards Dicketts, except when he tried to drag him out of one of his drinking bouts. Once, aided by a Jewish refugee called Knapmann, Dicketts had to rouse him up with wet towels.

On the second night of his return to Lisbon, Dicketts was with Owens and some other people at a bar when he spotted Mrs Quenall from the Madrid to Valencia train. It was obvious she had been listening into their conversation and had heard Dicketts speaking English with an English accent, instead of the American one she had heard him use on the train. Dicketts excused himself from the others, went over to speak to her and invited her to dinner, which she rather reluctantly agreed to.

He took Mrs Quenall to a car, and once inside said he was sorry to be unpleasant, 'but I want your passport'.[39] Mrs Quenall appeared a little frightened by this, and said it was obvious to her that Dicketts was an Englishman. Dicketts told her it was none of her business, and since she was reliant on her weekly allowance from the British Consul during her stay in Lisbon, he strongly advised her to forget anything she may have seen or heard. Then he took down all the details from her passport, including her various foreign visas.

During dinner, Mrs Quenall told Dicketts she was not a fool, and thought he must be working for the British Secret Service on account of what she had seen on the train. She said she had applied to work for them in Paris but had been turned down. Dicketts said he would see what he could do to help, so long as she gave him her word that she would forget the whole episode, which she agreed.

Dicketts discovered she had a high fever and no money to pay for medical attention, so he gave her 200 escudos and took her to see a doctor. He also paid for her fruit and medicine. The next time he saw Mrs Quenall, she said she had been questioned by a man called Regnault who claimed to be working for Dicketts' employer (Owens) doing work for the British and German Secret Services.

Dicketts immediately reported this conversation to Owens and warned him again of his foolishness.

'I will attend to them both and they will be in a concentration camp within twenty-four hours,' said Owens.[40] 'Don't speak to them again.'

Dicketts returned to the embassy on Monday, taking a circuitous route involving three taxis to make sure he wasn't being followed. He unlocked his bag in the presence of Mr King, the consul-general (his real role was the Commercial Secretary), who approved his papers, which were then sealed inside a foolscap envelope and placed in the embassy bag addressed to 'T.A.R., Room 055, War Office'.[41]

The night before they left Lisbon, Dicketts was invited to dinner by Hans Ruser, who had driven him to Madrid, and his mother at their place in Estoril. Dicketts took Owens with him because Dobler thought it would be good policy, but although Owens was rather coldly received, the Rusers invited him to dinner nonetheless. Owens declined, saying he was sorry but he had other arrangements, and joined Madame Fernanda at the English Bar instead.

Dicketts noticed a Union Jack and a swastika flag flying outside the Rusers' house, and asked if it wasn't rather dangerous. 'No, so and so [expletive] the Nazis. I am a German and I am working for my country. I have much influence and will entertain my friends of any nationality as and when I choose,'[42] said Ruser.

At the end of their very pleasant dinner, Ruser asked Dicketts to post a letter to their relatives in England and offered him the letter to read. Remembering how Ruser had refused to censor Dicketts' letters to his wife and parents in Madrid, Dicketts in turn declined to read Ruser's.

When he returned to England, Dicketts told MI5 that Ruser wanted to come to England, and 'could be of great value' to any of their people who found themselves in difficulty in Lisbon.[43] Dicketts said Ruser and his mother were sincere people who loved England and the English, and vehemently hated the Nazi regime.

A year later, Ruser approached SIS in Lisbon and offered to reveal all in return for being allowed to come to England. Ruser was rebuffed for fear of jeopardizing Tricycle, one of MI5's most important double agents with whom Ruser had been in contact. When Ruser was transferred to Madrid in 1943, he tried again, and this time he was successful in being recruited and became double agent Junior.

As word spread that Dicketts and Owens were leaving Lisbon, Owens' coterie of dependants became increasingly desperate. As Dicketts was playing the role of Owens' secretary, it was left to him to sort it all out. The manager of the Metropole Hotel approached Dicketts and said Owens had told him to get 6,000 escudos from Dicketts to pay Regnault's bills.

The night before they left, Regnault confronted Owens in the hotel lounge with the news that he was going to commit suicide that night. Owens told him not to talk such nonsense and asked him why he told such lies about him to Dicketts. 'You know very well that they are not lies, but I thank you for the money you have given me,' said Regnault.

'Don't talk nonsense,' said Owens, and turned to Dicketts. 'Pay this man's bills for two nights and keep the receipt for me,' he said.[44]

Regnault was madly in love with Mrs Nolan, who was only staying with her husband until they got their children out of France and then planned to run away with Regnault. Regnault had accused Owens of ruining his life, as Owens had initially sympathized with him and Mrs Nolan, but had since changed sides and was giving Nolan money, often going out drinking with him at Owens' expense.

Dicketts later described Nolan to MI5 as a weak man, a sponger of the worst kind, and said he was certain Owens had revealed to him his involvement with British intelligence. Dicketts also recommended that Regnault should not work for British intelligence under any circumstances, as he was unreliable in every way and an inveterate gossiper. MI5 carried out their own investigations, which confirmed Dicketts' view, and asked the British Repatriation Office to help them get Regnault out of Lisbon so he couldn't damage Owens' or Dicketts' status within the Abwehr.

Dicketts didn't know that after he and Sessler arrived back in Lisbon, Owens had introduced Nolan to Sessler as a potential recruit. Nolan told Sessler that he and his wife had to flee France after he got into trouble with the police, and were forced to leave behind their two young children, aged just 18 months and 2 months. The Nolans had walked over the Pyrenees and arrived in Lisbon, where they were being paid around £2 a week by the Repatriation Committee until they could be resettled in Ireland. Sessler recruited Nolan and made arrangements for their children to be sent from Nice to Dublin, where Nolan was to work under Owens' instructions. The Germans intended to send agents into Ireland and would ferry them from the Channel Islands into England in the boat driven by Dicketts. Owens was to take over at this point and make sure they reached Ireland safely.[45]

Owens had also become friendly with a Jewish-looking man called Knapmann, who claimed to be down to his last £30 but was clearly getting money from somewhere. Dicketts strongly suspected Owens may have revealed his connection to British intelligence to Knapmann, just as he had done with Regnault. Despite Owens' assurance 'Absolutely not', Dicketts suspected otherwise and carried out further investigations into Knapmann's background. When he discovered it was quite different to what Knapmann had told them, Dicketts went to see Mr King at the embassy and asked him to arrange a passage for Knapmann. King agreed that it was best if Knapmann was out of the country, and said he would see to it immediately.

Finally, on 27 March, after a week of anxious waiting, Dicketts and Owens got a seat on a flight back to England. Owens had asked Dicketts several times in the preceding few days if he had any worries or doubts in his mind. 'You must tell me everything, and then I can help you,' said Owens.

'Why are you asking?' said Dicketts.

'You are only a novice at this game. If you knew what I know you would be very worried,' Owens replied.[46]

'Please don't worry me as I have had a sufficient nerve strain,' said Dicketts. 'Tell me what it is about.'

Owens refused, saying all he could tell Dicketts was that he was in a dangerous position and that Dicketts should put his trust in him and do nothing without talking to him first.

Shortly before they left, Owens told Dicketts he had just received a cable from England saying Dicketts would be arrested on his return. He would have a very bad time back in England, said Owens, adding: 'I think you can trust Robbie [Tar], but no one else.'[47]

'I've kept my promise and got you back,' said Owens. 'I'm the only person you can rely on, so [do] you want to go back [to England] or not?'

Chapter 9

Who to Believe?

'He that has eyes to see and ears to hear may convince himself
that no mortal can keep a secret. If his lips are silent, he chatters
with his fingertips; betrayal oozes out of him at every pore.'
Sigmund Freud

At Portela airport north of Lisbon, Dicketts and Owens boarded their
Douglas DC-3 aircraft to return to England at last. They were looking forward to seeing their wives and families again, but Owens knew
the strain of the past six weeks wasn't over yet. He had been through enough
MI5 debriefings after he returned from his *treffs* with the Germans to know
what to expect. This time, however, it was different. Owens didn't know what
Dicketts had discovered in Germany or the contents of that top-secret envelope he was carrying. Whatever it was, Dicketts seemed a bit intense, perhaps
even excited about it. Used to being the centre of attention, Owens wondered
if Dicketts was about to become more significant to MI5 than he had previously thought possible.

As their plane took off from Lisbon on 27 March, Dicketts felt some of
the strain ease from his body, and the fatigue he had fought for so long
threatened to overcome him. He knew he had done all he could, and more,
and the prospect of delivering his vital information about troop preparations
he saw in Hamburg gave him a boost of energy as he anticipated Tar's reaction to the news.

Tar Robertson's feelings towards their return were very different to what
Dicketts could have expected. Tar knew Owens had blown the party to the
Germans, and if the information was correct, the entire British double-cross
system was facing collapse. Ralph Jarvis, a merchant banker in peacetime,
had told Tar he thought Owens appeared to have had a good time in Lisbon,
but believed Owens' current situation had rather gone to his head. 'But, I'm
sure you'll bring him to his senses on his return,' said Jarvis.[1]

Tar wondered if there was anything that could be salvaged from this disaster, and made careful plans for their arrival. Dicketts and Owens would be segregated immediately, and great care would be taken to prevent either of them from coming into contact with the other. The plan was to search each man separately, then take them in two different cars to separate locations where they would be interrogated. Stenographers would record everything they said during interrogations and privately, and this would be compared to future interrogations. One cannot help but feel sympathetic towards Dicketts, who had just been through an intensive interrogation in Germany, and would now have to go through it all over again in England.

As soon as Dicketts' and Owens' aircraft taxied to a stop at Bristol's Whitchurch Airport at 2.30 pm, they knew something was wrong. MI5 hadn't sent anyone to meet them, and the Security Control Officers appeared to have no idea who they were. If Dicketts had expected a hero's welcome, this certainly wasn't it.

Owens declared £10 and various papers, and was informed that he would be searched. Owens immediately asked to speak privately to Major Stratton, the SCO (Security Control Officer) in charge, and said he was employed by Major Robertson of MI5. Stafford knew this of course, but told Owens he would get in contact with Robertson for confirmation, and in the meantime the search would continue.

Owens was found to be carrying £10,000 in notes (around £454,500 today) and explosives hidden inside a fountain pen and a pencil.[2] They found further explosives in his baggage, hidden inside a torch, shaving soap and various toiletry items, which had been given to him by Hauptman Rudolf, the Abwehr's explosives expert in Lisbon, for sabotage purposes.[3]

Dicketts was examined next and appeared to be very nervous and ill at ease. 'I can't understand why you haven't been informed of our arrival,' he told Major Stratton. Realizing there was going to be a delay in getting his important intelligence to Tar, Dicketts asked Stratton to get in touch with Tar immediately and give him the message: 'Three 12,000 ton transports leaving Elbe [the major river that flows through Hamburg] 28th probably early morning. Carrying troops to assemble in Netherlands. Troops were to assemble March 26th.'[4]

They had just finished Dicketts' search when officers from MI5 arrived, and Dicketts, who had most resented his treatment, was placated. He was absolutely astonished when Stratton told him explosives had been found in Owens' bag, as 'he had no knowledge of it'.[5]

Dicketts and Owens were escorted to two separate vehicles, and their personal effects were placed in Dicketts' car, driven by MI5's most trusted chauffeur, the pre-war Aston Martin racing driver 'Jock' Horsfall. Also in the car was William 'Billy' Luke, an MI5 officer and owner of a linen thread company in Glasgow. He was also the case officer assigned to Duško Popov, the Serbian playboy who became one of MI5's most important double agents, Tricycle.

Owens asked if his belongings were in his vehicle, as he had no wish to travel with the explosives. It was a curious statement to make, as he had just flown from Lisbon to Bristol with them onboard, and Owens knew you had to fit the detonators hidden in the soap to the time clocks hidden in the flashlight to set off the explosives.[6] It may have been Owens' way of reminding MI5 about the risks he had just taken on their behalf and how courageous he had been.

Owens was taken to senior MI5 officer John Bingham's flat in Chelsea, and Dicketts to Billy Luke's flat in Mayfair. The following morning, Tar and his deputy, John Marriott, a young solicitor and Cambridge graduate, turned up to see Owens with a stenographer. Their strategy was to ask 'as few questions as possible' as Owens loved to talk, in the hope that Owens would say something in the relaxed environment that he wouldn't in a formal interview.[7] These notes would then be compared to future interrogations.

Owens wasn't well, and said he had been ill in Lisbon for some time. Although he was quite forthcoming, Tar thought there were definite moments where Owens was holding back, particularly when Owens introduced the fact that he had been blown. Owens told them much the same story he had given Jarvis in Lisbon, except for a few very important details.

Owens told MI5 that as soon as he arrived, Ritter had accused him of working for British intelligence, and Owens had replied that he had been trying to tell Ritter this for the past two-and-a-half months. Owens told Ritter that he had sent an SOS over the radio, but the operators in Hamburg 'were so lousy' Ritter never got it. Owens thought someone had given him away in England, as British intelligence had walked in on him and said they knew all about him and had given Owens two choices. 'I either helped them, or … What else could I do?'[8] Owens had asked Ritter. He had said he wanted to get to Lisbon to warn Ritter.

According to Owens, Ritter had accepted this explanation and said it didn't matter as he had come up with a new plan. Owens was to continue sending his messages as before, and Ritter would give him a code to indicate when a message was false.

Tar was itching to ask more questions but held back, knowing they would be digging into this story a lot deeper later on, but even he didn't expect what came next. Owens said he had told Dicketts that the Germans knew 'all about it' as soon as Dicketts arrived in Lisbon, and that Dicketts had gone into Germany regardless. Owens had apparently told Dicketts at the time that it was a very, very dangerous situation and asked Dicketts what he thought about it. Dicketts had replied that 'he thought it would work out all right'.[9]

If Owens was telling the truth that he warned Dicketts before he went into Germany, then why didn't the Germans execute Dicketts as a spy?

How was it that Owens, having made his admission to Ritter that he worked for British intelligence, was then given £10,000, a new radio code, some sabotage equipment and instructions to keep the game going? It just didn't ring true. The whole affair would need a lot of sifting, thought Tar.

One of the questions Tar did ask Owens was how Ritter viewed the other agents in Owens' network. It would give them an insight as to whether the whole party was blown as far as Ritter was concerned. Owens said GW and Charlie were fine with the Doctor, and although he was suspicious about Gösta Caroli's (Summer's) disappearance, Ritter thought Caroli would use his seaman's papers and eventually find his way back to Germany.[10] But as far as Biscuit (McCarthy) was concerned, 'he should be washed out altogether', said Owens. 'His name is mud with the Doctor. He thinks he is a complete mad man.'[11] It sounded like Owens' own view of McCarthy, not Ritter's, who had only met McCarthy once for a couple of hours in Lisbon. McCarthy would have been on his best behaviour in front of the Doctor, particularly as it was immediately after the failed North Sea rendezvous incident.

According to Owens, Ritter had become suspicious by the ease with which Biscuit managed to get his wireless set back into England, and thought he had 'made himself look ridiculous' by getting drunk and throwing away money. Ironically, this is exactly what Owens appeared to have been doing during his time in Lisbon.[12]

During an unrecorded lunch with Owens after Tar left them alone for a few hours, Marriott discovered two soft spots in Owens' story which he thought they could use during future interrogations. The first was that despite Owens' complete ignorance and indifference to the most important of current affairs, he now believed that Britain would win the war. Until now, Owens had always expressed profound admiration for German efficiency, which he believed nothing could stand against, and 'therefore on psychological grounds alone he would be likely to play on the German side, if he thought he could get away with it'.[13] The other was his extreme jealousy of Dicketts and the great treatment he received in Germany.

Owens told Marriott he couldn't understand how someone like Dicketts, who had come out of the blue, had no hesitation at all about going into Germany, after what Owens had told him about the Germans knowing all about their connection to British intelligence. To him, it was proof Dicketts was double-crossing MI5: 'Take it from me he's working for Germany. He's an extremely dangerous man. Very dangerous. He's money mad and takes dope.'[14]

What's more, Dicketts had told him he would receive a telegram when the invasion was about to take place, so they could get themselves and their wives out of England in time. 'By the way he talks, he's been sleeping with Hitler, and he's been talking in his sleep,' said Owens.[15]

The thing that seemed to be irritating Owens the most, was the way Dicketts had been treated in Germany:

> He went to Berlin, and he had an apartment at the Adler Hotel, which I've never had. He went to Hamburg, and he had the best hotel there, and he was treated like a king. It was remarkable to me. I have an extraordinarily good standing over there, as you know, but I've never had treatment like that.[16]

Although it was obvious to MI5 that Owens was extremely jealous of Dicketts, they also had to consider the possibility that Dicketts had been turned by the Germans, and the treatment he received was a reflection of the value they placed on him. Alternatively, given Owens' history in diminishing the importance of other double agents such as GW to someone 'who was too nervous' and Biscuit 'to a complete madman', Dicketts may have appeared to Owens to be his greatest threat yet. Someone who, for the first time, could potentially be of more value to the Germans, and therefore to MI5, than him.

* * *

Meanwhile, at Billy Luke's flat, Dicketts was writing down the details of the observations he had made in Hamburg regarding troops, submarines, shipyards and bomb damage. Lieutenant Commander Ewan Montagu from Naval Intelligence came to interview him twice, and wrote afterwards that he believed Dicketts was telling the truth, 'that he wasn't being stuffed with a story for this country' and that George Sessler from the Abwehr spoke to him as man to man, or as one German agent to another. Montagu thought Dicketts 'was rather too intelligent to have been deceived'.[17]

John Masterman and a stenographer arrived after lunch and took down Dicketts' reports on Germany's invasion plans, along with Ritter's relationship with Owens. Dicketts told Masterman about all the people he had met, describing them as best as he could, and gave him the surprising news that half of them used drugs to help deal with the stress. He handed Masterman a pill of Veronal (which survives in his file today) for MI5 to analyze, and said the Germans used it to help them sleep. 'They use cocaine in the morning to wake them up, and when they go on breaks they use a drug called Veramin which helps counter the effects of the Veronal,' said Dicketts.[18]

Information would emerge after the war that drug-use under the Nazi regime was extensive. Hitler was injected with Coramine (amphetamine) by his personal physician whenever he was overly sedated with barbiturates, and according to a new book by German author Norman Ohler, *Blitzed*, over 35 million German soldiers and bureaucrats were popping Pervitin (amphetamine) pills every day by May 1945. It was an army that marched on amphetamines; an estimated 200 million Pervitin pills had been distributed to German troops by the end of the war.[19]

By 5.15 pm, Dicketts was too tired to continue, so was allowed to rest.

* * *

Owens and Dicketts were given Sunday off, and on Monday morning Tar and Marriott went to see Owens, intending to take his statement apart point-by-point until they got a coherent story out of him. It led to some heated exchanges and a great deal of frustration.

'I want you to describe in the minutest detail what happened when you got into the car with Dobler, to the time you got into the flat,' said Tar,[20] who added:

'And you all went up to the flat together?'

'Yes, the three of us.'

'Who opened the door? ... Which floor was the flat on?'

And so on, until Owens eventually reached the point where Ritter confronted him with the belief that he was working for British intelligence. 'Didn't it come as rather a shock to you?' Owens agreed that it had, and he had wondered what was going to happen next.

'Did you colour up?' asked Tar. Owens said he hadn't at all, and neither did he hesitate in answering Ritter as he knew the game would have been up in two seconds flat if he hadn't.

Tar was suspicious. Why didn't Owens try to deny it or bluff his way out of it? Owens said his experience of the Doctor was that he never made any statements to him unless they were correct. Also, Ritter said he had a list of passengers and knew Owens had come over by priority on the flying boat, and the only way he could have done that was with the help of British intelligence.

Tar scoffed at this. He said Ritter was lying that he had a list. Besides, there was a waiting list of 1,000 people, and the only way you could get out of the country was to have some sort of priority, either a business or a Government priority. 'And you had a perfectly good business priority,' he told Owens.

'You think that would have got me out?' said Owens.

'Certainly. I mean, are we fools?'

'I didn't understand that. I mean, there's such a mix up. I was not sure of the man who was going too, Dicketts,' said Owens.

'It has absolutely nothing to do with Dicketts,' said Tar. 'I just want you to give me an absolutely true account of the whole thing.'

'I don't understand you, Major. Do you think I'm trying to double-cross you?'[21]

'It wouldn't surprise me.'

Owens said he was surprised Tar doubted his word. 'You have always been a little mysterious, and I want to clear this question up, and this is the time to do it,' said Tar.

It was like trying to squeeze blood out of a stone, and three hours later, everyone needed a break.

* * *

Masterman's interview with Dicketts, conducted at the same time as Owens', focused on his side of the story and what took place immediately after Dicketts arrived in Lisbon.

'How much did Owens tell you about his previous conversations with the Doctor before you arrived?' asked Masterman.[22]

Dicketts replied:

> Absolutely nothing. I begged Owens to tell me what I should do before meeting the Doctor and what he had told him so far. I asked him what I should do when I got into Germany, and the only thing he could tell me was that I would be safe. Owens gave me his word and said he wasn't like these people in England who sent me out here blindfolded and to my death had he not been here before me.

Dicketts said he then made several remarks to try to elicit further information from Owens, but to no avail. 'Owens never actually told me anything at all.'

'He didn't give you even a line or a hint as to what he had been discussing with the Doctor?' asked Masterman.

'No. Nothing at all.'[23]

'Was it deliberate?' asked Masterman. Dicketts said Owens was a very secretive person, and despite all his promises to Dicketts before they left, Owens behaved exactly the same way in Lisbon. Even if he took a girl out, Owens said it was business. One evening he told Dicketts he had a very important meeting and would be out all night, when in fact Owens simply went to bed and had forgotten all about it the next morning.

'I think he is a maniac and lives in an atmosphere of mystery,' said Dicketts.[24]

* * *

At the end of several interrogations with Owens, Marriott would have been inclined to agree with Dicketts. Over the course of the same interview, Owens contradicted himself so many times it was obvious he was lying.

'Why didn't you tell Dicketts as soon as you saw him, exactly what you had told the Doctor?' asked Marriott.[25]

'I did tell him,' said Owens.

'No you didn't.'

'I told Dicketts the Doctor was wise to everything. He knew exactly what I was doing. No, it is wrong, definitely wrong. I can't have told him.'

Marriott asked him why not – he was a friend of his after all?

'No, I am sure I didn't tell him. I can't remember anyhow.'

'It is the single most important thing of your trip,' said Marriott. 'Did the Doctor tell you not to tell Dicketts?'

'He didn't say that at all.'

'I suggest that the Doctor said you should not tell Dicketts anything until he had seen him.'

'I cannot swear to that, I don't remember.'[26]

Marriott wrote in his report afterwards that Owens gave every appearance that he was telling the truth and appeared to believe this was exactly what he was doing. 'I am more than ever convinced that Owens is a case not for the Security Service, but for a brain specialist,' he concluded.[27]

* * *

Meanwhile, suspicion began to fall on Dicketts. His report that there was limited air-raid damage to the Blohm & Voss shipyard in Hamburg was contradicted by recent aerial reconnaissance, which showed around a third of their shipbuilding yards were damaged.

Montagu phoned Tar to warn him, saying Dicketts' report was so inaccurate that he must have known it to be untrue.[28] The inference was that Dicketts had been 'turned' by the Germans.

The problem MI5 faced had less to do with determining which agent was telling the truth, than with the secrecy of their operation. Even if Dicketts or Owens were telling the truth as they knew it, there was always the possibility that the Germans had deliberately planted misinformation on them.

MI5 suspected this was the case with what Dicketts had been allowed to see of the Blohm & Voss shipyard, but seemed to have missed the fact that Dicketts was taken to the docks on the morning of 11 March, whereas the RAF air raid which had damaged the shipyard so extensively had taken place that evening. Dicketts had reported this air raid and said he was sheltering in the underground beneath Hamburg's main train station between 4.45 am to 7.20 am.

Extracts taken from MI9's interrogations of prisoners of war later confirmed Dicketts' statement that there was little damage to the town and harbour. They said 'the damage was negligible, and there was no dislocation of public services.'[29]

Some of the suspicion directed at Dicketts was to do with his criminal background, and some of it with his information, which may have been planted on him by the enemy. Shortly after Owens arrived in Lisbon, SIS intercepted a telegram sent by the Abwehr asking for information about the whereabouts of Dicketts' ship, the SS *Cressado*.[30] Local Abwehr agent Kuno Weltzien said he had an important agent onboard who was considered to be a 'valuable medium for planting false information on the British'.[31] The fact that this cable was sent shortly after Owens' arrival – and before Dicketts' arrival in Lisbon – is important as it provides insight into what Owens told Ritter at their first meeting.

The significance of the contents and timing of this cable would not be realized until many months later. The source of these cables was Ritter, although this fact appears to have been missed. In a small note in Dicketts' file, dated 31 March 1941, is a suggestion by Dicketts that the cables sent by Ritter to Madeira and other neutral ports, asking if the *Cressado* had landed there, could be checked to find out 'the German agents' [spies'] addresses' in those ports.[32]

Dicketts realized he was being treated with a great deal of suspicion, but wasn't told why until much later in the interrogation process. To his credit, Dicketts insisted on giving MI5 what he referred to as the 'correct information' regardless. There were some in MI5 who thought Dicketts had been stuffed with propaganda by the Germans, and others who believed he had been overly impressed by German efficiency and had in fact been 'turned' by the enemy.

Mrs Burton, who recorded Dicketts' interviews and private conversations, put her concerns in writing. She said Dicketts was 'all praise' for Germany:[33]

> They had more food than we, their rations were bigger than ours, the Germans he met were of a better type than they used to be, and the women were much nicer and smarter looking. He said you could get meat five times a week in a restaurant and fish the other two days.

Mrs Burton added that she could not understand Dicketts' mental process: 'Surely if one was fond of their own country, and came to the conclusion that everything was better in the other country, you would find something negative to say about it without having to have it dragged out of you?'

You could equally argue that a real traitor would not want to highlight his suspected admiration so diligently.

Dicketts said:

> I made it my business to go into various restaurants alone and have conversations with normal people. I saw no food queues, no shortage in butcher-shops or grocer shops. There is no coffee, citrus fruit is cheaper than here. I don't want to be obstinate about this but I must give you my opinion. The quality and the quantity are both very good indeed.[34]

Dicketts' observations were confirmed by the British military attaché in Athens, who reported that a Greek merchant of high standing who had lived in Hamburg for many years, said German morale was good, and their food supply and organization was perfect.[35]

Dicketts' biggest problem, though, was that Owens, although he didn't realise it yet, was doing his best to discredit him, as he had done so before with GW and Biscuit.

The other significant factor was Owens' importance to MI5 at this stage in the war. Their double-cross system had begun with Owens and he was their first double agent – the one from whom they learned and practised the skills of deception, that would ultimately lead to one of history's greatest military deceptions, complete with fake radio chatter, rubber tanks, body doubles and double agents, that successfully duped the Nazis into believing that the D-Day landings would take place in Calais and not Normandy.

The difficulty for MI5 at the time was not only that they might lose Owens, but that they might also lose his replacement (or co-agent) Dicketts and all the other agents who had been in contact with the Snow network.

Owens' extreme jealousy of Dicketts could only be that he feared Dicketts would become more useful to the Germans than him, and consequently also to MI5. The question was how far was Owens willing to go? If he betrayed Dicketts to the Germans, he was effectively sending him to an almost certain death.

Owens behaved in an openly competitive manner, seemingly unaware how this would be viewed by MI5. He told MI5 that after Dicketts returned from Germany, he had information about Ritter that Owens hadn't known – and Owens thought he knew Ritter really well. Dicketts said Ritter's 'best friend and the only person he had to account to was Herman Göring'. Owens had replied, 'Well, that's nice for me. The only man I'm responsible to is the Doctor.'

Owens told Tar:

> Anyway, I got £5,000 out of them and an extra £5,000 for my loyalty. Actually, it's more than that, as I had very heavy expenses in Lisbon, approximately £10,000.[36] Dicketts is a most expensive man. I had to go out and buy gold watches for both of us and our wives just to keep him in a good frame of mind.

'What is your feeling towards him at the moment?' asked Tar.

Owens replied: 'That man is a double-crosser, an extremely dangerous man, and what's more, whoever's got the most money, he'll work for him.'[37]

* * *

It was time to tell Dicketts that Owens had given the game away before he even arrived in Lisbon.

Tar and Masterman met with Dicketts and told him that Owens claimed that he had told Dicketts this before he had gone into Germany. The fact that Dicketts had gone into Germany regardless was viewed by Owens as proof that Dicketts was double-crossing MI5.

Tar was watching Dicketts very closely when Masterman told him this, and explained why they had decided not to tell Dicketts this news until now.

'My impression was that Dicketts took this exceedingly calmly, and in fact his first remark after Captain Masterman had finished was that he believed that Owens was lying when he said that he had told the Doctor,' wrote Tar in his report afterwards.[38]

Dicketts was 'absolutely emphatic that Owens had never mentioned a word to him about this, and never hesitated to say that if he had known he would not have gone into Germany'.[39]

Once Dicketts grasped the full implications of what MI5 had told him, he realised that Owens had effectively sent him to his death by allowing him to continue into Germany.

They talked around the subject for a while and came to the conclusion that Owens had probably been threatened by Ritter to say nothing to Dicketts. If Dicketts refused to go into Germany, then Ritter would know Owens had broken his word. In the end, Owens had preferred the security of his own neck to that of his friend.

'I would like to confront Arthur [Owens] with this information as I don't believe he could maintain his assertions in my presence,' said Dicketts.[40]

The following day, Masterman came to see Dicketts again and asked him if he had any further thoughts or reactions to Owens' story. Dicketts said he had tried to put himself in Owens' shoes to try to work out his motive, and had a number of ideas which he thought were worth exploring.

Had it been Owens' intention to damage Dicketts' credibility with MI5 by inventing a conversation that never took place, so he could then say that despite Dicketts knowing the Germans knew he was a British agent, Dicketts had willingly gone into Germany and sold himself to the Germans?

'Was there any animosity between the two of you, before you left?' asked Masterman.[41] Dicketts said there wasn't, but Owens was jealous of him in a social sense. For example, Owens would study the wine lists and menus in restaurants and then ask Dicketts to order. Sometimes Owens cancelled the order and chose something else instead; Lily would tell him to mind his own business, saying 'Dick knows so much more about this than you.' Dicketts said he thought Lily was very tactless.[42]

Dicketts was certain Owens had no idea of the extent to which he was in Tar's confidence, as he had encouraged Owens to believe that Tar didn't trust him and was just using him. To give credence to this view, he had shown Owens some of his earlier correspondence with Tar (with Tar's full agreement), to prove how poorly he had been treated and justify why he was so disgruntled.

'If he sent me into Germany to my almost certain death, why?' asked Dicketts. 'He knew Lily was a hostage for us, Tar had told him at their last meeting that both wives would be arrested if anything went wrong, or if we failed to return.'

Dicketts added:

Perhaps Owens had made these remarks about me because he thought I had found out a lot about him in Germany and was going to report it. Therefore, Owens did whatever he could to damage what little credit he believed I had, so that when I gave my report, it would be, if not entirely disbelieved, at least doubted.'[43]

Dicketts suggested to Masterman that they arrange for interviews to be carried out with Knapmann, Regnault, Mrs Quennall and the Nolans in Lisbon. They could then find out what Owens had told these people about his roles within the British and German Secret Services.

Dicketts requested a private meeting with Owens at some future date, and made a surprising comment: 'I did not like the little man and his wife but in spite of that I still do not think that he is a major traitor.'[44]

This point was picked up in a later interrogation by MI5's Dick White, who asked Dicketts to clarify what he meant.

'As far as I can reasonably think, I don't think the little man is a major traitor, he is a money-grabber, he is sitting on the fence. In case anything happened, he might probably fall over to the other side,' replied Dicketts.[45] It was the same conclusion MI5 would eventually make.

* * *

Owens was complaining of stomach pains, saying he was suffering from a duodenal ulcer. Tar made arrangements for him to see a Harley Street specialist on Friday, 4 April, so that he could find out how sick Owens really was, and also obtain a professional opinion about how reliable a person Owens was.

Tar attended the consultation with Owens and Lily in the guise of a friend. Tar recalled: 'Owens made a terrific song and dance about his various ailments saying that he was sick and had a pain in his left side and had been told by his local Doctor that he was suffering from a weak heart.'[46] The specialist told Lily she shouldn't worry about his health too much, but she should try to persuade him to cut down on his drink.

After Owens and Lily had gone, Tar stayed behind to speak to the specialist, who said there was really nothing wrong with Owens at all, and if he had been drinking as much as he said he had, then he had the constitution of an ox. In his opinion, Owens was a 'malingerer who was mentally absolutely sound, but very sly indeed, and he would not trust him as far as he could see him'. Owens' X-rays later revealed no internal troubles and the specialist very much doubted if he had ever had a duodenal ulcer in the first place. The specialist thought Owens was 'a consummate liar whose word could not be trusted in anything he said'.[47]

On Sunday, 6 April, Owens made an urgent request to meet Tar at his club. He said the barman at the Otter public house had told Ronnie Reed, Owens' radio operator who was living with Owens at the time, that some of his customers believed he and Owens' party were working for British intelligence, and a known wireless was being operated from their premises.

Owens was in a frightful state, saying the game was up, and he and his family's lives were in jeopardy, but Tar thought it was all just a 'smoke screen', embellished by Owens for his own purposes, and sent him home still protesting.[48] Tar thought he would soon get over it.

Tar also believed that the fact that Dicketts knew the pub manager may have had something to do with it. Owens had it in for Dicketts, that much was clear, and was probably trying to advance the idea that Dicketts was pro-German and therefore a risk to him personally.

Nonetheless, an officer was sent to interview the pub manager, a Mr England. It turned out that England and Dicketts had served together in the same unit in France during the last war, and had become good friends. England hadn't seen Dicketts until a few months ago, when he recognized him in the pub, and although they frequently spoke about matters of general interest, Dicketts never gave any indication of what he was doing at the present time. When England asked Dicketts what he was doing, he said he was engaged in secret work, the nature of which he could not mention.

'I don't know where you are getting your information from,' the officer said to Tar afterwards, 'but there was no ground for you to feel any concern at all.'[49]

* * *

The decision was made to interview Dicketts again, and if there was 'no wilful departure from the truth', MI5 would conclude that he was generally speaking the truth.[50] Owens and Dicketts would then be brought together for the first time since they had landed back in England, and questioned over the significant disagreements in their two stories.

It was decided that Dick White, the future chief of both MI5 and MI6, would interview Dicketts with Commander Montagu from Naval Intelligence and focus on his trip to Hamburg. In the meantime, John Masterman had produced a thorough sequence of four hypotheses (see Appendix II, p. 233) which would be compared against interrogations and other sources to establish motive and guilt.

White wondered what Dicketts would say about his comment that 'he didn't believe Owens was a major traitor' if Dicketts subsequently discovered that Owens really had told the Doctor that both he and Dicketts worked for British intelligence?[51]

'I say that is an absolute blank lie,' said Dicketts.

'You say that the Little Man is not a major traitor?' asked White.

'If he had said that, yes. But I was never queried.'

'You don't think the Little Man did say that to the Doctor?' asked White.

'I would not like to say,' said Dicketts.

'What motive could you see for his saying this? Why should he say that to the Doctor?'

'There is only one reason I can think of, is that the Doctor actually knew it before.'[52]

Had Owens given him any indication before they left that he wanted to throw his hand in, asked White? Dicketts said he had complained about how bad his stomach was and how much he 'wanted to go to Canada' as he had so many worries. This had cropped up again in Lisbon on several occasions.

White next turned up the heat on Dicketts. White said that the conversation Dicketts claimed to have had with Ruser during the car journey from Lisbon to Madrid struck him as extremely odd. Ruser wasn't as violently anti-Nazi as Dicketts had said he was – 'Ruser was an important Nazi official',[53] a Landesgruppenleiter (the title given to a leader of a Foreign Organization branch of the Nazi Party).

Dicketts said he didn't know what that was, but he didn't believe it. He had gone to dinner at Ruser's house with just him and his mother, a simple, pleasant and kindly woman who demonstrated great affection for her son. Mrs Ruser told Dicketts she detested the Nazis, and her son had agreed with her. Dicketts told White that he didn't believe Ruser was living a double life with his mother as he was extremely devoted to her.

'Ruser was not the only pro-British, Sessler is too. He wants to come to England,'[54] Dicketts continued.

'Do you think this fellow was genuine?' asked White.

'Yes. He says the most dangerous things. He is Dr Schacht's [Hitler's President of the Reichsbank until 1939] nephew. He is either the most superb liar or else he is absolutely true.'

Unfortunately, Dicketts would never be informed by MI5 that his assessment of Ruser as pro-British would later prove correct. On 19 May 1942, White's boss, Guy Liddell, wrote in his once-secret war diary, 'there had been several indications recently that Dr Hans Ruser, who had been connected with German espionage work in Portugal since 1937, is now in disfavour with the German authorities. Recently there has been a suggestion that he was preparing to break away altogether from his German associates and attempt to seek refuge in this country.'[55]

Ruser escaped Madrid in late 1943 with the assistance of SIS and arrived in England, where he was taken to Camp 020 for questioning.[56] His mother was also given assistance and later rejoined her son in England.

MI5 then confronted Dicketts with the news that his information about bomb damage and activity at the shipyards wasn't accurate. Dicketts said he was disappointed to hear this, but insisted that his information about the destroyers, submarines and transports 'was definitely, absolutely correct'.[57]

'We may be wrong, we don't think we are, you may be lying and you may have had the wool pulled over your eyes. I am not in a position to take responsibility to say that I am convinced beyond doubt that you are not lying,' said MI5.[58]

Dicketts then said:

But you should be. I do resent one thing. I went out with the specific purpose, because I wanted to go, the whole adventure is odd. But I want you to take back from your Department's point of view, leaving out any question of lying, the Hohe Brücke Ferry – those destroyers were there and those transports. They were not brought up for my own benefit. It was a brilliant sunny day and it is absolutely correct.[59]

Towards the end of their interrogation, White asked Dicketts to consider that they were confronted with two completely different stories: Owens' claim that he told Dicketts immediately he arrived in Lisbon, and Dicketts claim that it was a complete lie.

'But I am working for the Department,' said Dicketts.[60] In other words, Dicketts saw his role as having been instructed by MI5 to go to Lisbon to find out what side Owens was really working for and to get himself recruited as a German spy, so he could obtain information for MI5 that they would not otherwise be able to obtain.

White said he was ready to agree with him, but he could see no motive for Owens to say what he did. Dicketts agreed with White and said it had been puzzling him too. The only thing he could think of was that Owens thought Dicketts had discovered something about him in Germany and wanted to discredit him.

'We will accept that he did not tell you, but in fact told the Doctor,' White told Dicketts.[61]

* * *

At last it was time for the two men to confront each other, on Wednesday, 9 April. Dick White pointed out the seriousness of the situation, and asked Owens to repeat what he had just told them about the nature of his warning to Dicketts in Lisbon.

'Dicketts knew exactly, that the Doctor knew I was in touch with the British Intelligence before he left for Germany. That is right isn't it?' Owens asked Dicketts. [62]

Dicketts: 'I had gathered as much but I didn't know.'

Owens: 'You didn't know?'

Dicketts: 'You never told me anything about it. You never mentioned it to me.'

Owens: 'You didn't know?'

Dicketts: 'I had very grave suspicions but I didn't know.'

Owens: 'You mean to tell me that you didn't know?'

Dicketts: 'I'm telling you. I have been told after working out my whole report that you had blown the whole project with the Doctor. And you warned me accordingly. You never made any such statement. When did you break it to me?'

Owens: 'I believe I warned you when I saw you in the room.'

Dicketts: 'You believe you did. I don't want to know what your beliefs are – I want to know exactly.'

After days of contradicting himself, Owens said he now remembered telling Dicketts in front of the Doctor at Dobler's flat in Lisbon. Dicketts replied:

> I say that you didn't, and I am also informed that you warned me personally that you had blown the entire party to the Doctor, that your own advice to me when you tried the last two or three days when I was with you [was] to assure me that you were the only person who could look after me, to put my whole trust in you and that you would see me back again as you had given your word of honour.

Dicketts reminded Owens that as he was getting into the cab to go to Germany, Owens appeared to be very nervous and shook his hand about a dozen times, saying, 'you are a very brave man, Dick, don't go if you don't want to'.[63] In Dicketts' opinion, Owens was wavering and trying to decide whether to tell him not to go.

'No, I wasn't,' said Owens.

In that case, said Dicketts, Owens was effectively sending him to his death, as there was nothing Owens could have done if something went wrong. Dicketts reiterated that he would never have gone into Germany had he known Owens had blown the whole game to the Doctor.[64]

'Dick, you knew perfectly,' said Owens.

MI5 interrupted and asked Owens if he told Dicketts all about the radio transmissions, and he said, 'Yes certainly.'

Dicketts said he knew nothing at the time. All he knew was that Owens had a relationship with the Doctor, who knew a great deal about him, but he had no conceptual knowledge that the Doctor knew all about the radio, or that Owens was controlled or anything like that.

'You were supposed to know nothing about the radio that was being worked by ...,' said MI5.

Dicketts interrupted: 'Neither did I, you see my presumption was that the Doctor knew something about Owens' connection here, but he didn't know about the major point that the radio was being controlled.'[65]

MI5: 'What did you suspect was the extent of the Doctor's knowledge? Can you be more precise?'

Dicketts: 'Well, that Owens was in touch with the British Secret Service here.'

MI5: 'For what purpose?'

Dicketts replied that the general idea was that Owens was double-crossing us (MI5) and working for Germany while pretending to work for us, and that the reason he was sent to Lisbon was to verify which side Owens was working on. Dicketts said that the one thing that both of them had had drummed into them by Tar, was to never mention the radio.

'Is that correct?' MI5 asked Owens.

'As far as I can remember,' Owens agreed.[66]

Dicketts explained that any remarks he made to Owens about being 100 per cent for the Doctor was all part of his role. He was to follow Owens wherever he went, and to get as close to the Doctor as he could, until he was sure which way Owens was working.

Dicketts said he had never had any discussion with Owens about his role, and Owens always refused to give him any information on the basis that he was an amateur, and that if he knew everything that was going on it would upset him, and he might fall into traps.

'Did you say that to him?' asked MI5, and Owens agreed he had.

'But you still say that you told him quite clearly that everything was known to the Doctor including…'

'Yes I told him,' Owens interrupted. He said he distinctly remembered telling Dicketts in front of the Doctor that the whole shooting match was known and to tell the Doctor what he knew.

Dicketts denied this: 'You made no such remark, because it doesn't match with the fact that we agreed before I left for Germany, which you have agreed with me [just] now, that I was never in any circumstance to mention the radio. I could say anything else. You've just agreed that. These two statements …'[67]

'Well are you, are you perfectly, let me see now, let me try and get this clear,' said Owens.

'You remember that agreement Mr Owens, don't you, you remember the reply to my question?' said Dicketts.

'Yes, I do,' Owens replied.

Dicketts continued: 'That we had agreed before I left that I should tell everything but not the radio, well then that doesn't bear out the statement that I knew the whole party was blown and the radio controlled…'

Owens asked Dicketts if the Doctor had ever mentioned that he knew Owens was in touch with British intelligence. Dicketts said he had never asked him about Owens, and neither was he interrogated about it.

MI5 noted that in spite of the unpleasant things Owens and Dicketts said about each other when interviewed separately, they did not embark on any serious recriminations when confronted with each other.

Towards the end of their joint interrogation, Owens said he liked Dicketts very much and thought he was a shrewd fellow. If he could be trusted, he thought Dicketts could be of great help to the country: 'There's no question about it. I'd like to work with Dicketts very much.'

'Personally, I think that Owens just regards the whole business as a money-making concern and gives a little to both sides,' wrote Guy Liddell on 19 May. 'Probably neither side really trusts him. He has not been in a position to give the Germans very much from this country, except information which we planted on him.'[68]

* * *

That evening, when Masterman called on Dicketts, he gave him a long list of notes which he wanted to put on record. Dicketts wasn't happy. After completing what he considered to be a dangerous and difficult task, he said he had been 'met with a great deal of suspicion'.[69]

Masterman explained that it was their duty to treat every agent's statement with reserve and to check up on every detail that they could. Somewhat reassured, Dicketts said that although he didn't like this sort of work, he would be willing to make any sacrifices to get back into one of the Services, including going back to Germany, provided this time he had the assurance of the department.

Dicketts said he had great confidence in Tar and had tried in all respects to carry out his instructions, and hoped he would be present at some stage in his future interrogations as he felt Montagu could not have been fully apprised of his instructions, judging by the questions he asked.

Despite the risks, Dicketts said he was still prepared to continue with the plan as proposed by Ritter. During his recent short break to Brixham, Dicketts had looked into the matter of hiring a motor launch and what sort of difficulties might arise. He said he was very well known on the River Dart, particularly at Dittisham, and would be able to obtain as much petrol as he wanted provided he had the money to pay for it.

Masterman thought it only fair to put on record that in both his interrogations and in every conversation he had had with Dicketts since he arrived, he was perfectly consistent in his statements:

> Though his memory is undoubtedly excellent I find it difficult to believe that he could repeat a story of this length and complexity on many occasions without introducing errors or contradictions, unless the story was substantially the truth.
>
> My own conclusion is that though he was obviously dangerously impressed by German efficiency and may have toyed with the idea of involving himself too deeply on the German side, yet he has in the main behaved with loyalty and done his best for us.[70]

Chapter 10

Aftermath

'Absence of evidence is not evidence of absence.' Carl Sagan

The time for Arthur Owens - Britain's first double agent, from whom all others evolved - was almost over. Members from MI5's counter-espionage division met on 10 April 1941, and decided that the only safe course to pursue was to assume that Ritter knew about their control of agents. In that case, Owens could therefore be of little, if any, further use to them.[1] The fact that Ritter wanted to keep the whole game going was a strong argument for closing it down, as Ritter clearly believed he could still learn a great deal from the information MI5 sent over.

Tar would tell Owens that they were going to close his network down, and if he accepted the news without comment or suggesting an alternative, Tar would say they believed Dicketts' account that Owens never told him – which they regarded as a foolish and dangerous act on his part. MI5 also realized they may need to 'shut Owens up or remove him from this country'.[2]

Tar and Masterman went to see Owens, and told him they had gone through his and Dicketts' statements very carefully and were unanimous in their opinion that Owens didn't tell Dicketts the game was blown before he went into Germany, and had therefore 'knowingly sent a man on a most dangerous mission, to his death probably'.[3]

Now that Ritter knew Owens' radio was under British control, Owens could no longer be of any use to them, and a message would be sent over Owens' radio, saying his nerve had gone and that he could not go on any longer.[4]

'Can't I do anything to help the country at all?' asked Owens.

'What do you suggest you do?' said Tar.

'I will do anything,' Owens offered.

'I mean, what description…'

'Well, I am not a fool,' said Owens. 'I have a good education, and I have had excellent experience, and if my education and my experience is wasted...'

'You have had ample opportunity all these months of doing jobs, haven't you? I mean, quite frankly, you have been tremendously idle,' said Tar.

'Oh, there is no doubt about that. I haven't bothered with anything,' Owens admitted.

'No. You have done nothing. You have just lived on the fat of the land with an enormous salary – a salary which would make a Cabinet Minister's salary look stupid at the present rate of taxation,' said Tar.[5]

'Quite,' said Owens, who added that in Ritter's view, he was in an ideal position now because he had a free hand and could go more or less where he liked, and could provide assistance to the agents Ritter sent over by motor launch.

'I'm not interested in Ritter's schemes,' said Tar. This latest scheme of his was like some sort of smoke screen like all the others before it, all of which had been of exceedingly little benefit to MI5.

'Does Ritter really believe British Intelligence is so full of saps that you would be allowed to return to England carrying a large sum of money and explosives without being searched? Does he regard our entire intelligence service as being decadent and incompetent?' asked Tar.[6]

Owens agreed Ritter didn't have a very good impression of the British Secret Service, but was unable to offer any suggestions of his own, other than those proposed by Ritter. With no further points to discuss, Tar told Owens that in future if he wanted to get in touch with them, he was to do so in writing.

Owens was sent to Stafford Prison for compromising Dicketts and betraying the radio traffic to Ritter. He was imprisoned among other full-blown enemy agents for the remainder of the war.

British codebreakers tracked MI5's message to Ast. Hamburg regarding Owens' ill-health, as it was relayed to Ritter at his new posting in North Africa, and Ritter's reply asking to be kept fully informed, as there was 'something wrong' with Owens' sudden illness.[7]

Owens' imprisonment brought about the end of the careers of Biscuit, the ex con-man turned MI5 informant, and Eschborn, the half-German photographer known as Charlie. GW, the retired Welsh policeman, was able to revive his own career through his contact with Del Pozo, a Spanish journalist and Abwehr spy (Pogo).

Wulf Schmidt (Tate), the Abwehr spy who had parachuted into England in 1940, continued to be accepted by the Germans and operated successfully under MI5's control throughout the war. Tate was awarded an Iron Cross for his espionage activities on behalf of Germany, and remained in England under the name of Harry Williamson for the rest of his life. His fellow German spy, Gösta Caroli (Summer), returned to Sweden at the end of the war, but he never fully recovered from his parachute jump and completely lost his memory.[8]

As for Dicketts, his future was now up in the air. Unable to use Dicketts in the same way as they had before, John Masterman wondered if they could use him somewhere else:

'If we decide that he cannot be used any more as an agent, it will be very difficult to find him a suitable job, and if a job is not found for him, he will become a disappointed and disgruntled man, capable of doing harm.'[9]

MI5 hoped to elicit a response from Ritter regarding his plans for Dicketts to smuggle agents into England by boat from the Channel Islands. Dicketts was instructed to send Ritter a letter as if it had been carried by a ship's steward or captain, saying he was trying to get over to Lisbon again, but it was becoming more and more difficult to obtain a seat on the plane. In the meantime, Dicketts would welcome further instructions.

* * *

Tar wrote to Sir David Petrie, MI5's recently appointed Director General (DG), and tried to secure Dicketts a job in the RAF. He said that during the entire time Dicketts had worked for him, he had no reason to doubt that Dicketts had made 'every effort to produce satisfactory results and had in fact been, on certain occasions, exceedingly useful'.[10]

Tar outlined Dicketts' previous career and his shady financial dealings, the last of which was ten years ago, and described his recent mission to Germany:

It is open to doubt whether during the period of this mission he did not go a very long way towards becoming a proper German agent. There is of course nothing in what he has told us to show this or to prove it, but there are certain sections of opinion among those people who have had an opportunity of interrogating him since his return which believe this possibility cannot be ruled out.[11]

Dicketts' employment in October 1940 came at a time when the Double Cross Committee was in the process of being established. Although weekly meetings were taking place, the first formal meeting under the chairmanship of John Masterman took place on 2 January 1941. Since it was very much a fledgling organisation, MI5 were extremely cautious, as John Masterman would later confirm:

> They had always supposed that the German network was much larger and more effective than it was, and their early treatment of the double-agents was conditioned by that belief. They were obsessed by the idea that a large body of German spies over and above those they knew, were checking up on their agents. It turned out to be untrue, but made them rather timid in the early days.[12]

In his letter to the Director General, Tar said he had sent Dicketts to Lisbon to test whether Owens was bona fide and if possible to get into Germany. Dicketts had achieved both of these tasks to Tar's satisfaction, but the information he managed to obtain in Germany 'was not in any sense of the word useful from a military point of view'.[13]

It is hard to imagine how MI5 expected Dicketts to obtain this information from right under the noses of the Gestapo. If the situation were reversed and MI5 had a German agent offering himself as a traitor, they would never have let him wander freely around London unobserved – just as the Germans had watched Dicketts in Hamburg.

Tar told the DG that he wouldn't recommend Dicketts for a job that brought him in contact with secret information to do with the RAF, but he was fully prepared to back Dicketts as far as his willingness to work was concerned:

'It will also be appreciated that whatever faults he may have had in the past, he has done a brave deed by going into Germany in wartime.'[14]

The solution to Dicketts' employment came from Dicketts himself. He was convinced Sessler wanted to defect, as he had told Dicketts several times that he hated the department he worked for and would like to come to England if that could be arranged, or to rejoin his father's relatives in Milwaukee.

MI5 were wary. Sessler's comments could have been a ruse to draw Dicketts out and declare his real purpose for going into Germany. On the other hand, there was a chance Sessler was telling the truth.

After much discussion, MI5 decided to send Dicketts to Lisbon to complete this one task only. As they had still not decisively proven Dicketts' reliability and loyalty, MI5 realized they would be no better off in their understanding of Dicketts if he succeeded in some tasks, and not in others.[15] If Dicketts was successful, then the gain to them would be considerable, as Sessler had an intimate knowledge of the whole German intelligence system.

Dicketts was instructed to send a message to the Germans, suggesting that Sessler should come and collect him from Lisbon and take him back to Germany in the first week of June. Although the Germans agreed to this suggestion, ISOS transcripts (signals intelligence) revealed Dicketts was being treated with some scepticism.[16] This is not surprising, as Owens had reported ill immediately after returning to England, which the Abwehr put down to something Dicketts told British intelligence.

MI5 briefed Dicketts that when Sessler turned up, Dicketts was to refuse to go to Germany with him because he was afraid he had been shadowed by the British. Sessler was to bring up the subject of defecting himself, and if he didn't, the whole thing was to be abandoned. Dicketts mustn't try to coerce Sessler into returning, and he wasn't to 'use drugs or force'.[17]

He was to offer Sessler $5,000 and promise that Sessler would receive a safe passage to England by sea in the disguise of a seaman. When they arrived in England, Sessler would not be placed in a prison or internment camp, and they would help him get to America in due course.

Sessler walked into Dicketts' hotel room in Lisbon on 5 June 1941, and said he had orders to bring Dicketts back to Berlin as soon as possible. They arranged to meet at the Rossio Restaurant in Lisbon's main square the following day, where Sessler paid Dicketts £400 and asked him when he was going to take him to England. Sessler asked this question three or four times before Dicketts could be drawn.

From the moment Dicketts made his offer, Sessler could have had no further doubt that Dicketts worked for British intelligence. Sessler thought $5,000 (around $81,500 today) wasn't very much for leaving everything behind, but he was willing to tell them all when he returned to Lisbon around 29 June. First, he had to return to Hamburg.[18]

At the end of their meeting, Dicketts was convinced Sessler would return as promised. Dicketts left Lisbon on 12 June and Sessler went back to his hotel room at the Grande Duas Nacoes and wrote a letter to Gerda Koch in Milwaukee, which he posted two days later. Sessler's letter was intercepted by the Imperial Censor in Bermuda, who passed it onto MI5 on 5 July.

'Gerda darling, I'm still alive!' wrote Sessler.[19] He said he had wanted to write to her in English but was so excited he had to lapse into German. 'Unfortunately, I have still no chance of coming, but today from here, I promise you that I shall come, and then you will be able to look after me for a long time.' Sessler enclosed a photograph, and asked Gerda to let an old lady in New York know that her daughter Lore was happy and in good health.

MI5 realized it was too dangerous for Dicketts to return to Lisbon, so they sent Cyril Mills of Bertram Mills' Circus fame instead. Mills had become a British agent by accident after spotting a railway disappearing into remote mountains when flying over Germany in his De Havilland Hornet Moth in 1936.[20] Mills reported this to MI5 on his return and they asked him to continue reporting anything suspicious during his flying adventures.

Mills remained in Lisbon until 5 July, but Sessler never showed up. His non-appearance caused a great deal of speculation back in England, that Sessler may have made his suggestion to Dicketts just to try him out. Masterman strongly believed that the most likely explanation for Sessler's absence was that his orders had been changed due to the crisis on the Russian Front. Although Sessler never did defect to England, Masterman's guess that he had been sent to Russia was correct, but it wasn't until several months later when he was transferred to Abwehr III headquarters in Smolensk.[21]

Sessler surrendered to Allied troops in Milan in 1945, and was taken to CSDIC, where he was described as a pleasant, intelligent type, who was fully cooperative and claimed his experience of seeing England when he was a merchant seaman long before the war convinced him that Nazi Germany did not offer the best way of life.[22] Sessler proved to be very popular with the Allies, and testified against his former colleagues at the Nuremberg Trials in November 1945.

* * *

The youngest journalist at the Nuremberg trials was Günter Peis, who, twenty-three years later, tracked down Sessler at his home in France and interviewed him for one of his books. Sessler told Peis he only met 'Dickitts', as he mistakenly pronounced his name, once. He said they were expecting Dicketts to turn up in Lisbon a second time, but he never showed up.[23]

Given the number of years that had passed since then, it is possible Sessler had forgotten Dicketts' second trip to Lisbon, and his excited letter to Gerda Koch in Milwaukee two days later, but this doesn't seem likely, given the account that follows.

Sessler told Peis that when he and Dicketts returned to Lisbon in early 1941, they went for a drink at the Avenida Palace, where Dicketts offered to treat him to a meal for all the hospitality he had been shown in Germany. They ordered lobster, and then Dicketts sat back in his chair and told Sessler he would pay him anything he liked to accompany him back to England (in fact Dicketts was only authorized to offer him US $5,000). Sessler asked him what protection there would be for his security and Dicketts assured him he would be treated with the same kindness as he had been shown in Hamburg. 'I told him that he should save himself the trouble, as I would much rather go back to Hamburg – I would manage somehow,' said Sessler.[24] Dicketts afterwards reported to MI5 that Sessler had accepted his offer, although he didn't think the money was very much, and said he would return around 29 June.

What Sessler told Peis next is either a fantastic story or a giant cover-up. He said he and Dicketts were enjoying their meal at the Avenida Palace in Lisbon, when Dicketts revealed that he knew that he had been drugged in Hamburg. 'It was unfair to have knocked me out with those sleeping pills, but I suppose it was all part of the game,' said Dicketts.[25] Their wine glasses were filled again and again, and each time they toasted each other German-style, saying *Prosit*, but from a certain point all Sessler could remember was getting up from the table and becoming violently sick in the toilet before passing out.

Sessler claimed he had been poisoned by Dicketts and lay recovering in the military hospital in Hamburg-Wandsbeck for three weeks. His symptoms were identical to the two German agents whom the Secret Service had tried to abduct via Gibraltar. Sessler was very disappointed that none of his colleagues visited him during that time, except 'Fraulein Rehder' (the secretary to Kapitan Wichmann, the head of the Abwehr station). 'I have never forgotten it!' said Sessler.[26]

Clearly Sessler was lying. What could be gained by Dicketts drugging Sessler, then leaving Lisbon? Dicketts had come to Lisbon to bring Sessler back to England, and SIS had made extensive preparations for them to escape by sea.

The head of Ast. Hamburg, Herbert Wichmann,[27] told British interrogators at the end of the war that Dicketts was supposed to have returned to Hamburg with a member of Ritter's staff (Sessler), 'but had left Lisbon by plane one morning without warning'. The reason for his sudden disappearance had caused great speculation within the Abwehr at the time.[28]

Could this 'great speculation' account for Sessler's voluntary statement at CSDIC in 1946, that 'he was instrumental in getting Dicketts to safety in Lisbon after Berlin had become suspicious of him, and had been confined to his rooms for three weeks until he managed to clear himself of the suspicion of having deliberately helped Dicketts'?[29] It certainly seems a more likely story than the one he told to Peis about Dicketts drugging him in Lisbon.

Sessler was obviously hiding something, but why lie about it all these years after the war? Ritter and perhaps Canaris appear to have been in on it too.

In his 1972 memoirs, written around the same time as Sessler gave his account to Peis, Ritter said that Sessler escorted Dicketts back to Lisbon from Germany. They had a long stopover in Madrid to change planes, and Sessler 'allowed Dicketts to step out without going along. Dicketts did not return. He was a communist and used this opportunity to get to Russia with the help of the Spanish communist underground. The street with the number from his ring did not exist in Madrid.'[30]

Dicketts' so-called links to communism were also mentioned by Sessler. When Peis asked Sessler in 1973 if he knew what had happened to Dicketts, Sessler asked: 'Have you heard of the Red Orchestra?' Before Peis could ask Sessler what the Red Orchestra had to do with Dicketts, Sessler began talking about another agent. Later in the interview, Sessler had laughed and told Peis he should make enquiries in Moscow, 'as they were most likely to know what had happened to Dicketts'.[31]

Earlier in their interview, Sessler told Peis that the SD had discovered that the Abwehr were holding a British spy at the Hotel Vier Jahreszeiten and wanted to get hold of him, and Sessler had helped Dicketts to escape.

He had gone to Canaris to obtain his permission first, who told Sessler to 'get that man back to where he came from'. Dicketts told MI5 on his return to England that he had travelled on a diplomatic passport, as Sessler was in a hurry to leave Hamburg. Could it be that by inventing a bogus link between Dicketts and the hated Bolsheviks, the Abwehr had a believable excuse to explain Dicketts' sudden disappearance to the feared SD? The Red Orchestra was a resistance group to Hitler with links to the Soviets.

Peis described an 'atmosphere of fear' at Sessler's home in Aix-en-Provence, where Sessler was protected by a fierce dog and a Tunisian body-guard.[32] Something was troubling Sessler, who placed a loaded gun on the table in front of Peis and explained rather dramatically that he might need it. 'I'm glad I got away with it last time, and I don't want anything more to do with the whole dirty business,' said Sessler. 'A lot of those people who survived the war, were in it again, and people who got caught up in that kind of business, do not get out of it again so easily.'[33]

Sessler had a genuine reason to fear reprisals as he had given evidence against his former colleagues at the Nuremberg trials, in particular against Nazi general Anton Dostler, who was found guilty of war crimes. Dostler was tied to a post and shot by the US Army on 1 December 1945.[34]

A large number of former Nazis and their supporters were still alive when Peis interviewed Sessler. It is estimated that around '9,000 war criminals' escaped to South America and other countries after the war, assisted by a broad coalition of people, including Bishop Alois Hudal at the Vatican, and these people were still at large.[35]

Sessler told Peis he was attacked at his home by unknown assailants a few months after their interview, but this may have been a ploy to prevent Peis contacting him again.

* * *

Although Ritter was held in high regard by his colleagues for his success in obtaining America's top-secret Norden bombsight in 1938, there were some who believed Owens was controlled. Others had problems with Ritter's personality and objected to his 'resounding self-esteem, and inexhaustible self-confidence'.[36]

Ritter was described by Joseph Starziczny, one of the men he trained as a pre-invasion LENA spy, as 'an ambitious individual who received the Iron

Cross for his work in sending agents to England'.[37] Vera Eriksen, an Abwehr agent who landed by flying boat and rubber dingy with two others in Scotland, told British interrogators that Ritter was inordinately conceited. When Drueke, a fellow Abwehr agent, pointed out to Ritter that he had sent three agents to England in the summer of 1940 in 'an extremely casual and unorganised manner', Ritter replied that he could always get plenty of agents to replace those who were captured.[38]

During the early part of the war, Ritter had for some time been having 'violent disagreements on points of policy' with the Gruppenleiter of the Abwehr's Air Intelligence Section, Major Brede, and his assistant Major Friedrich Busch.[39] Busch successfully campaigned for Ritter to be transferred from Hamburg, and by the time Owens and Dicketts turned up in Lisbon, Ritter had already been tasked with infiltrating German spies into Egypt.

Ritter obtained the assistance of Count László Almásy, the experienced Hungarian desert explorer, motorist and aviator, to help him spirit the pro-German General Aziz el Masri out of Egypt, so he could help Rommel take over Egypt. Almásy (who was the inspiration behind the character played by Ralph Fiennes in the film *The English Patient*) quarrelled with Ritter over plans to infiltrate two German agents behind the Egyptian-British front, so Ritter's Heinkel 111 aircraft took off alone.[40] The plane was forced to ditch in the sea near Derna in Libya, breaking Ritter's arm and killing one of his agents.[41]

In September 1941, Ritter was just about to leave Germany for a cushy job as assistant to the air attaché in Rio de Janeiro, when he was recalled to Berlin by Colonel Piekenbrock, the chief of Abwehr 1. Piekenbrock told him his entire US spy-ring of thirty-three agents had been broken, and Ritter was named as a co-conspirator.[42]

It was the end of Ritter's role with the Abwehr and he was transferred to active duty, becoming a battalion commander in the Hermann Göring Air Force Panzer Division and participated in the fighting in Sicily. Later, Ritter was in charge of various anti-aircraft defences, including for the city of Hanover.[43]

Colonel Nikolaus Ritter's last role in the Second World War was as acting anti-aircraft commander in the Harz Mountains, where the Germans hid their high-prestige V-2 rocket programme in tunnels buried beneath the mountains. When the war was over, Ritter was used as an interpreter and air defence expert by the British and the Americans until October 1945, and then transferred to the British interrogation centre in the spa town of Bad Nenndorf, near Hanover.[44]

The War Office's Combined Services Detailed Interrogation Centre (CSDIC) at Bad Nenndorf was under the command of Lieutenant Colonel Robin 'Tin Eye' Stephens, who previously ran Camp 020 in South London where Ritter's LENA agents were interrogated during the war. Stephens later described Bad Nenndorf as a 'brutally tough place, for brutally tough people', where detainees, including Nazis who had been involved with implementing the Holocaust, were subjected to every kind of 'mental pressure' short of physical violence, to break them during interrogations.[45]

In May 1946, MI5 sent one of their officers, John Gwyer, to CSDIC to interrogate Ritter for historical and operational reasons. Gwyer had a good understanding of the Snow case, as he and John Marriott had drafted a hypothetical 'Final Report', ostensibly written by Ritter himself after his meeting with Owens in Lisbon in 1941.[46] The strategy of writing a report as if it were written by the enemy was a useful tool to envision Ritter's short and long-term outcomes.

Five years later, Gwyer found himself face-to-face with the foe against whom he and MI5 had matched their wits, and came to the conclusion that not only had they overestimated Ritter's abilities, but Ritter had underestimated theirs.

Ritter told Gwyer he had 'very little confidence' in Owens before the meeting took place, as his faith had been shaken by the failed North Sea trawler rendezvous and the ease with which Owens managed to obtain visas for himself and Dicketts to Lisbon.[47] In his memoirs, Ritter explained that a man in Owens' position in Germany would never have been allowed to leave the country without the approval of the Secret Service, and Ritter thought it was bound to be the same in England, 'certainly not in time of war'.[48]

Gwyer asked Ritter if he had challenged Owens about working for British intelligence immediately after his arrival. 'No, but he would have guessed something was wrong by my manner,' replied Ritter. Owens told MI5 that Ritter *had* challenged him, saying they had to have a very important talk, as Ritter had evidence that Owens was in contact with British intelligence.

In his memoirs, Ritter said he didn't bother to read Owens the riot act because he knew Owens couldn't have got to Lisbon without the assistance of the British Secret Service. All he asked Owens was, 'How did you clear things up with the Intelligence Service?'[49]

Owens told MI5 he hadn't denied Ritter's accusation that he was in contact with British intelligence, but MI5 were suspicious. Why hadn't Owens tried to bluff his way out of it? According to Ritter's memoirs, he did. Owens said British intelligence had 'walked in on him' two and a half months ago, as someone must have given him away.

Owens told Ritter he had tried to get out of England as a blind passenger with a captain friend, but found he couldn't even approach the train station without a special identity paper. So he decided to take Ritter's advice and offered his services to British intelligence, where he was interviewed by an extremely suspicious captain who wanted to know why he was volunteering his services now. Owens said he tried to convince the captain with a patriotic approach, but he didn't believe him because he was Welsh and accused him point-blank of working for the Nazis:

> My god, *Doktor*, I can assure you I did not feel at all well when he said that. It might have been that they had really observed me in the past. I told him I had met the person I knew only as 'the Doctor' during a business trip, and had given him some information about Bristol airfield and the depot at Wolverhampton. The Captain had eventually said, 'Okay! If you are completely frank, then I will help you. Otherwise you're finished.'[50]

Ritter thought it was a first-class tale and told Owens so. Privately he felt very disappointed. He had trusted Owens completely for two years and liked him on a personal level. Could he still believe in him? Ritter was taken aback when Owens reacted passionately.

'Doktor! Don't you believe me? Did I deserve that?' Owens asked. 'Okay,' said Ritter. 'We will see. But how is this all going to play out now?'[51] Owens suggested they should carry on exactly as they had before, perhaps even better, as he would now be able to tell him 'what was genuine and what was bogus material'. Ritter said 'he was defeated'; either Owens was smarter than he thought or he was really honest. There was only one thing Ritter couldn't understand, and that was how Owens would be able to procure material in the future without being observed, but didn't let on what he was thinking.

Owens told MI5 it was Ritter who put forward the whole idea of carrying on as before, but MI5 hadn't believed him. 'Does Ritter really believe we are foolish enough to allow you to wander around freely without watching you very closely?' an incredulous Tar had asked Owens at the time.[52]

Gwyer asked Ritter about Dicketts, who said his opinion of Dicketts was 'confirmed by both his and Owens' statements', which was that he was a lllF (counter-espionage) agent who had been given the mission of penetrating Owens' network.[53] Dicketts had admitted his status in Hamburg and had offered his services to Germany, which had been accepted, 'not so much from any confidence in Dicketts, as in the hope that the case might after all be rescued from disaster in this way'. According to Owens, Ritter already knew Dicketts worked for British intelligence, because he had told Ritter he did.

What Dicketts had told Ritter, with MI5's full approval, was that he had worked in intelligence in the Air Ministry during the First World War.[54] It was part of Dicketts' cover story to increase his value to the Germans. So why did Ritter tell Gwyer that Dicketts had revealed his more recent connection to British Intelligence? Could it be that he was protecting Owens?

Ritter wrote in his memoirs that Owens was always his agent and he believed in him throughout his life. Owens' radio message to him after he returned to England saying he could not go on made Ritter suspicious. ISOS decrypts confirm Ritter asked Ast. Hamburg to keep him fully informed as something was wrong. Could it be that Ritter suspected Dicketts' involvement in Owens' demise and effectively squared up with him by informing British intelligence that their agent, Dicketts, had admitted his role with them?

With the collapse of Owens' network, Ritter not only lost his star agent, but the prestige that had come with it. The rumour in the Abwehr was that Ritter had been posted to North Africa shortly afterwards.

Major Friedrich Busch from the Abwehr's Air Intelligence section in Berlin, told the Allies he had successfully campaigned for Ritter to be transferred from Hamburg, after he realized Owens was controlled: 'After Owens wired Ritter that a friend of his [Dicketts] was travelling to Lisbon and should be met, Ritter went to Lisbon and brought the man back to Hamburg in triumph.' Busch said he was so sceptical that he gave Dicketts 'the covername *Hades*, short for Hamburg thistle'.[55]

According to Sessler, Dicketts had successfully duped Ritter, exactly as MI5 had intended:

> When I realised how naively the officers responsible had estimated the triumphs of their interrogations, I told Ritter about Dicketts' unmistakable offer to take me back to England, but Ritter had remained adamant.
>
> 'That man is never a double agent! I am absolutely certain that he gave his information voluntarily, otherwise he would never have dared to come to Hamburg.'[56]

Sessler said Ritter also pressed £10,000 into Owens' hands, explaining 'he was a poor devil and somehow, I felt sorry for him'.[57]

During his interrogation with Gwyer, Ritter said he had given Owens and Dicketts a sum of between £300 and £400 in Lisbon, and had been challenged by Gwyer. 'The sum was much larger than that, £9,000 or £10,000,' said Gwyer. Ritter had feigned the greatest surprise and protested that he had never in his life ever given Owens more than £500 at a time. Gwyer assured him that Owens had indeed returned with £10,000.

'I can only suppose that the money came from Abteilung II in Madrid, whom I now recall had been in touch with Owens during his stay in Lisbon,' said Ritter.

Gwyer came to the conclusion that Ritter didn't try to withhold the truth, and neither was his memory especially bad, because what he did remember, he remembered clearly and in great detail despite the lapse in time. However, Ritter's knowledge was strictly confined to the parts he had handled personally, which was limited by his extremely slack handling of his cases from the very outset. Whenever Ritter 'could leave a case, or part of a case' to some other section, he had done so.[58]

Ritter's tactic of wining and dining Dicketts, and accommodating him in the best hotels, also made MI5 suspicious, and allowed Owens to promote the view that Dicketts would do anything for money. The information Ritter and his colleagues planted on Dicketts also backfired, as MI5 soon discovered the information was useless. It was a valuable reminder to MI5 of how not to play the game of deception. If they didn't provide their agent with genuine information as well as chicken feed, the enemy wouldn't believe him. In Dicketts' case, the Germans had unsuccessfully tried to plant misinformation on British intelligence, and discredited their agent in the process.

* * *

According to Ritter's son-in-law, Colonel Manfred Blume, Ritter did mislead Gwyer. Ritter feared being prosecuted with war crimes if his time with the Abwehr was deemed to be a success. 'It was not the time to reveal the truth, nor his achievements,' said Blume.[59]

Ritter had been in prison for eight months by the time Gwyer interviewed him, and according to his memoirs, his two-year internment was a traumatic experience. One of the reasons Ritter said he didn't write his memoirs until 1972, was that 'it had gone against his principles to reveal his feelings and those of his comrades about the mistreatment of German intelligence officers by the British after the war. The time had not yet come to talk about that without bitterness.'[60]

In 1968, Ritter was approached by Herbert Wichmann, the former head of Ast. (Abwehrstelle) Hamburg, who asked Ritter if he would be willing to see Ladislas Farago, the military historian and journalist, who was in Hamburg at the time. Wichmann told Ritter to be careful, as Farago was interviewing former members of the German, British and American Intelligence Services for his book *The Game of the Foxes* - about German espionage in Britain and America during the war.[61]

Farago had stumbled upon a remarkable find in the National Archives in Washington DC. Inside a metal footlocker which looked like it had never been opened were

> hundreds of little yellow boxes containing rolls of microfilm. Dozens of the rolls, with about a thousand frames in each, contained the papers of the Hamburg and Bremen outposts of the Abwehr, the two branches of the German senior military intelligence agency that specialized in the clandestine coverage of Britain and the United States.[62]

Ritter was astonished when Farago showed him some of the documents, including a series that addressed his own activities. Until then, Ritter believed all their records had been destroyed, and he had kept silent about his activities during the war, despite encouragement that he should write his memoirs. Ritter wrote:

> Anyone who at one time or another belonged to the Intelligence Service – or so I thought – has a natural disinclination to talk about things that were previously confidential and whose secrecy he was expected to honor. In addition, there was the fact that any reports on espionage might easily expose a former co-worker who has not yet been revealed.[63]

Could this explain why Ritter had protected Owens during his interrogation with Gwyer? Ritter wrote in his memoirs he had no doubt that Owens would have come to live in Germany if he had allowed it. He was also genuinely fond of Owens, as Dicketts had observed in Lisbon.

If Ritter had intended to appear somewhat of a failure at CSDIC, he succeeded. Gwyer wrote in his report afterwards: 'I gathered that Ritter had not found it prudent to pass on to Abteilung II any suspicion of Owens or Dicketts that he might himself have entertained.'[64]

* * *

One of the questions the double-cross team asked themselves during the war, was whether the Abwehr considered it better to have a spy than none at all. In his book about the British double-cross system during the war, Masterman described how any member of the Abwehr could start and control an agent, whereas MI5 operated in a very tightly knit team, coordinating their efforts and cross-checking information. They maintained very detailed records and were in direct communication with SIS and the heads of the three armed services, who met regularly during XX Committee meetings to decide what information could go through to the Germans and what was to remain secret.

Masterman wrote:

> Not unnaturally the prestige, and presumably the income, of many Abwehr personalities depended upon the reputation of their own particular agents. If then the reliability of a double agent was questioned, his chief defender always turned out to be his own

spy-master, who could go to almost any lengths to protect him against the doubt and criticisms of rival persons or of Berlin.[65]

Naturally, Section B1 (a) were very proud of their success with the double-cross system, and justifiably so. However, they weren't alone in taking control of an enemy's radio and continuing to operate it. This concept was called *funkspiel* (radio play) in Germany, and the Gestapo used it in France with deadly effect. The Gestapo captured numerous British SOE agents and their radios and pretended to be a resistance movement, and by the time their *funkspiel* was discovered, almost the entire British organization in France was revealed and dismantled. By May 1944, the British had established new agents and networks elsewhere and the German operation was no longer a success.

Unable to resist a parting shot, the German operator's final message was: 'Thank you for your collaboration and for the weapons that you sent us.' Not to be outdone, the British operator replied: 'Think nothing of it. These weapons were a mere bagatelle for us. It was a luxury we could easily afford. We shall soon be coming to fetch them.'[66]

In 1974, perhaps the war's biggest secret was revealed by SIS's Group Captain Frederick Winterbotham in his book *The Ultra Secret* – the existence of a cryptographic operation based at Bletchley Park, home to British codebreakers during the war, where some of the daily keys of the ciphers generated on the Enigma machine, which gave '159 million, million, million, possible settings to choose from', were broken.[67]

These decrypted messages, referred to obliquely by Winston Churchill as his 'most secret sources', enabled Masterman to make the extraordinarily confident statement that the Double Cross Committee 'actively ran and controlled the German espionage system in this country'.[68]

Although Owens' radio messages had provided a window into the Abwehr's use of wireless encryption, British codebreakers had been unable to crack the special version of the Enigma machine used by the Abwehr. This changed on 8 December 1941, when Mavis Lever, a 19-year-old girl working under the eccentric codebreaker Dilly Knox at Bletchley Park, managed to break a message which allowed them to reconstruct one of the Enigma machine's wheels.[69] Within days, Knox had cracked the Abwehr Enigma, and from then on the double-cross team were able to monitor exactly how the Germans were responding to their agents, and the information they were feeding them.

Ritter, who died a few years after the publication of his 1972 memoirs, may never have learned about the existence of ULTRA, but had he done so, there could be no further denying that all his pre-invasion spies had been turned and his entire network controlled.

Although Ritter didn't know about ULTRA before he published his memoirs, he did manage to read John Masterman's book about the British double-cross system. His immediate reaction was to defend the loyalty of Owens. When Ritter read that the British believed Owens was a double agent, it only 'enhanced the value and the honesty of this little man for me'.[70]

He said Owens had sold his contact with British intelligence to the Abwehr, and 'occasionally supplied them with information while he was working loyally for us'. Ritter said the British were correct that Owens was working for them, but what they didn't know was that it all happened with Ritter's full consent and total support: 'If the English claim that we did not use him as a double agent then that is not in keeping with the facts. Johnny often asked me for bogus material so he could consolidate his position against the English.'

Ritter also said that the information Owens supplied him was of the utmost value for Germany.[71] Surely Ritter realized this information came from MI5?

'No, I am firmly convinced that he was always honest with me,' wrote Ritter.

> Our little Johnny had played his restless and fascinating game to the very end. But when I met him the last time in Lisbon, it was certain that he had become worthless for us, and I found myself forced to cut off the connection with him.[72]
>
> Today there is no further doubt that Johnny was a master spy. Unfortunately, I have no further personal contact with him, but I learned from my reliable source that he is alive and healthy and that he lives somewhere in Ireland under a false name with Lily and his children.

* * *

Years later, in 1971, Tar Robertson, like Ritter before him, was contacted by Ladislas Farago. Before they met, Farago said he was 'going to conjure up the shadows of the past', and achieved just that. Unsurprisingly, Tar was hugely interested in the information Farago told him. Tar wrote to John Masterman on 1 August that year:

> It seems incredible that the Germans never smelt a rat throughout the whole four or five years of the operation and that they never once suspected any one of our scatter-brained actions, such as sending Celery to Lisbon, Snow into the North Sea and so on. However, he assures me that is the case, and who am I to disbelieve him?

Tar said he couldn't help feeling that the anti-Nazi feeling was strong among German intelligence officers of the pre-Hitler vintage, and didn't think 'they cared whether their agents were good or bad or produced good or bad information'.[73]

MI5 were not aware until the end of the hostilities that their surmise was correct about some Abwehr officials wilfully shutting their eyes to suspicions about their agents. The interrogation of Major Friedrich Busch, who demanded Ritter's transfer, made it plain that these officials 'thought it better for selfish reasons to have corrupt or disloyal agents than to have no agents at all'.[74]

In the summer of 2000, CIA historian Benjamin Fischer wrote in *A.k.a. 'Dr. Rantzau'*:

> No one represented the Abwehr's ambiguous record of occasional success and repeated failure better than Major Nikolaus Ritter. He was intimately involved in one of the service's greatest successes [the Norden Bombsight] and its two greatest disasters – the compromise of all Abwehr agents in the United States and Britain.[75]

Ritter's daughter, Katharine, told me in 2013 that her father never joined the Nazi Party: 'He considered himself a gentleman working for his country, and didn't even think of himself as a spy.' In his private life, away from the stress and horror of war, her father's nature was 'somewhat immature and playful. He enjoyed parties, games, art and music, good food and drink and mostly American apple pie.'

As to which side Owens was on, John Masterman makes a very valid point about how we think of a double agent, compared to the way in which the agent regards himself:

> We think a double agent is a man who is supposed to be an agent of say England, when in fact he is working in the interests and under the direction of say Germany. But the agent, particularly if he started work before the war, is often trying to work for both England and Germany and to draw payments from both.[76]

This was probably the case with Owens, wrote Masterman:

> Perhaps he was seventy-five per cent on our side, but I should need a lot of evidence to convince me that he has not played for both sides. But it was also possible that Ritter had always regarded him as someone who was working for both sides, but knew he could be bribed or frightened into doing better work for Germany.

At the end of the war, an anonymous MI5 officer wrote a summation of the Snow case and described Owens as a vain and untruthful man:

> He has a perpetual itch to inform other people of his importance and when he does (which is usually when he is rather drunk), he has no regard for truth or discretion. Owens was probably not completely aware on these occasions that he was telling a lie or grossly exaggerating, and alternated between viewing himself as a patriot genuinely doing dangerous and valuable work for his country, or as a daring spy, clever enough to outwit British Intelligence.[77]

Yet in the end, Owens was outwitted by the man he considered to be an amateur. Dicketts' word was believed over his, and Owens was sent to prison, where he remained among other enemy agents until the end of the war.

Chapter 11

South America Beckons

'The bravest are surely those who have the clearest vision of what is before them, glory and danger alike, and yet notwithstanding go out to meet it.' Pericles

After Dicketts' unmistakable offer to Georg Sessler in Lisbon, Ast. Hamburg knew Dicketts' loyalty was to Britain despite his claims to the contrary, and MI5 needed to find him a new role. He was considered for a role with SO2, the Foreign Office's clandestine sabotage and subversion department,[1] in France, and MI5's Director of Counter-Espionage, Guy Liddell, wanted his counterparts in SIS's Section V to use Dicketts in Brazil.[2]

Britain was dependent upon the vital supplies of food, resources and equipment from South and North America, and Germany was attempting to starve Britain into defeat by attacking its merchant vessels on their journey across the Atlantic Ocean. The Battle of the Atlantic, as it came to be known, was a fight for Britain's very survival, and 'the U-boat peril' was the only thing that Winston Churchill said really frightened him during the Second World War.[3]

The role of intelligence was crucial. If the British knew where the U-boat wolfpacks were patrolling, they could divert their convoys into safer areas. But the reverse would apply if the Germans knew the route and date when the Allied convoys were sailing; they could send U-boats to destroy them. One of the problems for British intelligence was the large number of Italian and German immigrants who had settled in South America for over 100 years before the outbreak of the war. Their descendants now held important positions within society and the administration, and assisted the Abwehr in building up extensive spy networks. These networks gathered information about the type and quantity of cargo being sent to Britain and the dates of arrival and departure of ships and convoys - then forwarded it to the U-boats, who would seek out and destroy these vessels. The task for the Allied intelligence agencies in these countries was to prevent the enemy spy-networks from supplying information. First of all they had to identify enemy agents and informers, and then infiltrate their networks and destroy them.

Dicketts was not the type of man to sit around waiting for things to happen, so he began seeking opportunities where he could be of value to MI5. In July 1941, he received an offer to go to work in Brazil, and MI5 was interested – the commercial cover was ideal for Dicketts to continue operating as a British spy. MI5 told Dicketts 'to continue his negotiations with Pereira [unidentified codename] and go to Brazil, even if SIS didn't employ him',[4] and they would give his employer a guarantee of £500 (around £22,720 today).[5]

From that moment on, Dicketts' activities with MI5 are missing from his file at the National Archives. SIS's files will never be released to the public, so it is fortunate that the wartime diary of the Chairman of the Double Cross Committee, Sir John Masterman, has recently come to light, containing numerous entries involving his meetings and conversations with Dicketts until mid-1943, after which Dicketts disappeared into the world of business.[6]

Dicketts' role with MI5 had been as a penetration agent, and it is reasonable to assume that he would do the same thing in South America. An important consideration was his knowledge of the Abwehr, particularly Ast. Hamburg, as they ran one of the largest spy networks in South America, called *Bolivar-Netz*, which operated around forty agents and eight wireless stations.[7] Wohldorf-Hamburg, the receiving station for their signals intelligence, was under the control of Kapitän Trautmann and his assistant, Leutnant Richard Wein, whom Dicketts had met in Hamburg in March.[8]

Guy Liddell, MI5's Director of Counter-Espionage, who backed Dicketts' trip to South America, was concerned that 'German agents were bribing' allied seamen in South and North America not to rejoin their ships.[9] Enemy agents could then be placed on board to carry out acts of sabotage, gather intelligence or enter Britain illegally. It was also fairly clear that the 'Germans were collaborating with the Japanese in building an intelligence service' in South America which would link up to one in North America.[10]

In late October, Walter Dicketts, travelling as a manufacturer's agent, and his wife, Mrs Kathleen Dicketts, set sail from Liverpool, travelling first class aboard the SS *Andalucia Star* to Rio de Janeiro. MI5 had obtained a passport for Kay in the name of Mrs Dicketts, despite being fully aware that Dicketts was legally married to Vera.[11] Kay was an important part of Dicketts' cover, and already knew a great deal about his activities with MI5.

It was a dangerous time to be crossing the Atlantic, never knowing if your ship was about to be sunk by a U-boat. The Dicketts were lucky; one year later, the SS *Andalucia Star* was en route from Buenos Aires to Liverpool carrying a cargo of 5,374 tons of meat and 32 tons of eggs, when she was torpedoed by *U-107* and sunk. Three crew members and one passenger were killed in the attack.[12]

Dicketts and Kay left England in the cool of autumn, and around thirty days later arrived in the steaming, tropical heat of Rio de Janeiro in spring. Their first sight of this huge seaside city couldn't have failed to impress, from the sandy beaches of Ipanema and Copacabana to the incredible views of Sugarloaf Mountain and the nearby granite peak of Mount Corcovado. Compared to the austerity of Britain at war, Rio was different in every way: tanned men and women in swimwear strolled along the boardwalk and played ball on the beach; there was samba and tango, brightly coloured birds and tropical fruit, numerous races and skin tones, dialects and languages, and a happy carnival-like atmosphere compared to the blackouts, rations, bomb damage and stress of life at home.

Kay and Dicketts were still at sea, when the Japanese bombed the US Pacific Fleet at Pearl Harbor on 7 December, after which America entered the war. Within weeks, many Latin American countries broke relations or declared war on Germany. Although Brazil didn't declare war on Germany until August, it allowed America to set up air bases along the north-eastern coast and played an important role in the campaign against the U-boats in the South Atlantic.

The Allies persuaded the local police authorities to 'arrest, intern, or deport' enemy agents, and with the arrest of the leaders of the Brazilian spy rings in March, Germany was never again successful in establishing an effective espionage service in Brazil.[13]

Dicketts and Kay were in Montevideo, the capital city of Uruguay, when the country declared war against Germany on 15 February 1942, and left shortly afterwards. They travelled aboard the New Zealand Shipping

Company's SS *Ruahine* and arrived safely in Belfast, Northern Ireland, on 7 March 1942.[14]

Dicketts met with John Masterman and John Marriott in May, and asked to be free 'of all claims of contract' and to be able to take on other jobs as required.[15] Dicketts had come up with a plan to import oranges from South America, but there was a possibility he might be sent back to Brazil again.

In June, Dicketts met with Mills and Wright from SIS, who told Masterman afterwards that Wright was very impressed with Dicketts. 'Considering the short amount of time he was there, Dicketts had shown a remarkable knowledge of South America,' said Wright. 'He made contacts and provided information that was of primary importance to me.' Wright was going to ask Felix Cowgill, head of SIS's counter-espionage Section V, to employ Dicketts if he went back to Brazil again.[16]

Dicketts never did go back to Brazil, but he continued to pursue his orange juice idea and called Masterman in July to say he was having lunch with the Brazilian Ambassador.[17] Further details are not available, but according to an article in the *Daily Telegraph* in 1949, Dicketts had '£20,000 in pesetas frozen in a Brazilian bank account'.[18]

Masterman and Dicketts remained in regular contact until 1 April 1943, after which Dicketts disappeared into the world of commerce.

Chapter 12

A New Life

**'I've known several spies who have wanted to become novelists. And
novelists who became spies, of course.' Christopher Koch**

espite the shared bond of their wartime experiences, Dicketts and
Kay's relationship ended when they returned to England in March
1942. It was a year of romantic endings, as Vera, his legal wife,
obtained a decree nisi in December so she could marry someone else.

Their parting left Kay with an identity problem. The name Kathleen
Mary Dicketts in her passport was false, she had no marriage certificate
to Dicketts and the name on her birth certificate was Holdcroft. Kay was
bound by the Official Secrets Act and couldn't tell her future husband who
she really was, or explain to her father why she called him Arthur Lionel
Dicketts on her wedding certificate instead of Holdcroft. When she became
Mrs David Rose in June 1946, her conundrum was solved.[1]

Interestingly, other than the official records, the only surviving account of
Kay's wartime past is an anecdote from one of her surviving relatives who
remembers his grandmother saying Kay had given her a pair of tights after
she returned from South America. Before the war, no well-dressed woman
would be seen in public without silk stockings, but nylon and silk were used
for parachutes and other essential wartime products, so women resorted to
painting fake stocking seams on the back of their legs with eyebrow pencils.
No wonder Kay's gift was remembered.

At a West End party in June 1943, Dicketts met a beautiful young
Hungarian woman and was absolutely smitten. If ever there was a love of
his life, it was Judit Rose Kalman. Judy was 20 years old and looked like
a film star; she had thick brown hair, curled just under her ears, arched
eyebrows, high cheekbones and big brown eyes. She was slim and elegant,
and twenty-three years younger than her admirer, Richard 'Dick' Dicketts,
as he liked to be known then. I'm certain he didn't tell Judy she was the same

age as my mother Effie – Dicketts' only daughter, who was born in the same year and the same month as Judy, although he hadn't seen his daughter (if he ever did) since.

Judy's father, a top Hungarian concert pianist, died in 1936, and she was on a grand tour of Europe with her mother in 1938 when Hitler took over Austria, with a wave of street violence towards Jews and Jewish property following in its wake. Anti-Jewish sentiment spread throughout Germany and Austria, and culminated in the event commonly known as *Kristallnacht*, or the 'Night of Broken Glass', on 9 November. Members of the Nazi party burned synagogues, looting Jewish homes and businesses, and the Gestapo and uniformed police arrested around 30,000 Jewish men and imprisoned them in concentration camps. Judy's mother left her in England, while she returned home to Budapest to sort out their affairs and returned to London a few days before the outbreak of war.

After a whirlwind romance of just three months, Dicketts and Judy were married on 8 September 1943, and held their wedding breakfast at the Savoy, London's first true luxury hotel.[2] Dicketts' profession at the time, according to his marriage certificate, was 'Director of Companies', but as Judy would soon find out, things were not quite as they seemed.

Judy was three months pregnant when Guy Liddell, head of MI5's Section B, wrote in his secret wartime diary on 1 February 1944 that there was 'a warning out for Celery's arrest for embezzlement. Celery has apparently disappeared.'[3]

Dicketts' request to be released from his obligations with MI5 and SIS was agreed to when he returned from Brazil, and he had since become involved in several businesses as an agent. In 1943, he was introduced to Sir Maurice Bonham Carter, a liberal politician and chairman of two aviation companies, General Aircraft Ltd and Aero Engines Ltd, by a Dr Joseph Sagall. Dicketts attended the meeting in the company of a 'marquess whom he introduced as Don Pedro', and discussed purchasing a block of 430,000 two-shilling shares in Aero Engines Ltd.[4] As far as Bonham Carter was concerned, nothing ever came from these discussions, but that didn't stop Dicketts acting as if they had.

Over a number of apparently successful business deals, Dicketts had gained the confidence of two investors, Mr Jacob Goff and Mr William Forbes. Dicketts told them about a highly profitable scheme for the amalgamation of several aircraft companies, and said the transactions would 'yield a profit of £40,000 to £50,000'.[5] Eager to make some serious money, Goff gave Dicketts £2,500 and Forbes gave him £4,000 [around £165,100 today] to purchase some shares, but unbeknownst to them their money went straight into Dicketts' bank account and was used to pay them the profit from earlier schemes. It was a typical Ponzi or pyramid selling scheme, whereby money which had just been invested was used to pay people who had invested previously, instead of using real profit (if there was any in the first place) to pay them. In this case, the new investors and the previous investors were the same. No shares were ever purchased, and Goff and Forbes lost their money.

When Goff and Forbes realized they had been swindled, they reported Dicketts to the police, but he claimed the whole share venture had been genuine and blamed the collapse of a 'whiskey deal' in Birmingham for his financial situation.[6] Dicketts had undone all the good he had worked and risked so much to achieve. Sadly, no one at MI5 and SIS was that surprised; it simply confirmed their belief that 'once a criminal, always a criminal'.

What they didn't expect was what Dicketts did next. After attending his initial proceedings in court, Dicketts used his skills as a conman and a double agent to disappear. After jumping bail, he and his pregnant young wife Judy fled, but only as far as East Grinstead, around 24 miles south of London. Starting from scratch, Dicketts assumed a new identity as Charles Stewart Pollock, a wealthy public benefactor, and began carrying on business transactions of a similar nature. To pull off deals of the magnitude he had in mind, Dicketts needed to adopt a suitably upper-class name like 'Charles Stewart Pollock', which he may have sourced from the 107th Edition of *Burke's Peerage*, where a person of the same name is listed as having died in March 1890 at the age of 25.[7]

Charles, as he was now known, built himself up into one of the most honoured and respected citizens of the district. He purchased two estates, Brockhurst and Horne Park with 893 acres, for £70,000 [around £2,270,000 today] and became a rich country gentleman, who was well known at social gatherings. 'People were impressed. Property deals went through, and thousands of pounds changed hands,' wrote a *Daily Express* journalist in 1949.[8]

He drove around in a white Rolls Royce, which he liked to change every six months, and sometimes wore old clothes - remarking that 'only a wealthy man could afford the luxury of appearing shabby'.[9] He had a chauffeur, servants and beautiful homes, but underneath the suitably eccentric Charles, was Walter Dicketts pulling his strings.

Whilst his countrymen were struggling in a near bankrupt post-war Britain, Charles bought a country club with forty acres, whose 250 members were all wealthy. He had a beautiful wife, a young son and was generous to charity, donating a cup for local boxers and another for a horse show, and nobody suspected that there was anything suspicious about the 45-year-old squire of Brockhurst.

Charles became interested in British Ores Development Ltd, a genuine concern connected with a mine in Wales, and was given complete power of attorney over a period of six weeks to get the company back on its feet.[10] He persuaded Mr Albert Batchelor to part with over £8,000 to buy shares in the company and received a further £10,000 (around £390,000 today)[11] from Mr Ernest Burrows for the same purpose. Once again, no genuine shares were ever purchased and Dicketts simply paid the money into his own account and 'just frittered' it away.[12] Poor Mr Batchelor was financially ruined as a result.

By December 1948, Dicketts knew his carefully constructed world was about to come crashing down. Just before Christmas, he travelled to Bristol to see Richard, his 14-year-old son with Vera, and said he had come to say goodbye as he was going to work in Australia for a while. When he got home, he wrote Richard a farewell letter and enclosed 'a souvenir, with our crest, with my dearest wishes for your future life and happiness'.

Dicketts' letter reflects the deep sadness he felt at his certain imprisonment and future inability to see his son. The advice he gave Richard in his letter was what he should have followed himself: 'Be honest and straightforward in everything you do, and have a kindly and generous heart – these are the only things that count.' Richard didn't know his father had gone to jail, and was in his seventies when he discovered the truth, and a whole lot of other surprising truths as well.

Having settled his affairs as best as he could, Dicketts gave himself up to the police after nearly five years on the run. His life of luxury ended at Knightsbridge police station on 4 January 1949, where he spent his first night in prison on a hard bed, and ate a 'simple supper of sausage and cocoa'.[13] As Dicketts was being charged, he inquired after 'poor Mr Batchelor', said he felt sorrier for him than any of the others and hoped he would be able to get some money back for him.[14]

Dicketts pleaded 'not guilty' at his trial at the Old Bailey on 15 March 1949, and was released on bail of 'cash and sureties' totalling £3,000 (around £97,270 today).[15] Mr James Burge, his defence barrister, described Dicketts as 'a man of remarkable character, whose work in the last war was certainly above the average'.[16] Burge told the court that he could only give the barest of details under the Official Secrets Act, but Dicketts had undertaken 'the most hazardous type of work possible for any man to be engaged upon in war time'.[17]

Detective Inspector Gillan of Scotland Yard said that during the First World War, Dicketts 'had served with distinction', and by the time he was 21 had risen to the rank of captain.[18] In fact, Dicketts was only 18, but during a trial in which he was being charged for dishonesty, nothing could be gained by saying he lied about his age to enlist. Gillan said that during the next war, Dicketts had carried out his mission entrusted to him by a government department 'with courage and dignity'.[19]

'Although Dicketts was known to be a convicted criminal during the 1930s,' said Gillan, 'he was given a position as secretary of the Social Services where he rose to an executive position.' The scheme was sponsored by the Prince of Wales, whom Dicketts regularly entertained with other notable personalities at the Dorchester and other leading hotels.

Burge made the point that given his training as a British agent, Dicketts could easily have fled abroad without going through the usual channels, but had chosen instead to remain in England, where he became involved in a number of successful property deals.

'Where did he obtain the £70,000 [around £2,270,000 today] to purchase the two estates?' asked Judge McClure.[20]

'He purchased a block of flats in London for £20,000 which he sold for a profit of £2,000, and sold a house in East Grinstead for £9,000. He had also invested £27,000 in a hotel at Eastbourne, and purchased other property for £48,000,'[21] replied Burge.

'He also owns £1,400 worth of shares in a new midget car which was receiving great publicity, and has 4,000 export orders for it already,' added Burge.[22] The car referred to is probably the legendary Morris Minor, as Dicketts worked for the Morris Car Company in Cowley in the early 1950s after his release from jail.

'Recently,' Burge continued, 'Dicketts had come up with a scheme to build the first new town to be constructed after the war, to house 7,000 people.'[23]

Dicketts' idea and expertise had been taken seriously by the authorities, and he had recently given evidence for three days before the government inspector, at a public inquiry held at the Ministry of Town and County Planning regarding the scheme. The only reason it had fallen through was because the recently elected government decided to build their own new town at Crawley.

'It does not look as if he was living from hand to mouth by swindling people – by simply milking the public of money and being a persistent fraudster,' summed up Burge.[24]

Dicketts pleaded 'guilty' to fraudulently converting to his own use or benefit, cheques for £2,500, £2,500 and £1,500, and two charges of recklessly making false statements to induce two men to enter into agreements to purchase shares.[25] In sentencing Dicketts to four years' penal servitude, Judge McClure said he felt he had to make a note in his favour, especially with regard to his war service, but felt sure that 'had the true picture been painted to the people he was dealing with, he would not have been able to get any money from them at all'.[26]

As Dicketts was led away, he stretched out his hand to his young wife Judy, mother of his 4-year-old son Robert.

'I will wait for you,' promised Judy.[27]

She told waiting reporters afterwards that 'you cannot help loving that man', but she must now go back to her son and four years of loneliness.[28] 'I must get a job for the boy and I must live.'

Judy said her husband had run from police five years ago because she was pregnant with their son. He had intended to go to work and begin a new life, so that he could repay the people he owed money to, 'but he became too clever and got involved in so many business deals at one time, that he got them all mixed up'.[29]

She added: 'Now I am penniless, selling his suits to keep me and our four-and-a-half-year-old son.'[30]

By the time Judy got back to the bed-sitting room in Kensington which was now her home, she had decided that their son Robert would never discover the truth about his father's criminal past. Judy succeeded in her goal, as Robert wouldn't find out until fifty-six years later that his father had been in jail.

The morning after Dicketts' trial, the newspapers – both local and international – were full of stories about Walter Dicketts the charming spy. The

Daily Herald reported that the 48-year-old Dicketts had been 'a company director, financial agent, promoter of dinner and dances for debutantes, soldier, welfare worker, orange-juice importer, whiskey dealer, estate agent, designer of the first satellite town (which was shelved), acquaintance of the Duke of Windsor, convict and wartime Allied Agent'.[31] Was there anything he hadn't done?

Whilst the newspapers were declaring him an odd mixture of hero and crook, Dicketts was taken to Wandsworth Prison, from where he was later transferred to Leyhill Open Prison in Gloucestershire. Dicketts wrote several letters to his family from Leyhill, calling it Thornbury Castle due to its proximity to the jail. Judy visited him regularly, and so, surprisingly, did Vera, his ex-wife, whose new husband sat in the car until she returned.

Dicketts served two years of his four-year sentence, and was released for good behaviour in 1951. Judy had waited for him as promised, and they moved into a large basement flat in Wilton Crescent, just off Belgrave Square, London. Unable to start his own business until bankruptcy proceedings against him were over, Dicketts became a salesman for the Morris Car Company in Cowley, but this was never going to be enough for a man like him. There were many favourable employment opportunities throughout the British colonies after the war, so Dicketts left Judy and Robert behind in England and travelled to Singapore to manage a rubber plantation.

Robert remembers receiving a letter from his father describing the monkeys he could see outside his window and the difficulties of dealing with terrorists during the period known as 'The Troubles', which began after the withdrawal of the Japanese at the end of the Second World War. The revenue from Malaya's tin and rubber industries was vital to Britain's post-war recovery, and a conflict between the communist guerrillas and Commonwealth forces soon began. When three European plantation managers were assassinated in 1948, a state of emergency was declared until 1960, when the British and Commonwealth forces succeeded in defeating the uprising.

In an extraordinary coincidence, my mother and father were in Malaya at the same time. Tonie (as she now called herself) and her husband Freddy Witt had been posted to Malaya in 1947 by his employer, the Commercial Union Insurance Company. The expatriate community were a tight-knit group, particularly up-country where Tonie, Freddy and her father Dicketts were based. They may even have met, but neither would have guessed they were father and daughter.

There's no doubt that if by some extraordinary fate they did meet, Dicketts could not have failed to notice her. His daughter Tonie was outgoing and gregarious, tall, slim and shapely with a narrow waist. A widow's peak framed her forehead and her dark, slightly wavy hair bounced softly above her shoulders. Her eyes were deep blue, sometimes almost violet, and she had dramatic facial expressions like raising her right eyebrow in mirth or query, or lightly pouting her lips when thinking or after one too many gins. The expatriates lived it up after the war; food, alcohol, clothing and cheap labour was readily available, and they were mostly young and glad to be alive. It was a long way from the rationing and struggle of most British citizens as their country recovered from war.

Dicketts had returned to England by September 1953, where his son Richard managed to track him down and get in contact. In doing so, he had gone against his mother Vera's wishes that he should never try to contact his father, but Richard, who was 19 at the time, thought otherwise. Richard remembers his father and Judy taking him to dinner and then to the theatre afterwards. He was struck by how beautiful Judy was, and how well she and his father looked together.

A year later, Judy and Dicketts separated with much sadness. On their wedding anniversary, Dicketts sent her a card on which he crossed out the printed words and added his own. Dicketts was clearly deeply affected by their break-up and referred to the early part of their relationship 'as the one abiding memory in my heart':

> So, darling, may the future be very kind to you, God bless you in every way and give you real happiness and security. I send you all my worldly worth and health to drink to the dog-days gone by, and to the good days ahead for you. Cheerio! My sweet lamb, with much sadness but most enduring affection. Charles. Perhaps on future anniversaries, we may meet and drink together as the greatest of friends.

Less than a year later, Dicketts' beloved mother Frances died in June 1955, and his 85-year-old father Arthur moved in with his niece, Ada Amelia

Evans, so she could take care of him. Arthur died eighteen months later in January 1957, leaving a reasonable amount of money to various members of his family, and especially to Ada - but to his son Walter Dicketts, he bequeathed only his gold watch and signet ring. Due to the bankruptcy proceedings currently being undertaken against his son, Arthur may have realised that any money he left him would have gone straight to his creditors.

A few weeks after his father's death, the hearing for Dicketts' application for discharge from bankruptcy was begun, and may perhaps have been the only bright light in his year of misfortune.[32] His and Judy's divorce was finalized in May 1957, and ever the gentleman, Dicketts had admitted to adultery so Judy could be free to pursue a new relationship, begun shortly after their separation.

On 28 July 1957, with the trials and sorrows of the last few years behind him, Dicketts 'took lodgings at 13 Craven Hill Paddington'.[33] A few days later, a guest on the same floor as Dicketts complained to the housekeeper, Mrs Olive Teugels, that there was a strong smell of gas coming from his room and she immediately went to investigate. Mrs Teugels knocked on his door and, after receiving no reply, attempted to open it and found it was unlocked, but coats and other clothing had been used to seal it. Lying with his head on a pillow in front of the gas fireplace was Walter Dicketts, who did not respond when she spoke to him. 'I suppose he was dead, I didn't look very long,' Mrs Teugels told the Coroner later.[34]

Dicketts was taken to St Mary's Hospital Paddington, where the pathologist, Dr Camps, said he had died of 'coal gas poisoning, and had no significant natural disease'.[35] Judy identified his body, and at the inquest said she only occasionally saw her 57-year-old ex-husband, 'who could be despondent at times'.[36] She said he was in 'rather a nervous state. His health was "fair" but he was always inclined to complain.'[37]

The Coroner, W. Bentley Purchase, said 'he had no doubt that Dicketts had taken his own life and he would record that verdict'. On his death certificate, he stated Dicketts' profession was a 'writer'.[38]

The day after his death, on 7 August, Judy wrote a very brief letter to Vera and Richard saying that she was sorry to have to tell them 'that Charles (as Judy called him) passed away yesterday morning'.[39] That was it ... Judy gave no explanation for his death, and Vera told Richard (then 23) that his father had been assassinated as a result of his wartime activities. Richard was absolutely shattered to learn that his father had committed suicide when he learned the truth in later life, but he didn't believe it: 'Father was not the sort of person to kill himself. He had tremendous personal courage as is evident by the actions he took during both wars. He was also the type of person who would pick himself up and begin again.'

Judy's son Robert was just shy of his thirteenth birthday when his father died. Judy didn't give him any explanation for his father's death, but he remembers going to the funeral. 'I can still remember driving along with the hearse and people standing on the side of the road doffing their hats and caps as they did in the 1950s,' he told me.

Dicketts' ashes were scattered in the Kensal Green Cemetery's Garden of Remembrance on 10 August, and from that moment on, Judy was extremely reluctant to discuss his father with Robert on any occasion. 'It was obvious she didn't want to talk about him, and after a while I gave up,' said Robert, who today wishes he had pushed her harder.

Despite his parents' separation, Robert remembers them being very civil and almost loving towards each other. He didn't see a lot of his father because he was at boarding school and Dicketts was away a lot, but there was one thing that continues to stand out in his mind today – his father's imposing character: 'One was always aware of his presence. If he walked into the room, everybody noticed him, especially the ladies.'

Robert remembers a few holidays with his father, and in particular a holiday in 1955 when they went mackerel fishing together in Dorset: 'Overall, he was a good father but, as was often the case in those days, a slightly distant person but he could also be very affectionate.'

Judy got on with her life after Dicketts' death and married Bill Bentley, the well-known restaurateur and founder of London fish restaurant Bentley's, which was particularly famous for its oysters. Regrettably, Judy systematically destroyed all Dicketts' remaining possessions, leaving their son Robert with very few photographs, just one or two personal letters and no business documentation of any kind. Judy seemed hell-bent on hiding all evidence of his activities (and her compliance with them), and sadly, for a man who was described on his death certificate as a writer, not a single scrap of Dicketts' writing has survived.

When Dicketts was arrested in Austria for swindling in 1930, *The Yorkshire Post* reported the following:

Writing of Stories: Imposter to Try New Way of Making A Living

Since his arrest in Austria, Dicketts had written a number of stories
and he expressed his intention of trying to earn his living in that
way. [40]

Judy wasn't the only one of Dicketts' wives to destroy all evidence of him.
Vera, his third wife, tore Dicketts' image out of every one of her photographs. Richard found a couple that his mother must have missed, but sadly
all that remains of Dicketts' personal effects today are a few silver toiletry
items and a leather suitcase.

In December 1975, Oliver Muldoon, one of Dicketts' closest friends,
wrote to Dicketts' son, Rodney, who had lost contact with his father, saying
Dicketts was:

attached to British Intelligence in the war and spoke French and
German fluently. After the war he complained that the War Office
had placed an embargo on his plan to publish his memoirs, a ban
which had contributed to the great financial difficulties he experienced towards the end of his life - difficulties I may say, in which I
tried to assist. [41]

The publishing of memoirs at the end of the war was deeply frowned on
by MI5 due to the secrecy of the information, particularly the existence
and use of ULTRA, the British codename applied to highly secret signals intelligence obtained by breaking the Germans' 'unbreakable' Enigma
code. According to MI5's B Division Director Guy Lidell, 'Even an innocuous foreword penned by Tommy Robertson for a wartime history of
MI5 was banned on the basis that his contribution would set a precedent
and enhance the status and credibility of a book that did not have official
approval.' [42]

Only five double agents managed to pen their own memoirs: Zigzag
(Eddie Chapman), Garbo (Juan Pujol), Tricycle (Dusko Popov), Treasure
(Lily Sergueiev) and Mutt (John Moe). Chapman was prosecuted under the
Official Secrets Act when he tried to publish his memoirs in Britain in 1945,
and although he was let off with a small fine due to his bravery during the

war, his version of his adventures, *The Real Eddie Chapman Story*, wasn't released until 1956.

John Masterman, the Chairman of the Double Cross Committee, received both support and intense criticism over the 1972 publication of his book *The Double Cross System of the War 1939-1945*. Among Masterman's private papers is a letter from Sir Martin Furnival Jones, the Director General of MI5 (1965-1972): 'I consider your action is disgraceful and have no doubt that my opinion would be shared by many of those with whom you worked during the war.'[43]

A second letter from Furnival Jones points out that MI5 would have given the double-cross agents an undertaking that their roles would never be revealed without their consent, and that two agents had already sold their own stories: 'There was a leakage through a Chief Constable about two others, but by prompt action we were able to contain the damage. One at least of the agents is dead.'[44] I wonder if he was referring to Dicketts?

In an interesting twist, the name of the Coroner on Dicketts' death certificate was Mr Bentley Purchase - the same Coroner who falsified the death certificate of Owens' business partner, ex MI5 officer William Rolph, in 1940. Concerned the Germans would interpret Rolph's death from suicide as proof that he had been blown, MI5 asked Bentley Purchase to confirm Rolph died of a heart attack.[45]

Bentley Purchase also supplied a corpse from the morgue for the successful deception known as Operation MINCEMEAT, which duped the Germans into believing that the planned Allied invasion of Sicily in 1943 would take place in Greece.[46] The body of a Royal Marines courier with a briefcase attached to his wrist containing fake documents, was released from a submarine off the Spanish coast so it would come ashore and be discovered by the Abwehr. The ruse worked and saved thousands of lives, and was later immortalized in the 1956 film *The Man Who Never Was*.

* * *

In October 1957, *John Bull* magazine featured an article written by Austrian journalist Günter Peis and British journalist Charles Wighton, who worked for Reuters during the Second World War, with the headline-grabbing title *Hitler's Wartime Spies in Britain*. It told the story of how Nazi agents stole Britain's war secrets. 'They lurked in cities, masqueraded in country towns and even posed as farmers,' wrote Peis and Wighton, unaware that nearly every one of those agents had been captured by MI5 and operated under their control.

The article was based on high-ranking Abwehr official General Erwin Lahousen's diaries, and revealed the identity of the Abwehr's master-spy in London as being a fiercely anti-British Welshman called Arthur George Owens. It gave an account of Jack Brown's (Dicketts) trip to Hamburg, and described how the Abwehr had drugged Brown before removing his signet ring.

Although Dicketts wasn't identified by name, and had died two months previously, Owens was still alive and living in Ireland. When Owens was released from prison on 31 August 1944, Lily and their baby, Jean, had disappeared, but Owens soon found love again with Hilda White, who lived in Dollis Hill; their son Graham was born in November 1946. Owens changed his surname to White by deed poll in October of that year, which was fortunate in light of the *John Bull* article which would later name Owens as Germany's master spy in Britain.

Owens was in a fuel additive business with his older son, Robert, in March 1948, when he borrowed £5 from him and without any explanation moved to Wexford, Ireland, with Hilda and baby Graham. In Wexford, Owens repaired radios and sold batteries, along with a liniment he mixed together called Zing Salve. He 'attended Sinn Fein meetings' and would clap enthusiastically at the end of each, despite not being able to understand Gaelic.[47]

Graham told author Madoc West, who was writing a book about his father called *Snow*, that Owens had received a letter from one of his fellow prisoners in Dartmoor, a pro-German Dane called Borreson, saying that he was pleased to have heard from Owens, 'thus seeing that nobody has cut your throat'. 'I suppose you are having a good time in Ireland. Perhaps you are writing your memoirs. Now let me hear how you are getting along.'[48]

When Graham and Madoc met many years later, they found themselves speculating about the mysterious circumstances of Snow's death. Graham recalled that on Christmas Eve, two months after the publication of the *John Bull* article, Owens had given him a £5 [around £110 today] note - a large sum for an 11-year-old boy to be given at the time. Graham later wondered why he had not given it to him in the morning on Christmas Day, as was traditional. Owens died later that night from myocarditis on the way to the hospital. He had been experiencing breathing problems since November.

A few days later, Owens was buried in an unmarked grave in Crosstown, just outside Wexford. After his death, without receiving any warning, Hilda received a visit from a representative from the Royal British Legion, who said he was checking to see if she qualified for a war pension. After discussing Owens' war record, he told Hilda she was not entitled to one, but omitted to tell her how he knew that Arthur Graham White was Arthur Owens the double agent – and neither could the man from the British Legion explain how he had traced their family.

Graham and Madoc speculated whether Owens had been on an undercover mission to infiltrate the Irish Republican Army. He certainly had the right cover, as a suspected German spy who had been interned during the war. Perhaps he had been spirited away to Canada after his cover was blown by the *John Bull* article? This is not as wild a guess as it sounds.

Madoc's co-author Nigel West tracked down another double agent, Juan Pujol Garcia (codenamed Garbo), who had received both an Iron Cross and a British MBE for his wartime efforts, who was supposedly dead. Fearing reprisals from surviving Nazis, Pujol had faked his death in Angola, allegedly from malaria, but was in fact very much alive and living in Venezuela.

Was the *John Bull* article, which would almost certainly have been cleared by MI5 beforehand, a catalyst for the deaths of both Dicketts and Owens? They died in the same year of its publication, 1957. Or was this just a coincidence?

Chapter 13

Lost and Found

'History keeps her secrets longer than most of us. But she has one
secret that I will reveal to you tonight in the greatest confidence.
Sometimes there are no winners at all. And sometimes nobody
needs to lose.' John le Carre

W hen the Luftwaffe flew their Heinkel bombers and Messerschmitt
fighters over Lancashire during the war, Harry Butcher, like a lot
of young boys, would rush outside and aim two fingers at them
as if he was firing a gun. He wondered what sort of people would come to
England and bomb their cities and kill people like him. As Harry grew older,
his interest in the German view of the conflict continued to develop, and he
decided to write a book about the Abwehr. Harry used a false name to carry
out his research, because some of the people he met were the kind of people
who had done some terrible things during the war.

In the early 1990s, Harry was at the German Archives in Freiburg, where
he began chatting to a young German student and told her what he was
doing. It was pure luck, as she gave him the very break he needed - the name
and address of a former Abwehr member in Hamburg. Harry called at the
house of Mr Auerbach, who initially thought Harry was a radio ham (amateur radio operator) from England. He was more than willing to share information and gave him an introduction to Rudolf Staritz, another member
of the Abwehr involved in clandestine radio operations during the Second
World War.[1] Staritz was also very helpful and informative, and introduced
him to another Abwehr member, and so on ...

It was in this manner that Harry came across a man called George
Sessler in 1995.[2] Sessler, who was 78 at the time, told Harry a fascinating
tale about how he had escorted a British agent called Walter Dicketts from
Lisbon to Hamburg in 1941, and helped him to escape 'after Berlin had
become suspicious'. Sessler had always wondered what had happened to

Dicketts, and asked Harry if he could try to find him when he got back to England.

Harry was intrigued and began searching for Dicketts immediately. He searched phone books, census records, birth, marriage and death certificates, but there was nothing – Dicketts seemed to have disappeared, a perhaps not unsurprising consequence of being a spy. However, Harry was persistent and began searching for Dicketts' descendants, and in 1996 came across his youngest son, Robert, who was then 52.

He called Robert at home, and while cautious, Robert was greatly interested in everything Harry had to say. His mother was Judy, Dicketts' last wife, who had always refused to talk to him about his father. As a result, Robert was hungry for information and relieved to hear his father was a spy; he had always secretly believed he was, and in fact was rather proud of it. He wished he could share this information with his mother, who was ill at the time, but knew it would only upset her if he did. So Robert kept the secret to himself, and sent a photograph of his father for Harry to show to Sessler.

The next time Robert heard from Harry, it was to confirm that his father was the same man Sessler had known in 1941. Although it was very exciting news, it also raised a lot of questions. Who had sent his father to Germany, and what was so important that his father had risked his life to go there? As there was no way of finding out any further information at the time, Robert told Harry about his older brother, Richard, whom he hadn't seen for fifty years, who might know more about his father. 'If you ever come across him, please ask him to contact me,' said Robert.

* * *

Richard Tudhope was gazing out of the window at his beautiful cottage garden in Herefordshire in 2002, when he noticed a short, grey-haired man striding purposefully up his garden path carrying a folder under his arm. He opened the door and noticed the name on the folder was Dicketts. He was immediately wary, thinking he was someone from his father's fraudulent past. Harry Butcher introduced himself and said he had information about his father. He was a British double agent called Celery, whose file KV 2/674 was now open to the public at the British National Archives in Kew, and Harry showed him a few documents he had copied from this file.

Richard, who was 68 at the time, was completely stunned by the news, but he was also enormously relieved as it removed some of the negative after-taste of his father's criminal past. He wished he had been able to discuss this with his father, whom he had last seen in 1949 shortly before he gave himself up to police. His mother, Vera, was dead and the only person who had known Dicketts was an elderly aunt whose memory was fading. He wished he had someone with whom he could share it.

With perfect timing, Harry gave Richard the piece of paper on which Robert had jotted down his name and address. Richard hadn't seen his half-brother since he was a teenager. It was one of those moments in life that is both bitter and sweet: regret that they had not seen each other for so long, and excitement that they might at last meet again.

A few days later, Richard called Robert and they agreed to meet, never expecting that their connection would be instantaneous, or that they would develop a deep friendship, spending future Christmases and holidays together with their wives.

They soon discovered an interesting and rather perplexing similarity – that both their mothers had destroyed almost everything belonging to their father. Richard's mother had even gone to the extraordinary length of tearing him out of every photograph, whereas Robert's mother, Judy, had simply got rid of them. Both women had destroyed all Dicketts' business correspondence, property deeds, contracts, letters, bills, correspondence with lawyers – all of it had gone.

Richard knew a little bit about their father's background as a fraudster and told his uninformed brother all that he knew. He explained to Robert that the reason he had changed his name by deed poll to Tudhope, his stepfather's name in 1956, was to avoid any connection to their father's criminal past. In the class-conscious society of the times, there was an enormous social stigma attached to being the son of a criminal, and their mothers had tried to protect them from that. For all they knew, a disgruntled creditor might one day turn up on their doorstep and threaten them for money.

Did their mothers know or suspect Dicketts was a spy, they wondered? Although Dicketts was bound to secrecy by the Official Secrets Act, his absences and the fact he wasn't wearing a uniform was certain to have raised questions in their minds.

The two brothers shared what little information they had about their father, hoping to find answers. They examined his few remaining personal effects as if they still retained some essence of him - one silver box smelt of sandalwood, his favourite cologne. They found a postcard Dicketts wrote to Vera's parents in 1937 when he and Vera travelled to Singapore to buy silk. It was a simple postcard with a photograph of their ship, the *Haruna Maru* - but it opened up an entirely new world they never knew existed. On it was written:

> Cheerio! Folks – many thanks for wire received this morning in Naples (Sunday). I am just going to have a double gin and ginger beer (price 2½ pence) – Wish you were here. Love to all, Dick.

In 2003, the brothers traced the owners of the *Haruna Maru*, the Nippon Yusen Kaisha Shipping Line, who put them in touch with the editor of their monthly passenger magazine *Seascope*. Incredibly, the editor found three photographs of Dicketts and Vera on board the ship in 1937 in the magazine's archives, and then published a series of three articles about Dicketts in *Seascope* in late 2003. She included a photograph of his sons Robert and Richard having tea and biscuits in her office.

Robert was in his early fifties, tall, dark and well-built. His hair was brown and he had an oval-shaped face with strong features, brown eyes and thick eyebrows. His half-brother Richard was nearly 70, but you would never have guessed it. He had a slim, medium build with blue eyes, fine features and a fair complexion which was lightly tanned.

They may not have looked like brothers, but judging by the width of their smiles, they were clearly enjoying each other's company.

* * *

Thousands of miles away in Bangkok, Thailand, 56-year-old Mike Adair read the *Seascope* articles online with astonishment. The man featured in the articles had the same name as his grandfather, Walter Dicketts. Could he be the same person, wondered Mike?

Mike's father, Rodney Adair, was diagnosed with cancer in 1976 when he was 55. Facing his own mortality, Rodney wanted to connect with the father he had never known, and placed a series of advertisements in

The Times asking for information about Walter Arthur Charles Dicketts, hoping to receive a reply. Rodney was Dicketts' second son to his 1918 marriage to Phyllis, and after he deserted her in August 1922, their two sons never saw him again. Phyllis remarried and changed their surnames to that of her new husband, Adair.

After Rodney succumbed to cancer in 1979, his secret search for his father was revealed. His eldest son, Mike Adair, was going through his personal effects when he came across two mysterious letters written to his father in 1976. The first was from a close friend of Dicketts called Oliver Muldoon and the second was from Dicketts' ex-wife, Judy Bentley, who had a son by Dicketts. Mike couldn't understand why his father hadn't told him this. After all, Rodney had found out what happened to his father after all these years, and discovered he had a half-brother. Intrigued, Mike decided to find out why Rodney hadn't said anything.

Mike had been conducting family research for a number of years by the time the *Seascope* articles appeared in 2003 - but he still hadn't found the (unnamed) son Judy Bentley described in her 1976 letter to his father Rodney. When Mike looked at the photograph of Robert Dicketts and Richard Tudhope in *Seascope*, he wondered if he had found him. The problem was, where did the other brother come from?

* * *

In late October 2003, Robert Dicketts was at home in Kent reading an email from Mike Adair, who claimed to have information about his father, Walter Dicketts. The *Seascope* articles had only recently been published, so Robert wasn't entirely surprised to receive Mike's email, but he was shocked by what Mike had to tell him.

Mike said he had a letter in his possession written by Robert's mother, Judy, to his father, Rodney Adair, in 1976. Mike went on to explain that Rodney was Dicketts' son to his first marriage to Phyllis in 1918, and therefore his father Rodney was Robert's half-brother. Robert was stunned. Even though Judy had always refused to discuss his father with him, he could never have believed she would have gone so far as to hide other siblings from him; but that was exactly what she had done.

'The second letter my father received was from a man called Oliver Muldoon,' continued Mike. 'Have you heard of him?' Robert was taken aback, as he knew Muldoon well. Muldoon was a very close friend of his father and mother, and it seems that he too had hidden from him the existence of Dicketts' other children.

When Robert read these letters, it was hard not to feel sympathetic towards Rodney. Here was a man who had reached out to try and find his father after fifty-five years of absence, and when he finally found him, the news he received was grim. 'Your father died in 1957 and I was one of the very few people at his funeral, which had been strictly private,' wrote Muldoon.[3] He continued:

> I was very fond of Charles as he liked to be called, and knew him to be a most erudite, very widely-read man-of-the-world and above all a most charming person. ... He had such a personality that even after twenty years, he lingers in my mind as one of the most likeable men I have ever met.

In 2003, Judy had been dead for six years when Robert read the letter she had written to Rodney Adair in 1976. She would have turned in her grave had she known this letter would one day end up in the hands she least wanted it to. It was an emotional letter, full of anger and heartbreak, and exposed her sheer determination to make sure Robert had only happy memories of his father:

> Charles was a remarkable man, a dynamic character, highly intelligent, knowledgeable in every way, a socialite with great charm and most amusing. He had such vitality one was never bored in his company. He made a lot of people very happy for a time, but he also caused a great deal of heartache and distress to many people including his own parents, who believed in him until the day he died. Charles was his own worst enemy. He used his charm and talent of persuasion in such a way that time and time again it destroyed him and some of those around him.[4]

Writing the letter, she said, had brought up a lot of happy memories for her, but also some bitter and angry ones: 'Charles had the personality and brains to have a wonderful life, but through his own folly threw it all away and died in misery.'

Judy's principal aim appears to have been to deter Rodney from ever contacting her son. She said he (Robert) was 30 at the time, married to a girl from an old English family and had a good career ahead of him: 'If he were to discover the truth about his father after all these years, it would be an emotional disaster with far reaching consequences.'

In fact, Judy had her own secrets to hide. She had gone on the run with Dicketts after he skipped bail in London in 1943, and had settled in East Grinstead under an entirely false identity, as the wife of wealthy philanthropist Mr Charles Stewart Pollock. To be fair to Judy, war was raging across the world, and she was young, pregnant and in love with a fascinating older man who seemed to have a good future ahead of him. Who knows what and how much Dicketts told her about what he was doing? Like any good conman, he probably believed in it himself.

'Perhaps you will come to the conclusion that it would be better for you to leave things as they are,' Judy wrote to Rodney in 1976. 'I will understand it if you do not wish to reply.'

Mike Adair believed Rodney took Judy's advice and never contacted her again. His father was dead and the reconciliation Rodney had hoped for could never take place. His mother's warning to never try to contact his father had probably been correct, as Dicketts had obviously caused a great deal of heartbreak to others, as well as his own family. It was time to move on.

* * *

In October 1945, Flight Lieutenant Eric 'Dick' Dicketts was awarded a Distinguished Flying Cross (DFC) for his wartime role in flying bombing missions against the Germans, Italians and Japanese.[5] In the early part of the war, he had flown daylight low-level sorties at just 50ft against enemy shipping off the French and Dutch coast. German flak ships fired on them at sea-level as they attacked, and they were too low to take evasive action. Unsurprisingly, losses were extremely high and it is a miracle anyone survived.

Dick later saw action with No. 6 Squadron in the Middle East, and No. 113 and 194 Squadrons in India and Burma, and was 23 when the war ended. By his reckoning, 80 per cent of the young men he started out with didn't make it.

He always knew he had been given away at birth and that his father's name was Walter Arthur Charles Dicketts, and his mother was Dora Viva

Guerrier, so when Dick received a letter from Mike Adair (who had written to every Dicketts in the phone book), his principal interest was in finding out what had happened to his mother and sister, whom he believed had gone to Canada (which they hadn't) shortly after his birth.

He wrote to Mike Adair in 2006 when he was 84 years old, and explained who he was. He attached his birth certificate and a copy of the letter Dora had written in giving him away at birth. When Mike saw Dick's date of birth, there could be no question that Walter Dicketts had been carrying on with Dora at the same time as he was married to his grandmother, Phyllis - they were born within months of each other.

Dick told Mike that he had read about his father's imprisonment at Leyhill Prison, which was close to where he lived, 'and had decided to have nothing to do with him'.

'Do you have any information about my sister?' wrote Dick. 'I'd really like to get in touch with her or her descendants.'

* * *

In Sydney, Australia, on 27 June 2008, my beloved mother Tonie (Effie) died of cancer at the age of 87. I knew she was illegitimate and ashamed of it, and although I knew Dora Guerrier was her mother, they had fallen out in the late 1960s and we had lost contact with her and her entire family. Dora had made up the name Arthur Dicketts on my mother's birth certificate, so I knew there was no point in searching for him.

I tried and failed to contact other members of the Guerrier family. It was all rather depressing, and I struggled with the fact that my lovely mother had died and no one in her family would ever know or seemingly care. They would never find out what a wonderful woman she had been. She was beautiful, funny, theatrical, entertaining, loving and caring; I felt so angry that she had been abandoned and betrayed by those closest to her and wanted to find out why.

Fortunately, my eldest daughter, Holly, felt the same way, and was so convinced that I had missed something that she took over the search. I was so glad that she did, as she quickly found Mike Adair's post on a genealogical forum asking for information about Dora and her daughter, Effie Winifred Sinclair Smith [Dicketts].

This was a name that only we, her most immediate family, knew, and I was very suspicious and even a bit angry that a stranger had this information.

Since Mum's legal identity was Dora's invention, whatever it was that this man Mike Adair wanted couldn't possibly relate to her. Yet, was it possible he had information about Dora's family?

When Mike and I spoke, I told him my mother had died just ten days earlier. Naturally, he was very sympathetic and tried to be as sensitive as possible, but the information he had to give me was so overwhelming. It was like being struck by bullets from a machine gun: the real name of my mother's father (she had spent her whole life not knowing who he was), and that he was a spy, a crook, a hero, a conman, a bigamist, a cad and father of six children. It was all way too much to absorb.

But Mike hadn't finished yet. Did I know Mum had a brother who had been given away at birth? I felt like shouting, 'No, of course I don't,' but managed to control myself. Deep down I was thinking, 'What a load of nonsense.' I was wrong.

When we finished talking, I felt an unbelievable sadness. It was so soon after my mother's death and I had discovered the secret she had wanted to know all her life, but I couldn't share it with her. Her father's surname had been on her birth certificate all along – she wasn't a non-person (as she had once referred to herself) after all. Her name wasn't Effie Smith, it was Effie Dicketts, and it always had been.

Thinking of her loss in never knowing this information during her lifetime made me think of her brother, Dick, who had never met anyone from his blood family. At least my mother had known Dora and the Guerriers. I decided that if I could no longer do anything to help her, I would help her brother instead.

I flew to England armed with a DNA kit and knocked on the door of Dick's house in Wales. I felt very emotional and a little bit afraid, of what I had no idea. I didn't expect Dick to be the way he was. At 89 he was upright, bursting with energy and vitality, and there was absolutely no question he was my mother's brother. Despite having spent an entire lifetime apart, he had the same mannerisms as my mother and the same quirky sense of self-deprecating humour. They both raised the same eyebrow as if to say, 'Come on now— really?' and when they laughed they threw their heads back with glee.

Dick, who had seen and done so much during the war, came straight to the point, with a humorous glint in his eye: 'I suppose you want my DNA …'

Postscript

by Katharine Ritter

In November 2011, I received a surprise email from a total stranger, Carolinda Witt, from Australia. I live in Virginia, in the United States, and yet we had a serendipitous connection. She told me that her grandfather and my father, Nikolaus Ritter, were entwined under rather unusual circumstances during the Second World War – a fact of which I had no knowledge. An exceedingly multifarious and entangled relationship developed between my father, an officer in the Abwehr, and her grandfather, a British double agent.

It is rather inconceivable and nostalgic that after more than seventy years, a granddaughter and daughter of two very controversial agents on opposite sides of the battlefield would share the same interests. Each of us is engaged in separate publications, yet writing about the same topic at the same time, but bringing different perspectives. Over the years, it has been a pleasure to collaborate with Carolinda. We have shared many thoughts, references and publications to untangle an intriguing web in a search for truth.

Acknowledgments

I have greatly benefited from the immense support and kindness I have received from the well-known author and intelligence expert Nigel West, who never failed to assist me in every way. Madoc Roberts who co-wrote *SNOW* with West, was equally generous in sharing information and was more than willing to provide assistance and advice.

It was rather surreal be in contact with Katharine Ritter, the daughter of Nikolaus Ritter of the Abwehr, who ran most of the agents mentioned in this book, including my grandfather. Katharine has been more than generous in giving me access to private information, photographs, audio recordings and her translation of her father's work.

Many people have helped me with research, including family members, professional researchers and amateur sleuths. A special mention to businessman and writer Harry Butcher (alias), who met Dicketts' bodyguard, Georg Sessler, in Germany, then tracked down Robert Dicketts to let him know his father was a spy. Also to Mark Williams (alias) for his enthusiasm and remarkable talent in research, who provided me with missing evidence regarding Dicketts' trip to South America and his ongoing relationship with MI5 and SIS. To Mike Osborn, who seems to be able to find anything, and is a mine of information regarding aviation; Phil Tomaselli, author and independent researcher at the National Archives, who was responsible for identifying Celery as Walter Dicketts in 2001, and later obtained new information on my behalf; Nick Barratt and Amber Strang of Sticks Research Agency, Susan Watkins at the Colindale Newspaper Archives and Danny Howell of Solo Syndication. Special thanks also to Henry Wilson, Katie Eaton, Tony Walton, Matt Jones, Jon Wilkinson and the great team at Pen & Sword; my writer friends, Amanda Hampson, Richard Woolveridge and Libby Harkness, for their professional feedback and advice; and to Mary Cunnane, my wonderful ex-literary agent, who fortunately still consults. Also to Frances Francis, with whom I had the best proof-reading fun ever! Thanks to my early readers for their encouragement, feedback, and suggestions: Angela Crowe, Sissy Katz, Dr Lorna Scott, Julian Canny, Danica Fehrenback, Mark Williams and David Ruthven. And finally to family members who read through my manuscript to make sure Dicketts and other relatives were depicted accurately.

It was an emotional and profound experience to meet members of my family whom I had never met before: my cousin Mike Adair, who put information on the internet for me to find, and my daughter Holly Moroney, who found it. Without Mike's enormous skills in research, his tenacity and his compassion, Walter Dicketts' descendants would not be in contact today, and this book would not exist. Despite never having met my uncles Dick Tudhope and Robert Dicketts before, they generously shared photographs and personal memories of their father with me, and provided details of his relationships with their mothers, Vera and Judy. My mother's unknown brother, Dick Dicketts, the son of Walter Dicketts and my grandmother, Dora Guerrier, we are all so grateful you are back in our lives. Thank-you for sharing the letter Dora wrote giving you away at birth, as this was the heart-rending proof to my family and the Guerrier/Olsen family that Dora really had given her secret children away. Thanks also to Dora's niece, Jacqueline Guerrier, who kept Dora's secret confession until this letter made it unnecessary; and to my cousins, Catherine Henderson and Dominique Charrier, who came with me to meet Dora's son and welcome him into the family. In addition to the above, I was warmly welcomed into the family by Gerry and Mark Smith, Sam and Will Sawyer, Vicky and Paul Carter, Sue and Ceri Llewellyn, Katie and Ceri Llewellyn, Sally Dicketts and partner Lee, Isabel Miao, Richard and Helen Dicketts, Richard, Fran and Rosie Dicketts, Bon Adair, Geoffrey Adair, Richard, Robin and Timothy Adair, Beryl Tudhope, Priscilla Dicketts, Karsten Laursen, Danielle Guerrier, Peter and Sonja Guerrier, Conrad and Jill Guerrier, Amelia and Harry Jonas and family, Sean and Sandrine Henderson and family, Dominic Henderson and family, Philippe, Louise and Léonie Charrier, and Patrick Charrier and family.

My biggest thanks of all are reserved for my family, who put up with my dedication, enthusiasm, and withdrawal. My partner Andrew Russell, my children Holly, Joss and Tess Moroney, and my brother Michael Witt have been pillars of strength throughout the writing process, as well as during the personal odyssey of discovering our long-lost family.

Finally, to my mother Tonie Witt, who was and is my inspiration – I only wish I could have found this out before you died.

Appendix I

Abwehr accounts

The accounts of former members of the Abwehr began appearing between the late 1950s and early 1970s. Unlike MI5's extensive, cross-referenced files, written in real time, the German accounts are mostly anecdotal or drawn from memory of events that took place many years earlier. The information cannot be verified as most of the people mentioned in those accounts are deceased, and a degree of caution should be exercised as to their accuracy.

This book has drawn upon the following accounts:

- *Hitler's Spies and Saboteurs* (New York: Henry Holt, 1958) by Günter Peis and Charles Wighton. Based on the Abwehr Secret Service war diary of one of Admiral Canaris' most intimate confidantes, General Erwin von Lahousen. Lahousen, chief of the Abwehr's Section 11, testified against the Nazis at the Nuremberg Trials. Günter Peis was an Austrian investigative journalist present at the Nuremberg Trials, who later conducted a number of interviews to reveal the in-depth stories behind Lahousen's entries.
- *Deckname Dr. Rantzau* (Hamburg: Hoffmann und Campe Verlag, 1972) by Nikolaus Ritter. Ritter's autobiography has recently been translated from German to English (*Codename Dr Rantzau*) by his daughter Katharine, whose insights into her father's character have been most revealing and are included in this book with her kind permission. Ritter was an egotistic and self-opinionated man who was responsible for some of the greatest espionage successes of the war and some of its greatest failures. Recordings of Ritter dictating his memoirs in English are held at the Howard Gotlieb Archival Research Centre at Boston University (Collection: Farago, Ladislas, 1906-1980).

- *Mirror of Deception* (London: Weidenfeld & Nicolson, 1976) by Austrian investigative journalist Günter Peis, who tracked down Dicketts' Abwehr bodyguard, Georg Sessler, to his home in France and interviewed him. Sessler still feared retribution from the Nazis after having testified on behalf of the Allies at the Nuremberg Trials. Peis' account is identical to the one Sessler gave British writer 'Harry Butcher', who tracked down Sessler in 1996. Harry gave me the full account of his meeting with Sessler when I met him in England in 2012.

- Files held at the British National Archives containing Allied interrogations of German prisoners relevant to this book, include the accounts of Nikolaus Ritter (KV 2/86-88); Captain Herbert Otto Wichmann, head of the Hamburg Abwehr Station (KV 3/204); and Ritter's recruit Major Julius Boeckel (KV 2/1333) who trained many of the German pre-invasion spies. One of Ritter's major opponents, Major Friedrich Busch (KV 2/529), the Berlin head of Abwehr 1 Luft/E (E = England), believed both Dicketts and Owens were controlled.

Appendix II

John Masterman's hypothesis regarding Snow and Celery's meeting with Ritter in Lisbon in February 1941.

Hypothesis No. 1

Owens had not given away the whole show to the Germans as he alleged he had. This would explain Dicketts' interrogation and their cautious acceptance of him, as well as the £10,000 Owens brought back. Owens was finding the risk and danger of playing for both sides was taking its toll, and planned to go into retirement with a foot in both camps. If Germany won the war, he would be able to point to his years of service on their behalf, and likewise he could say he had served Britain well until the Germans discovered his role in their double-cross system.

He may have made the whole story up after he discovered the great treatment Dicketts received in Germany. He had therefore destroyed his usefulness to both sides due to his consuming jealousy of Dicketts, whom he perceived to be usurping his place. This would explain his extraordinary inability to say when or if he warned Dicketts.

Hypothesis No. 2

That the story Owens told was true. However, Ritter realized that he had nothing to gain by losing Owens, other than his considerable prestige, and had bribed Owens with sufficient money to ensure he remained on their side. Ritter told Owens not to say anything to Dicketts, so he could interview him and find out for himself how much he knew about Owens' position in England. If Dicketts followed his orders to return, he would know his bribe had been sufficient to prevent Owens from telling Dicketts what had happened and Dicketts could then be run as a separate agent to Owens.

Hypothesis No. 3

Owens did inform Ritter and warned Dicketts on his arrival. Alternatively, Ritter told Dicketts he knew about their connection with British intelligence at the meeting and gave him the choice of going back to England to earn

£3 per week or get paid big money like Owens. If this was the case, then Dicketts had been turned and planted back on MI5 as a double agent working for Germany.

Hypothesis No. 4:
Owens had really gone over to the Germans a long time ago, and may have had other means of communicating with them. It explained the very brief questioning he received from Ritter after he had revealed all. In this case, Owens was probably a major traitor who had always been working for Germany.

Endnotes

Files held at the British National Archives, Kew: Citations marked KV refer to the Security Services Files, ADM to Admiralty Files, AIR to Air Ministry files and CRIM and HO to the After-Trial Calendars of Prisoners of the Central, North London and South London Criminal Courts. These files contain public sector information licensed under the Open Government Licence v3.0. http://www.nationalarchives.gov.uk/doc/open-government-licence/version/3/

www.measuringworth.com has been used to calculate the historical value of money compared to 2016 using the Retail Price Index (RPI).

Prologue

1. Celery's interrogation, Part 5, 29/3/1941, KV 2/674, p.20.
2. Police Report, 27/3/1941, KV 2/674.
3. Celery's interrogation, 3/4/1941, KV 2/674, p.1.

Chapter 1: A Fateful Meeting

1. Description of Dicketts by MI5 Watchers, 23/3/1940, KV 2/674.
2. Colonel Edward Peale's description of Snow, 8/10/1936, KV 2/444.
3. *Codename Dr Rantzau*, by Nikolaus Ritter (Hamburg: Hoffman & Campe, 1972), trans. Katharine Ritter, p.90.
4. Description of Kay Dicketts, KV 2/674, and Kay's Brazilian immigration card, 6.10.1941, https://familysearch.org/ark:/61903/1:1:KC65-ZR9.
5. Dicketts' statement to Police, 16/3/1941, KV 2/674.
6. Ibid.
7. Anonymous MI5 officer regarding Snow's character, KV 2/452.
8. *Kitchener's Army: The Raising of the New Armies 1914–1916*, by Peter Simkins (Barnsley: Pen and Sword, 2007), p. 38.
9. Southend-on-Sea during the First World War, http://www.southendtimeline.com/1914.htm

10. Dicketts' war records, ADM 273-17-106.
11. http://www.historylearningsite.co.uk/boy_soldiers.htm
12. Dicketts' war records, ADM 188-567 and AIR 76 133 111.
13. Dicketts' cousin Billy's letter to Sue Llewellyn (nee Dicketts), private collection.
14. Dicketts' letter to Air Commodore Boyle, 27/5/1940, KV 2/674.
15. Dicketts' war records, ADM 273-17-106.
16. http://www.history.com/news/londons-world-war-i-zeppelin-terror
17. Dicketts' letter to Air Commodore Boyle, 27/5/1940, KV2/674.
18. Dicketts' war records, ADM 273-17-106.
19. http://www.tanks-encyclopedia.com/ww1/gb/tank_MkI.php and http://
    www.longlongtrail.co.uk/army/regiments-and-corps/tank-corps-in-the-
    first-world-war/.
20. Dicketts' war records, ADM 273-17-106.
21. Ibid.
22. *Country Life Magazine*, 11/11/1916, p.570.
23. Dicketts' war records, ADM 273-17-106.
24. *Bloody April*, by Peter Hart (London: Hachette, 2012), Epilogue.
25. http://www.bbc.com/news/entertainment-arts-36712829.
26. http://www.usaww1.com/World_War_1_Fighter_Pilots.php4
27. Dicketts' war records, AIR 76 133 111.
28. Dicketts' war records, ADM 273-17-106 and AIR 76 133 111.
29. Marriage certificate, Phyllis Hobson and Walter Arthur Charles Dicketts,
    13/5/18.
30. Dicketts' birth certificate, 31/3/1900.
31. Bristol Archives: File of correspondence re appointment of Mr R.A. Dicketts,
    1/3/1933, 40183/CI/12.
32. Ibid.
33. *The Times*, Dicketts, Captain (late RAF) Diplomatic Service, mother Phyllis,
    formerly Hobson, 8/8/1919.
34. ELTA - http://www.europeanairlines.no/e-l-t-a-the-first-aviation-exhibition-
    amsterdam-1919/ and *ELTA*, by Rob Mulder (Norway: European Airlines,
    2009).
35. *The Mad Major*, by Major Christopher Draper DSC (London: Air Review
    Limited, 1962).
36. Note in Snow's file, 10/9/1936, KV2 /444.
37. Snow's letter to Mr Sanders, 8/9/1936, KV2/444.
38. Celery's interrogation 1, 8/4/1941, KV 2/674, p.1.
39. Ibid.
40. Bristol Archives: File of correspondence re appointment of Mr. R.A. Dicketts,
    1/3/1933, 40183/CI/12.

41. Image: Dicketts with RAF and Argentine officers: private collection.
42. *Joy Bells*, Programme Albert de Courville production, March 1919, private collection.
43. *Tiller's Girls*, by Doremy Vernon (London: Robson, 1988), p.23.
44. *Women on the Home Front in World War One*, by Professor Joanna Bourke. http:// www.bbc.co.uk/history/british/britain_wwone/women_employment_01.shtml
45. *Daily Mail*, 'Condemned to be virgins', 7/9/2007.
46. *Singled Out*, by Virginia Nicholson (London: Oxford University Press, 2008), p.182.
47. Dicketts' war records, AIR 76 133 111.
48. http://www.nationalarchives.gov.uk/pathways/firstworldwar/aftermath/ brit_after_war.htm
49. *The London Gazette*, 11/2/1921.
50. Birth certificate, Euphemia Winifred Sinclair Dicketts 17/9/1920. Father, Arthur Dicketts, occupation unknown (deceased). Mother, Dora Dicketts, formerly Guerrier.
51. *Derbyshire Courier*, 'The Worthless Cheques', 13/8/1921.
52. Ibid.
53. Ibid.
54. Birth certificate, Rodney Philip Arthur Dicketts, 13/10/1921. Father, Walter Arthur Charles Dicketts, General Importer and Exporter. Mother, Phyllis Dicketts, formerly Hobson.
55. *Daily Mirror*, 'Ex Officers' Joy Rides', 21/10/1921.
56. Ibid.
57. Dicketts' criminal records, HO140-367.
58. Birth certificate, Eric Richard Dicketts, 18/2/1922. Father, William Walter Arthur Dicketts, Music Hall Artiste. Mother, Dora Viva Dicketts, formerly Guerrier.
59. Ibid.
60. Marriage certificate, Dora Viva Guerrier and Cable Boville, 26/6/1922.
61. Personal account by Jacqueline Guerrier, niece of Dora Guerrier.
62. Personal account by Mike Adair, grandson of Walter Dicketts.
63. Personal account by Mike Osborne, whose grandmother was Hilda, sister to Dicketts' first wife, Phyllis.
64. Dicketts' war records, AIR 76 122 111.
65. *The Quest for C: Mansfield Cumming and the Founding of the Secret Service*, by Alan Judd (London: HarperCollins, 2000), p.470.

Chapter 2: From Batteries to Spying

1. Diary entry, 7.4/1940, *The Guy Liddell Diaries Volume 2, 1942-1945*, KV 2/185.
2. Tar report to file, 4/4/1940, KV 2/447.

3. Dicketts' statement to police, 16/3/1940, KV 2/674, p.2.

4. Ibid, p.5.

5. *Snow*, by Nigel West and Madoc Roberts (London: Biteback, 2011), p.8.

6. Wandsworth prison visit, 10/9/1939, KV 2/446.

7. Summary of the Snow case, KV 2/452, p.1.

8. Colonel Peal report to file, 9/1/1936, KV 2/444.

9. List of events, point 19, 23/9/1936, KV 2/444.

10. Notes on Snow's statement 2/12/1936, KV 2/444, p.2.

11. Colonel Peal report to file, 1/10/1936, KV 2/444.

12. Notes on Snow's statement 2/12/1936, KV 2/444, p.1.

13. Interrogations of Snow, 7/4/1942-10/4/1942, KV 2/451, p.2, item 4.

14. Snow's testimony, 2/12/1936, KV 2/444, p.2.

15. Notes on Snow's statement, 2/12/36, KV 2/444, p.2.

16. *Codename Dr Rantzau*, by Nikolaus Ritter (Hamburg: Hoffman & Campe, 1972), trans. Katharine Ritter, pp.6,7.

17. Letter to Mr Sanders, 8/9/1936, KV 2/444.

18. 'Dierks: An International Spymaster and Mystery Man', article by F.A.C. Kluiters and E. Verhoeyen, p.2.

19. Peale's report to Hinchley-Cook, KV 2/444.

20. Note in file re letter intercept, 9/10/1936, KV 2/444.

21. Description of Snow, KV 2/444.

22. Surveillance of Snow, 3/11/1936, KV 2/444.

23. Sanders letter to Snow, 9/12/1936, KV 2/444.

24. *Codename Dr Rantzau*, by Nikolaus Ritter (Hamburg: Hoffman & Campe, 1972), trans. Katharine Ritter, p.6.

25. File name: Interrogations of Snow, 7/4/42-10/4/42, KV 2/451, Point 8, p.3.

26. *Codename Dr Rantzau*, by Nikolaus Ritter (Hamburg: Hoffman & Campe, 1972), trans. Katharine Ritter, p.7.

27. *Aurora*, by K.F. Ritter (Bloomington: Xlibris, 2006), Chapter 2.

28. Ibid, p.547.

29. Ibid, p.557.

30. *Codename Dr Rantzau*, by Nikolaus Ritter (Hamburg: Hoffman & Campe, 1972), trans. Katharine Ritter, p.22.

31. Memorandum Peal, Hinchley-Cook, Major Whyte, 23/3/1937, KV 2/444.

32. Ibid.

33. *Hitler's Spies and Saboteurs*, by Charles Wighton and Gunter Peis (New York: Henry Holt, 1958), p.158.

34. *Codename Dr Rantzau*, by Nikolaus Ritter (Hamburg: Hoffman & Campe, 1972), trans. Katharine Ritter, p.128.

35. *Hitler's Spies and Saboteurs,* by Charles Wighton and Gunter Peis (New York: Henry Holt, 1958), p.160.
36. CSDIC interrogation Ritter, 16/1/1946, KV 2/451.
37. *Hitler's Spies and Saboteurs,* by Charles Wighton and Gunter Peis (New York: Henry Holt, 1958), p.160.
38. BUF letter, 6/7/1938, KV 2/445.
39. Outline of Snow network, 23/4/1946, KV 2/451, Vol.35.
40. Interrogation of Snow, 24/9/1938, KV 2/445, Vol.6.
41. Special Branch detective's report, 3/10/1938, KV 2/445.
42. *Codename Dr Rantzau,* by Nikolaus Ritter (Hamburg: Hoffman & Campe, 1972), trans. Katharine Ritter, p.121.
43. Special Branch report, 17/1/1939, KV2/445.
44. Special Branch report, 23/1/1939, KV 2/445.
45. Ibid.
46. Redacted letter to Air Ministry, 23/1/1939, KV 2/445.
47. Letter to Squadron Leader Plant, 30/1/1939, KV 2/446.
48. Ibid
49. MI5's Letter to Air Ministry, 2/2/1939, KV 2/446.
50. Inspector Gagan's report, 6/2/1939, KV 2/445.
51. Inspector Gagan's report, 24/3/1939, KV 2/446.
52. *Hitler's Spies and Saboteurs,* by Charles Wighton and Gunter Peis (New York: Henry Holt, 1958), p.160.
53. Gagan's report, 24/3/1939, KV 2/446, p.2.
54. *Codename Dr Rantzau,* by Nikolaus Ritter (Hamburg: Hoffman & Campe, 1972), trans. Katharine Ritter, p.90.
55. Ibid.
56. Jessie Owens police statement, 18/8/1939, KV 2/446.
57. Owen's Detention order, KV2/446
58. *Codename Dr Rantzau,* by Nikolaus Ritter (Hamburg: Hoffman & Campe, 1972), trans. Katharine Ritter, p.99.

Chapter 3: About Turn

1. The *Daily Mirror,* 'Shell Shock Defence', 6/9/1923.
2. The *Daily Mirror,* 'Airman in Dock', 6/9/1923.
3. Ibid.
4. The *Guardian,* 'Brilliant Young Airman's Downfall. Given His Last Chance', 6/9/1923.
5. *Now It Can Be Told,* by Phillip Gibb (EBook: Project Gutenberg, 2009).
6. *The Soldier's War,* by Richard Van Emden (London: Bloomsbury, 2009).

7. The *Daily Mail*, 11/11/2008. Edited extract from *The Soldier's War,* by Richard Van Emden (Bloomsbury), http://www.dailymail.co.uk/news/article-1084616/A-bitter-victory-Returning-WWI-soldiers-hatred-leaders-sent-die.html

8. The *Daily Mirror*, 'Ex-Officer's Frauds', 17/11/1921.

9. *Sagittarius Rising*, Cecil Lewis (London: Harcourt, Brace & Company, 1936), p.137.

10. The *Daily Mirror*, '23 Aliases', 29/5/1929.

11. Dicketts' criminal record, Seine, KV 2/674.

12. *The Police Gazette*, Confidential Supplement A. No. 6, 12/3/1926, Vol. XIII. Expert and Travelling Criminals.

13. Dicketts' criminal record, 7/4/1940, KV 2/674.

14. Bristol Archives: File of correspondence re appointment of Mr R.A. Dicketts, 1/3/1933, 40183/CI/12.

15. Ibid.

16. Ibid.

17. Ibid.

18. http://sanfelipe.com.mx/about-san- felipe/desert-soils/

19. Passenger List, SS *New York* travelling from New York to Southampton, 20/8/1928, www.ancestry.com.

20. National Archives, T161-252, and Passport Office, Foreign Office KV 2/674, 14/1/29.

21. Ibid.

22. Ibid.

23. *The Times*, 'Missing Southend Girl', p.16, 20/5/1929.

24. *Daily Express*, 'Swindler Who Married A Girl of Fifteen', 26/6/30.

25. The *Daily Mirror*, '23 Aliases', 29/5/1929.

26. *Daily Express*, 'Missing Bride Traced', 22/5/29.

27. *Lake Wakatipu Mail*, 'Romance Ended: Girl-Bride Returns', 9/10/1929.

28. *Daily Mail*, 'W.A.C. Dicketts' Many Names', 24/5/29.

29. Alma Wood Divorce Petition, National Archives, J77-2730-4682.

30. *Daily Express*, 'Hotel Proprietors, and servants', 17/1/1930.

31. *Daily Express,* 'Dicketts Bid For Freedom', 25/11/1930.

32. *Daily Mirror*, 'Divorce for Girl Wife', 18/12/1930.

33. *Daily Express,* 'Man Arrested in Germany', 21/6/1930.

34. *Daily Mirror*, 'Arrested at Hamburg', 21/6/1930.

35. Dicketts' Criminal Record, 26/6/1930, National Archives, KV2/674.

36. Bristol Archives: File of correspondence re appointment of Mr R.A. Dicketts, 1/3/1933, 40183/CI/12.

37. Ibid

38. Ibid

39. Dicketts' letter to Air Commodore Boyle, 27/5/1940, KV2/674.

40. *Western Daily Press*, Letter to Editor from Mrs N.B. Taylor, 13/1/1934.
41. Marriage certificate, Richard Arthur Dicketts and Vera Nellie Fudge. Profession of father Organising Secretary. His father's name was given incorrectly as Arthur Sidney Dicketts instead of Skinner. Profession is listed as Stock Broker and Vera's father as Musician.
42. Birth certificate, Richard Anthony Dicketts, 18/1/1934, (surname later changed to Tudhope by deed poll). Father's name Richard Arthur Charles Dicketts. Profession of father Area Administrator Land Settlement of Bristol.
43. Passenger List *Haruna Maru*, Japanese Shipping Line NYK from Southampton to Singapore, May 1937.
44. Private correspondence with Richard Tudhope.
45. Police report, Kathleen Mary Holdcroft, 16/3/1940, KV 2/674.
46. Private correspondence with Richard Tudhope.

Chapter 4: A New Kind of Spy

1. Inspector Gagan's police report, 6/9/1936, KV 2/446, p.2.
2. MI5's first controlled radio transmission to Germany, 9/9/1939, KV 2/446.
3. Tar Robertson's report, 9/9/1939, KV 2/446, p.1.
4. Ibid
5. Percy William Rapp, British, arrested on the outbreak of war, and interned, KV 2/700.
6. Owens' first radio transmission sent at 11.30 am and again at 4 pm, KV 2/446.
7. Tar's report to file, 14/9/1936, KV 2/446, p.2.
8. *The Double-Cross System in the War of 1939 to 1945*, by J.C. Masterman (London: Yale University Press, 1972), p.40.
9. Ibid, p.41.
10. *Snow*, by Nigel West and Madoc Roberts (London: Biteback, 2011), p.39.
11. *Gentleman Spymaster*, by Geoffrey Elliott (London: Methuen, 2011).
12. Ibid, p.28.
13. Ibid, p.49.
14. Ibid.
15. *The Double-Cross System in the War of 1939 to 1945*, by J.C. Masterman (London: Yale University Press, 1972) p.3.
16. *Double Cross - MI5 in World War Two*, by Nigel West, http://www.bbc.co.uk/history/worldwars/wwtwo/mi5_ww2_01.shtml
17. ISOS and ISK: Signals intelligence. The Enigma decrypts were circulated under the name ISK to distinguish them from the hand cypher decrypts issued by Oliver Strachey Section at GC&CS as ISOS. ISOS was sometimes used to cover all decrypts of German secret intelligence services traffic.

18. *The Double-Cross System in the War of 1939 to 1945*, by J.C. Masterman (London: Yale University Press, 1972), Foreword, p.xii.
19. Tar report to file, 21/9/1939, KV 2/446, p.5.
20. Tar report to file, 19/9/1939, KV 2/446.
21. Ibid, p.1.
22. Ibid, p.2.
23. Unknown MI5 officer's report to file, 17/10/1939, KV 2/446, p.3.
24. Tar report to file, 26/10/1939, KV 2/466, p.1.
25. https://www.measuringworth.com/ used to calculate relative value today.
26. *The Double-Cross System in the War of 1939 to 1945*, by J.C. Masterman (London: Yale University Press, 1972), p. 41.
27. Tar report to file, 20/12/1939, KV 2/446, p.3.
28. Tar note to file, 6/11/1939, KV 2/446.
29. *Spying For Hitler,* by John Humphries (Cardiff: University of Wales Press, 2012), p. 163.
30. Richman Stopford note to file, 4/11/1939, KV 2/446, p.1.
31. Ibid.
32. Stopford debriefing Snow, 10/11/1939, KV 2/446, p.1.
33. Tar report to file, 3/4/1940, KV 2/447.
34. Dicketts' statement to police, 16/3/1940, KV 2/674, p.3.
35. Ibid, p.4.
36. 'He's got away with an easy £50': Ibid.
37. Ibid, p.3.
38. Tar report to file, 4/4/1940, KV 2/447, p.2.
39. Dicketts' statement to police, 16/3/, KV 2/674, p.4.
40. Ibid.
41. Letter from Air Ministry to Tar, 5/4/1940, KV 2/674.
42. Dicketts' statement to police, 16/3/1940, KV 2/674, p.5.
43. Tar report to file, 4/4/1940, KV 2/448, pp.3,4.
44. Ibid.
45. *The Double-Cross System in the War of 1939 to 1945*, by J.C. Masterman (London: Yale University Press, 1972), p.47.
46. *Spiegel online*, 'Hitler's Drugged Soldiers' by Andreas Ulrich, 6/2005, http://www.spiegel.de/international/the-nazi-death-machine-hitler-s-drugged-soldiers-a-354606.html

Chapter 5: A Loyal Rogue

1. Extracts from telephone checks on Snow, 6/4/1940, KV 2/674.
2. Tar report to file, 6/4/1940, KV 2/674.
3. Tar report to file, 7/4/1940, KV 2/674.

4. Extracts from telephone checks on Snow, 6/4/19 40, KV 2/674.

5. Dicketts' letter to Tar, 11/6/1940, KV 2/674, p.2.

6. Dicketts' additional notes on Snow, Police report, 16/4/1940, KV 2/674.

7. Ibid.

8. Tar report to file, 9/4/1940, KV 2/674.

9. Statistics on Dunkirk from Rickard, J. (16 February 2008), 'Operation Dynamo, the evacuation from Dunkirk, 27 May-4 June 1940', http://www.historyofwar. org/articles/operation_dynamo.html

10. 'We must be very careful', http://www.churchill-society-london.org.uk/ Dunkirk.html

11. 'Hitler knows that he will have to', http://www.churchill-society-london.org. uk/FnstHour.html

12. 'We shall defend our island', http://www.churchill-society-london.org.uk/ Dunkirk.html

13. Tar report to file, 4/4/1940, KV 2/448, pp.3,4.

14. Tar report to file, 17/5/1940, KV2/448.

15. Tar report to file, 17/5/1940, KV2/448.

16. Tar report to file, 15/5/1940, KV 2/448.

17. Tar report to file, 23/5/1940, KV 2/448, p.1.

18. Ibid.

19. Ibid.

20. Ibid.

21. Diary entry 19/5/1940, *The Guy Liddell Diaries Volume 2, 1942-1945*, KV 2/185.

22. Report by Captain of *Barbados* trawler, 20/5/1940, KV2/448, p.1.

23. Sam McCarthy's handwritten report, KV 2/448, p.5.

24. Tar report to file, 23/4/1940, KV 2/448, p.4.

25. Ibid.

26. Report Snow, Biscuit, GW, Charlie & Summer, 23/4/1946, KV 2/451, p.4.

27. *Codename Dr Rantzau,* by Nikolaus Ritter (Hamburg: Hoffman & Campe, 1972), trans. by Katharine Ritter, p.120.

28. Tar report to file, 27/4/1940, KV 2/448, p.2.

29. *Codename Dr Rantzau,* by Nikolaus Ritter (Hamburg: Hoffman & Campe, 1972), trans. by Katharine Ritter, p.192.

30. Dicketts' letter to Tar, 29/4/1940, KV 2/ 674.

31. Tar's letter to Stammers at Air Ministry, 3/5/1940, KV 2/674.

32. Dicketts' letter to Air Commodore Boyle at Air Ministry, 27/5/1940, KV 2/674.

33. Dicketts' letter to Tar, 29/4/1940, KV 2/674, p.2.

34. Note from Air Ministry to Tar, 2/5/1940, KV 2/674.

35. Dicketts' letter to Tar, 11/6/1940, KV 2/674.

244 Double Agent Celery

36. Ibid, p.3.
37. Tar's letter to Dicketts, 20/6/1940, KV 2/674.
38. Tar report to file, 28/5/1940, KV 2/488, p.2.
39. William M. Rolph was a former MI5 officer from the First World War. He was also a senior member of PMS-2 (Parliamentary Military Security Department, Section 2), set up to investigate subversion and sabotage in factories supplying weapons to the Allies. It investigated suspected enemy saboteurs as well as politically motivated activists within the workforce. Source: Nigel West, *Historical Dictionary of World War 1 Intelligence*.
40. Tar report to file, 27/5/1940, KV 2/488, p.2.
41. Ibid.
42. Death certificate, William Mair Rolph, 64 years old, 29/5/1940, dies of rupture of aorta, atheromatous of aorta. Coroner was Bentley Purchase, 'after post-mortem without autopsy'.
43. Tar report to file, 27/5/1940, part 2, KV 2/488, p.2.
44. Ibid.
45. Dicketts' letter to Tar, 28/6/1940, KV 2/674.
46. Ibid.
47. Dicketts' letter to Tar, 5/7/1940, KV 2/674.
48. Tar's letter to Dicketts, 16/7/1940, KV 2/674.
49. Tar's letter to SIS, 9/7/1940, KV 2/674.
50. Ibid.
51. Valentine Vivien's letter to Guy Liddell, 1/7/1940, KV 2/674.
52. Tar's letter to Dicketts, 1/8/1940, KV 2/674.

Chapter 6: Parachutes and Dinghies

1. BBC Broadcast, 'The War of the Unknown Warriors', 14/7/1940, by Winston Churchill. http://www.churchill-society-london.org.uk/UnknWarr.html
2. Tar note to file, 19/6/1940, KV 2/448.
3. Tar note to file, 21/8/1940, KV 2/448, p.2.
4. *Codename Dr Rantzau*, by Nikolaus Ritter (Hamburg: Hoffman & Campe, 1972), trans. Katharine Ritter, p.99.
5. Summary of Snow case, KV 2/452, p.7.
6. *Codename Dr Rantzau*, by Nikolaus Ritter (Hamburg: Hoffman & Campe, 1972) trans. Katharine Ritter, p.131.
7. Ibid.
8. Ibid
9. Summary of Snow Case, KV 2/452, p.8.
10. *Codename Dr Rantzau*, by Nikolaus Ritter (Hamburg: Hoffman & Campe, 1972), trans. Katharine Ritter, p.140.

11. Ibid.

12. *Agent Tate,* by Tommy Jonason and Simon Olsen (London: Amberley, 2011), pp.20,21.

13. Interview of Tate by Major (later Lieutenant Colonel) Stephens, 21/9/1940, at Camp 020, Extracts KV2/61.

14. *Spooks,* by Thomas Hennessey and Claire Thomas (UK: Amberley Publishing, 2010), p.149.

15. *Agent Tate,* by Tommy Jonason and Simon Olsen (London: Amberley, 2011), p.193.

16. *Codename Dr Rantzau,* by Nikolaus Ritter (Hamburg: Hoffman & Campe, 1972), trans. Katharine Ritter, p. 141.

17. Tate's messages with regard to minefields at sea were instrumental in closing an area of 3,500 square miles to German U-boats. *The Double Cross System in the War of 1939-1945,* by J.C. Masterman (US: Yale University, 1972), p.52.

18. *Codename Dr Rantzau,* by Nikolaus Ritter (Hamburg: Hoffman & Campe, 1972), trans. Katharine Ritter, p. 143.

19. Diary entry, 13/1/1941, *The Guy Liddell Diaries Volume 2, 1942-1945,* KV 2/185.

20. *The Double Cross System in the War of 1939-1945,* by J.C. Masterman (US: Yale University, 1972), p.52.

21. Battle of Britain Historical Society, 15 August 1940, www.battleofbritain1940. net/0026.html

22. 'Luftwaffe', http://www.bbc.co.uk/history/events/britain_bombs_berlin

23. Dicketts' letter to Tar, 12/9/1940, KV 2/674.

24. Ibid.

25. Ibid.

26. Tar's letter to Dicketts, 17/9/1940, KV 2/674.

27. Dicketts' letter to Tar, 22/9/40, KV 2/674.

28. Tar's letter to Dicketts, 2/10/1940, KV 2/674.

29. Dicketts' letter to Tar, 8/10/1940, KV 2/674.

30. *The Double Cross System in the War of 1939-1945,* by J.C. Masterman (US: Yale University, 1972), pp.66-70.

31. Tar report to file, 28/8/1940, KV 2/448.

32. Tar report to file, 18/12/1940, KV 2/449.

33. Dicketts' letter to Tar, 28/6/1940, KV 2/674.

34. Dicketts' letter to Tar, 22/9/1940, KV 2/674.

35. Celery interrogation, 8/4/1941, KV 2/674, p.2.

36. Tar report to file, 17/12/1940, KV 2/449, p.1.

37. Tar report to file, 10/12/1940, KV 2/674.

38. Celery's report, 22/10/1940, KV 2/674.

39. *Agent Tate: The Wartime Story of Harry Williamson*, by Tommy Jonason and Simon Olsen (London: Amberley, 2011), p. 89.

40. Celery's report, 17/12/1940, KV 2/674.

41. Ibid

42. Tar's letter to Major Haylor, 15/10/1940, KV 2/449.

43. Major R. Haylor's letter to Tar, 20/10/1940, KV 2/449, p.2.

44. Celery's report to Haylor, with note to Tar, KV 2/675. p.4,

45. Celery's report to Tar, 25/11/1940, KV 2/675, p.1.

46. Bundesarchiv, Militararchiv, Freiburg im Breisgau.

Chapter 7: Penetrate the Abwehr

1. Tar report to file, 9/1/1941, KV 2/674.

2. Ibid.

3. Ibid.

4. Cowgill's questionnaire, 28/1/1941, KV 2/674.

5. Tar report to file, 29/1/1941, KV 2/674.

6. Tar report to file, 9/2/1941, KV 2/452.

7. *The Mirror of Deception*, by Günter Peis (London: Weidenfeld and Nicolson, 1977), p. 64.

8. Convoy, http://www.convoyweb.org.uk/og/index.html?og.php?convoy=52!~ ogmain

9. MI5 interview of Captain Stafford, 17/4/1941, KV 2/674.

10. *Codename Dr Rantzau*, by Nikolaus Ritter (Hamburg: Hoffman & Campe, 1972), trans. Katharine Ritter, p.129.

11. Owens' telegram from Lisbon, 22/2/1941, KV2/449.

12. Tar meeting Kay Dicketts, 26/2/1941, KV 2/674.

13. Diary visit of Mr Mills, Lisbon, June–July 1941, KV2/450.

14. Celery Interrogation 2, 8/4/1941, KV2/674, p.1.

15. *Hitler's Spies and Saboteurs: Based on the German Secret Service War Diary of General Lahousen*, by Charles Wighton and Gunter Peis (New York: Henry Holt & Co, 1958), p.168.

16. Celery Interrogation 2, 8/4/1941, KV2/674, p.3.

17. See Appendix i.

18. *Codename Dr Rantzau*, by Nikolaus Ritter (Hamburg: Hoffman & Campe, 1972), trans. Katharine Ritter, p.148.

19. Biscuit's description of Ritter, 21/8/1940, KV 2/448, p.2.

20. Celery interrogation, 31/3/1941, KV 2/674, p.4.

21. Celery's notes to report, 31/1/1941, KV 2/674, p.1.

22. *Codename Dr Rantzau*, by Nikolaus Ritter (Hamburg: Hoffman & Campe, 1972), trans. Katharine Ritter, p.149.

23. Ibid.
24. *The Mirror of Deception*, by Günter Peis (London: Weidenfeld and Nicolson, 1977), p.61.
25. Celery's report, 28/31941, KV 2/674, p.2.
26. Telegrams received at Homefields, 24/2/1941, KV 2/674.
27. Tar to Major (later Lieutenant Colonel) Stephens, 12/3/1941, TNA KV4/211, s.10a.
28. Orders in the event of an invasion, 3/4/1941, KV2/450, p.1.
29. Snow description of Dobler, 28/3/1941, KV 2/449, p.28.
30. Tar report on file, 21/8/1940, KV2/448, p.3.
31. Celery's interrogation, 31/3/1941, KV 2/674, p.3.
32. Interrogation of Ruser by MI5's R.T. Reed, 20/10/1943, KV 2/451.
33. *Hitler's Spy Chief*, by Richard Bassett (UK: Orion Books, 2005), p.164.
34. *The Unseen War in Europe*, by John H. Waller (New York: Random House, 1996), p.164.
35. Celery's report, 31/3/1941, KV 2/674, p.3.
36. Ibid, p.4.
37. *The Mirror of Deception*, by Günter Peis (London: Weidenfeld and Nicolson, 1977), p.68.
38. Ibid, p.61.
39. Celery's report, 31/3/1941, KV 2/674, p.1.
40. *The Mirror of Deception*, by Günter Peis (London: Weidenfeld and Nicolson, 1977) , p.70.
41. Ibid.
42. Celery's interrogation, 31/3/1941, KV 2/674, Part ll, p.3.
43. Snow and Celery joint interrogation, KV 2/450, Part III, p.25, Record 11.
44. Ibid.
45. Ibid, p.26.
46. Ibid, p.28.
47. Ibid, p.26.
48. Ibid.
49. *Codename Dr Rantzau*, by Nikolaus Ritter (Hamburg: Hoffman & Campe, 1972), trans. Katharine Ritter, p.150.
50. Ibid.
51. *The Mirror of Deception*, by Günter Peis (London: Weidenfeld and Nicolson, 1977), p.69.
52. Campaign Diary, RAF Bomber Command, webarchive.nationalarchives. gov.uk/20070706011932/http://www.raf.mod.uk/bombercommand/ diary1940_2.html
53. Celery's notes on report, 31/3/1941, KV 2/674, p.2, part 4.

54. http://ww2today.com/12th-march-1941-focke-wulf-factory-bombed

55. Celery's report, 28/3/1941, KV 2/674, p.2, part 3.

56. Celery's report on Snow, 29/3/1941, KV 2/674.

57. *The Mirror of Deception*, by Günter Peis (London: Weidenfeld and Nicolson, 1977), p.67.

58. Celery special note, 20/4/1941, KV 2/674.

59. *Aurora*, by Katharine F. Ritter (USA: Xlibris, 2006), p.608.

60. *Codename Dr Rantzau*, by Nikolaus Ritter (Hamburg: Hoffman & Campe, 1972), trans. Katharine Ritter, p.150.

61. Extract, *Codename Dr Rantzau*, by Nikolaus Ritter (Hamburg: Hoffman & Campe, 1972) trans. Katharine Ritter. Reproduced with permission, pp.151-52.

62. Celery's report, 28/3/1941, KV 2/674, part 4, p.2.

63. Celery's report, 28/3/1941, KV 2/674, p.1.

64. Celery's report, 28/3/1941, KV 2/674, KV 2/674, part 4, p.3.

65. Celery's report, German military invasion plans, 29/3/1941, KV 2/674, p.4.

Chapter 8: Escape from Germany

1. Celery's report, 28/3/1941, KV 2/674, part 4, p.4.

2. The payment of German agents by Bank of England notes, KV 4/465, p.21.

3. Celery's notes to his report, 31/3/1941, KV 2/674, part 4, p.4.

4. Celery's report, 28/3/1941, KV 2/674, part 4, p.4.

5. Celery's report, 29/3/1941, KV 2/674, part 5, p.16.

6. Diary entry 15/3/19, *The Guy Liddell Diaries Volume 2, 1942-1945*, KV 2/185.

7. *The Mirror of Deception*, by Günter Peis (London: Weidenfeld and Nicolson, 1977), p.74.

8. Ibid, p.75.

9. *Hitler's Spy Chief: The Wilhelm Canaris Mystery*, by Richard Bassett (UK: Orion Books, 2005), Chapter 8, note 34.

10. Introduction to Alfred Naujocks' file, TNA KV 2/280.

11. *The Mirror of Deception*, by Günter Peis (London: Weidenfeld and Nicolson, 1977), p.75.

12. Ibid.

13. Ibid, p.76.

14. Ibid.

15. Contents of Celery's envelope, KV2/674.

16. *The Mirror of Deception*, by Günter Peis (London: Weidenfeld and Nicolson, 1977), p.68.

17. Celery's interrogation, 8/4/1941, KV 2/674, p.13.

18. Celery's report, 29/3/1941, KV 2/674, part 5, p.16.

19. Diary entry, 23/8/1940, by William Shirer, American journalist, http://ww2today.com/25th-august-1940-berlin-bombed-for-the-first-time
20. Celery's report, 28/3/1941, KV 2/674, part 4, p.5.
21. *The Mirror of Deception,* by Günter Peis (London: Weidenfeld and Nicolson, 1977), p.76.
22. Ibid.
23. Celery's report, 28/3/1941, KV 2/674, part 4, p.5.
24. *The Mirror of Deception,* by Günter Peis (London: Weidenfeld and Nicolson, 1977), p.77.
25. Ibid.
26. *Codename Dr Rantzau,* by Nikolaus Ritter (Hamburg: Hoffman & Campe, 1972), trans. Katharine Ritter, p.193.
27. Interrogation of Julius Boeckel, 1/2/1946, KV 2/1333, p.2.
28. Celery's interrogation, 8/4/1941, KV 2/674, p.12.
29. Celery's report, 28/3/1941, KV 2/674, part 5, p.16.
30. Celery's report, 29/3/1941, KV 2/674, part 5, p.3.
31. Ibid.
32. Celery's interrogation, 8/4/1941, KV 2/674, p.9.
33. Snow's first interrogation, 28/3/1941, KV 2/449, p.30.
34. Celery's report 29/3/1941, KV 2/674, part 5, p.4.
35. Letter to Tar from SIS Lisbon, 21/3/1941, KV 2/449.
36. Note attached to Tar's letter to Cowgill, 28/3/1941, KV 2/674.
37. Snow's first interrogation, 28/3/41, KV 2/449, p.6.
38. Celery's interrogation, 8/4/1941, KV 2/674, p.8.
39. Celery's report, 29/3/1941, KV 2/674, part 5, p.2.
40. Celery's report, 3/4/1941, KV 2/674, p.2.
41. Celery's report, 29/3/1941, KV 2/674, part 5, p.5.
42. Celery's report, 29/3/1941, KV 2/674, part 5, p.6.
43. Ibid.
44. Celery's interrogation (1), 2/4/1941, KV 2/674, p.5.
45. Snow's first interrogation, 28/3/1941, KV 2/449, pp.10,30.
46. Celery's interrogation (2), 2/4/1941, KV 2/674, p.3.
47. Celery private note, 31/3/1941, KV 2/674.

Chapter 9: Who to Believe?

1. Jarvis letter to Tar, 25/3/1941, KV 2/449.
2. Police report, 27/3/1941, KV 2/674, p.1.
3. *Codename Dr Rantzau* by Nikolaus Ritter (Hamburg: Hoffman & Campe, 1972), trans. Katharine Ritter, pp.145-46.
4. Police report, 27/3/1941, KV 2/674, p.2.

5. Ibid.

6. Snow's first interrogation, 28/3/1941, KV 2/449, p.9.

7. Tar report to file, 30/3/1941, KV 2/450.

8. Snow's first interrogation, 28/3/1941, KV 2/449, p.2.

9. Ibid, p.3.

10. Ibid, pp.17,18.

11. Ibid, p.26.

12. Celery's report, 28/3/1941, KV 2/674, p.18.

13. Marriott notes, lunch with Owens, 30/3/1941, KV 2/675.

14. Snow's first interrogation, 28/3/1941, KV 2/449, p.5.

15. Ibid, p.23.

16. Ibid, p.7.

17. Transports at Hamburg, Commander Montagu NID, 28/3/1941, KV 2/674, p.2.

18. Celery's report, office routine, 29/3/1941, KV 2/674.

19. *Blitzed*, by Norman Ohler (London: Allen Lane, 2016)

20. Snow's second interrogation, 31/3/1941, KV 2/450, p.1.

21. Ibid, p.5.

22. Celery's interrogation, 31/3/1941, KV 2/674, p.4.

23. Ibid, p.5.

24. Ibid.

25. Snow's interrogation pm, 31/3/1941, KV 2/450, p.4.

26. Ibid.

27. Marriott's note to file, 3/4/1941, KV 2/450, p.3.

28. Montague phone call, 31/3/1941, KV 2/674.

29. MI9's interrogations of prisoners of war, KV 2/674.

30. Ronnie Reed report, 1/4/1941, KV 2/674, p.2.

31. Letter to Tar, 8/3/1941, KV 2/674, Vol.2.

32. Celery's note regarding cables, 31/3/1941, KV 2/674.

33. Mrs Burton note regarding Celery, 1/4/1941, KV 2/674.

34. Celery's interrogation, 8/4/1941, KV 2/674, p.2.

35. Military Attaché in Athens, 30/3/1941, KV 2/674.

36. Snow's interrogation, 28/3/1941, KV 2/449, p.12.

37. Ibid.

38. Tar report, 1/4/1941, KV 2/674.

39. Ibid.

40. Handwritten note. Ibid.

41. Celery's interrogation (2), 2/4/1941, KV 2/674, p.2.

42. Ibid.

43. Ibid.

44. Ibid, p.4.
45. Celery's interrogation, 8/4/1941, KV 2/674, p.7.
46. Tar report to file, 5/4/1941, KV 2/450.
47. Tar report to file, 18/4/1941.
48. Tar report to file, 6/4/1941, KV 2/674.
49. MI5 officer report, Mr England, KV2/674.
50. Masterman's four hypothesis, 4/4/1941, KV 2/450, p.4.
51. Celery's interrogation, 8/4/1941, KV 2/674, p.7.
52. Ibid.
53. Celery's second interrogation, 8/4/1941, KV 2/674, p.1.
54. Ibid.
55. Diary entry, 19/4/1941, *The Guy Liddell Diaries Volume 2, 1942-1945*, KV 2/185.
56. Diary entry, 10/10/1943, *The Guy Liddell Diaries Volume 2, 1942-1945*, KV 2/185.
57. Celery's second interrogation, 8/4/1941, KV 2/674, p.3.
58. Ibid.
59. Ibid.
60. Celery's second interrogation, 8/4/1941, KV 2/674, p.1.
61. Ibid.
62. Confrontation Snow & Celery, part 3, 8/4/1941, KV 2/674 p.1.
63. Ibid, p.2.
64. Ibid, p.8.
65. Ibid, p.21.
66. Ibid, p.20.
67. Ibid, p.22.
68. Diary entry, 19/5/1941, *The Guy Liddell Diaries Volume 2, 1942-1945*, KV 2/185.
69. John Masterman meeting with Celery, 10/4/1941, KV2/674, p.1.
70. Ibid, p.2.

Chapter 10: Aftermath

1. Meeting, 10/4/1941, GML, DGW, TAR, JHM, JCM, KV 2/450.
2. Ibid, p.2.
3. Final interview with Snow, 10/4/1941, KV 2/450, p.7.
4. ISOS decrypt, Snow's message to Ritter, KV 2/87.
5. Ibid, p.2.
6. Ibid, p.5.
7. ISOS decrypt, Snow's message to Ritter, KV 2/87, sheet 2.
8. *Codename Dr Rantzau*, by Nikolaus Ritter (Hamburg: Hoffman & Campe, 1972), trans. Katharine Ritter, p.191.

9. Celery's future, John Masterman, KV 2/674, p.1.

10. Tar's letter to the Director General, 28/4/41, KV 2/674, p.1.

11. Ibid, p.2.

12. *The Double Cross System in the War of 1939-1945*, by J.C. Masterman (US: Yale University, 1972), p.58.

13. Tar's letter to the Director General, 28/4/41, KV 2/674, p.2.

14. Ibid.

15. Celery's future, J. Masterman, KV 2/674, p.2.

16. Dairy entry, 6/5/1941, *The Guy Liddell Diaries Volume 2, 1942-1945*, KV 2/185.

17. Personal particulars, George Sessler, Celery final instructions, 14/5/1941, KV 2/528, p.5.

18. Ibid.

19. Sessler's letter to Gerda Koch, 11/6/1941, KV 2/528.

20. De Havilland Hornet Moth, http://www.circopedia.org/Cyril_Mills

21. Sessler's interrogation at CSDIC, 23/5/1945, KV 2/528, p.3.

22. Sessler's interrogation at CSDIC, 23/5/1945, KV 2/528, p.1, (d).

23. *The Mirror of Deception*, by Günter Peis (London: Weidenfeld and Nicolson, 1977), p.82.

24. Ibid, p.77.

25. Ibid, p.78

26. Ibid, p.79.

27. Naval Captain Herbert Wichmann had close ties to Canaris and members of the Stauffenberg group which planned to assassinate Hitler in July 1944. Historian Monika Siedentopf, author of *Operation Sealion*, argues that the botched spying mission was not the result of German incompetence, but a deliberate act of sabotage by a cadre of intelligence officials opposed to Hitler's plans. Her research was focused on a group of people around Herbert Wichmann, the officer in charge of the Hamburg intelligence unit.

28. Wichmann Memorandum, Camp 020, 10/8/1945, KV 3/204, pp.1,2.

29. Sessler's interrogation at CSDIC, 23/5/1945, KV 2/528, p.3 (iii).

30. *Codename Dr Rantzau*, by Nikolaus Ritter (Hamburg: Hoffman & Campe, 1972), trans. Katharine Ritter, p.153.

31. *Hitler's Spies and Saboteurs*, by Charles Wighton and Gunther Peis (New York: Henry Holt, 1958), p.177.

32. *The Mirror of Deception*, by Günter Peis (London: Weidenfeld and Nicolson, 1977), pp.61, 62.

33. Ibid.

34. Arrest and detention report: General Anton Dostler and Captain George Sessler (concerning murder of OSS agent), WO 204/12872.

35. http://www.dailymail.co.uk/news/article-2117093/Secret-files-reveal-9-000-Nazi-war-criminals-fled-South-America-WWII.html
36. *The Mirror of Deception,* by Günter Peis (London: Weidenfeld and Nicolson, 1977), pp.38, 39.
37. Memorandum re Ritter, 22/5/1944, KV2/87, p.4.
38. Extract of a report by Dr H. Dearden, 4/4/1941, KV 2/86, p.2.
39. Interrogation of Major Freidrich Busch, 13/8/1945, KV 2/451.
40. Extract from third detailed interrogation of Eppler, 2/8/1942, KV 2/87, p.1.
41. *Codename Dr Rantzau,* by Nikolaus Ritter (Hamburg: Hoffman & Campe, 1972), trans. Katharine Ritter, pp.167,168.
42. CSDIC, Ritter's activities at Hamburg, 16/1/1946, KV 2/88, p.10, no.37.
43. CSDIC, Final report on Ritter, 16/1/1946, KV 2/88, pp.2, 3.
44. CSDIC, Preliminary interrogation of Ritter, 20/11/1945, KV 2/88, p.4.
45. http://americanintelligence.us/the-bad-nenndorf-controversy/
46. Hypothetical: Major Ritter's final report on the Snow case, Gwyer and Marriott, 31/7/1941, KV 2/451.
47. Gwyer interrogation Ritter, May 1946, KV 2/88, p.1.
48. *Codename Dr Rantzau,* by Nikolaus Ritter (Hamburg: Hoffman & Campe, 1972), trans. Katharine Ritter, p.121.
49. Ibid, p.126
50. Ibid.
51. Ibid, p.127.
52. Tar report to file, 25/5/1940, KV2 /448.
53. Gwyer interrogation Ritter, May 1946, KV 2/88, p.2.
54. Confrontation Snow and Celery, part 3, 8/4/1941, KV 2/674, p.10.
55. CSDIC interrogation Major Friedrich Busch, KV 2/529, pp.4-5.
56. *The Mirror of Deception,* by Günter Peis (London: Weidenfeld and Nicolson, 1977), p.79.
57. *The Mirror of Deception,* by Günter Peis (London: Weidenfeld and Nicolson, 1977), pp.79,80.
58. Gwyer interrogation Ritter, May 1946, KV 2/88, p.1.
59. *Snow,* by Nigel West and Madoc Roberts (UK: Biteback, 2001), p.196.
60. *Codename Dr Rantzau,* by Nikolaus Ritter (Hamburg: Hoffman & Campe, 1972), trans. Katharine Ritter, p.1.
61. Ibid, p.1.
62. *Game of the Foxes,* by Ladislas Farago (New York: David McKay, 1971), p.xi.
63. *Codename Dr Rantzau,* by Nikolaus Ritter (Hamburg: Hoffman & Campe, 1972), trans. Katharine Ritter, p.1.
64. Gwyer interrogation Ritter, May 1946, KV 2/88, p.1.

65. *The Double Cross System in the War of 1939-1945*, by J.C. Masterman (US: Yale University, 1972), p.18.

66. *Funkspiel*, by Jacques Delarue (New York: Skyhorse, 2008), p.301.

67. Bletchley Park, https://www.bletchleypark.org.uk/our-story.

68. Actively ran, *The Double-Cross System In The War Of 1939–1945*, by J.C. Masterman (London: The History Book Club, 1972), Foreword xii

69. http://www.cryptomuseum.com/people/mavis_batey.htm

70. *Codename Dr Rantzau*, by Nikolaus Ritter (Hamburg: Hoffman & Campe, 1972), trans. Katharine Ritter, p.191.

71. Ibid, pp.192,193.

72. Ibid, p.193.

73. Tar Robertson letter to John Masterman, 1/8/1971, The Provost and Fellows of Worcester College, Oxford, diary covering 1941-45, WOR/PRO, 10/1/28/2.

74. *The Double Cross System in the War of 1939-1945*, by J.C. Masterman (US: Yale University, 1972), Note on p.86.

75. 'A.k.a. "Dr Rantzau", *Center for the Study of Intelligence*, Bulletin 11, by Benjamin Fischer (Summer 2000), pp.8-11.

76. John Masterman's response to memorandum drafted by Marriott and Gwyer, 17/11/41, KV 2/451, p.3, point e.

77. Summary of the Snow case, KV2/452, p.1.

Chapter 11: South America Beckons

1. SO2 later became SOE (Special Operations Executive). Diary entry, 4/7/41, *The Guy Liddell Diaries Volume 2, 1942-1945*, KV 2/185.

2. Ibid.

3. *The Second World War, Volume 2*, by Winston Churchill, CHUR 4/176.

4. Meeting Tar, Marriott, Mills & Masterman 9.7.41 – KV2/528.

5. Diary entry, 19/9/41, *The Guy Liddell Diaries Volume 2, 1942-1945*, KV 2/18.

6. *Diaries of John Masterman*, with permission from The Provost and Fellows of Worcester College, Oxford, diary covering 1941-45, WOR/PRO, 10/1/28/2.

7. 'Some aspects of the German Military Abwehr wireless service, during the course of World War Two', paper by Arthur O. Bauer, 15/9/2003, p.3. http://www.cdvandt.org/German%20Abwehr.pdf.

8. *The Mirror of Deception*, by Günter Peis (London: Weidenfeld and Nicolson, 1977), p.78.

9. Diary entry, 21/1/1941, *The Guy Liddell Diaries Volume 2, 1942-1945*, KV 2/185.

10. Diary entry, 23/9/1941, *The Guy Liddell Diaries Volume 2, 1942-1945*, KV 2/185.

11. Kathleen Mary Dicketts' Brazilian immigration card, 6/10/41, https://familysearch.org/ark:/61903/1:1:KC65-ZR9.

12. The *Andalucia Star*, http://uboat.net/allies/merchants/ships/2240.html

13. German espionage and sabotage, https://www.history.navy.mil/research/ library/online-reading-room/title-list-alphabetically/g/german-espio-nage-and-sabotage.html

14. UK incoming passenger lists, 7/3/1942, www.ancestry.com.

15. Diary entry, 29/5/1942, *John Masterman's Diary*, with permission from The Provost and Fellows of Worcester College, Oxford, diary covering 1941-45, WOR/PRO, 10/1/28/2.

16. Diary entry 4/6/1942, *John Masterman's Diary*, with permission from The Provost and Fellows of Worcester College, Oxford, diary covering 1941-45, WOR/PRO, 10/1/28/2.

17. Ibid, 15/7/41.

18. *Daily Telegraph*, 'Man Arrested After 5 Years', 5/1/1949.

Chapter 12 – A New Life

1. Marriage Kathleen Mary Dicketts and David Rose, 17/6/1946.

2. Marriage Judit Rose Kalman and Walter Arthur Charles Dicketts, 8/9/1943.

3. Diary entry 1/2/1944, *The Guy Liddell Diaries Volume 2, 1942-1945*, KV 2/185.

4. *Evening News*, 'Director Faces 1944 Charge', 20/1/1949.

5. *East Grinstead Observer*, 'Astonishing Story of a Plausible Trickster', 18/3/1949.

6. *News of the World*, 'Lord of Manor was a Trickster on the Run', 20/3/1949.

7. Burke's Peerage 107th Edition, p.3,163, http://www.burkespeerage.com/ search_results.php?results=1

8. *Daily Express*, 'While the Police Seek Him, Swindler Becomes Lord of the Manor', 16/3/1945.

9. Ibid.

10. Ibid

11. '£390,000', http://www.measuringworth.com/

12. *Guardian*, 'Director Guilty of Conversion. Hazardous Work in War', 19/3/1949, p.8.

13. *Daily Herald*, 'Fugitive Crook Lived for Years as Rich Squire', 16/3/1949.

14. *East Grinstead Observer*, 'Astonishing Story of a Plausible Trickster', 18/3/1949.

15. *Times Digital Archive*, Issue 51,285, 1/2/1949, p. 2.

16. *Daily Express*, 'While the Police Seek Him Swindler Becomes Lord of the Manor', 16/3/1949.

17. Ibid.

18. *News of the World*, 'Lord of the Manor Was Trickster on the Run', 29/3/1949.

19. Ibid.

20. *East Grinstead Observer*, 'Astonishing Story of a Plausible Trickster', 18/3/1949.

21. *Daily Mail*, 'Director Ruined Completely by One Man', 16/3/1949.

22. Ibid.

23. Ibid.

24. Ibid.

25. *Daily Telegraph*, 'Lord of the Manor Sent to Gaol', 16/3/1949.

26. Ibid.

27. *Daily Graphic*, 'The Secret Life of Walter Dicketts, Spy and Swindler', 16/3/1949, p.3.

28. *Daily Herald*, 'Fugitive Crook Lived for Years as Rich Squire', 16/3/1949.

29. *Daily Mail*, 'Man On Run From The Yard, Set Up As The Squire', 16/3/1949.

30. Ibid

31. *Daily Herald*, 'Fugitive Crook Lived for Years as Rich Squire', 16/3/1949.

32. *London Gazette* Issue 40,954, 2/12/1956, p.7,269.

33. *Paddington News*, 'Guest House Death', 9/8/1957.

34. *Middlesex Independent, W. London Star,* 'Nervous Lodger Gassed Himself', 16/8/1957.

35. Ibid.

36. *West London Observer*, 'Door of his Room was Sealed', 9/8/1957.

37. *Middlesex Independent, W. London Star,* 'Nervous Lodger Gassed Himself', 16/8/1957.

38. Dicketts' death certificate, No.385, 6/8/1957, Paddington.

39. His wives called Dicketts by two different names. Judy called him Charles, Vera called him Dick.

40. *Yorkshire Post*, 'Writing of Stories: Imposter to Try New Way of Making a Living', 26/6/1930.

41. Oliver Muldoon's letter of 11/12/1975 to Rodney Adair – private collection.

42. *The Guy Liddell Diaries*, edited by Nigel West (London: Routledge, 2005) Vol.1, p.19.

43. Letter to J.C. Masterman, 23/7/1971, from Sir Martin Furnival Jones; Diary covering 1941-45, WOR/PRO, 10/1/28/2.

44. Ibid, 4/8/1971.

45. Death certificate, William Mair Rolph, 64 years old, 29/5/1940, died of rupture of aorta, atheromatous of aorta. Coroner was Bentley Purchase.

46. *Operation Mincemeat, by* Ben Macintyre (London: A&C Black, 2010), p.52.

47. *Snow*, by Nigel West and Madoc Roberts (UK: Biteback, 2001), p.199.

48. Ibid, p.200.

Chapter 13: Lost and Found

1. Rudolf Staritz, of the Abwehr secret wireless intelligence service, Berlin-Stahnsdorf, born 1921.

2. George Sessler, Abwehr officer who escorted Dicketts from Lisbon to Hamburg and back, born 14/6/1916.

3. Oliver Muldoon's letter of 11/12/1975, to Rodney Adair – private collection.

4. Judy Bentley's (formerly Dicketts) letter of 12/3/76, to Rodney Adair – private collection

5. Eric Richard Dicketts DFC – *London Gazette*, 4th Supplement, 16/10/1945. pp.5, 121-22.

Select Bibliography

Andrew, Christopher, *The Defence of the Realm* (London: Heinemann, 1985)

Andrew, Christopher, *Secret Service* (London: Heinemann, 1985)

Bassett, Richard, *Hitler's Spy Chief* (London: Orion, 2011)

Crowdy, Terry, *Deceiving Hitler* (Oxford: Osprey Publishing, 2008)

Duffy, Peter, *Double Agent* (New York: Scribner 2014)

Elliott, Geoffrey, *Gentleman Spymaster* (London: Methuen, 2011)

Farago, Ladislas, *The Game of the Foxes* (London: Hodder & Stoughton, 1971)

Garcia, Juan Pujol, and West, Nigel, *Operation Garbo* (London: Biteback, 2011)

Harris, Carol, *Blitz Diary* (Stroud: The History Press, 2010)

Haufler, Hervie, *The Spies Who Never Were* (New York: New American Library, 2006)

Hilton, Stanley, *Hitler's Secret War in South America, 1939-1945* (Baton Rouge: LSU Press, 1999)

Hinsley, Sir Harry, *British Intelligence in the Second World War: Security and Counter-Intelligence*, Vol. IV (London: HMSO, 1990)

Holt, Thaddeus, *The Deceivers* (London: Weidenfeld & Nicolson, 2004)

Humphries, John, *Spying for Hitler* (Cardiff: University of Wales Press, 2012)

Jonason, Tommy, and Olsson, Simon, *Agent TATE: The Wartime Story of Harry Williamson* (Stroud: Amberley, 2011)

Kahn, David, *Hitler's Spies* (New York: Macmillan, 1968)

Leonard, Thomas, and Bratzel, John, *Latin America during World War II* (Plymouth: Rowman & Littlefield, 2006)

Liddell, Guy, *The Guy Liddell Diaries* (London: Routledge, 2005)

Lochery, Neill, *Lisbon: War in the Shadows of the City of Light, 1939-45* (New York: Public Affairs Books, 2011)

Longmate, Norman, *How We Lived Then: History of Everyday Life During the Second World War* (London: Pimlico, Vintage Digital, 2010)

Macintyre, Ben, *Double Cross: The True Story of the D-Day Spies* (London: Bloomsbury, 2012)

Marks, Leo, *Between Silk and Cyanide: A Codemaker's War, 1941-1945* (Stroud: The History Press, 2013)

Masterman, J.C., *The Double-Cross System in the War of 1939-1945* (Boston, Mass: Yale University Press, 1972)

McKay, Sinclair, *The Secret Listeners: How the Wartime Y Service Intercepted the Secret German Codes for Bletchley Park* (London: Aurum Press, 2012)

Miller, Joan, *One Girl's War: Personal Exploits in MI5's Most Secret Station* (Dingle: Brandon, 1986)

Miller, Russell, *Codename TRICYCLE* (London: Secker & Warburg, 2004)

Montagu, Ewen, *Beyond Top Secret Ultra* (New York: Coward, McCann & Geoghegan, 1978)

Nicholson, Virginia, *Singled Out: How Two Million Women Survived without Men After the First World War* (London: Viking, 2007)

Paine, Lauran, *The Abwehr* (New York: Stein and Day, 1984)

Peis, Gunter, *The Mirror of Deception* (London: Weidenfeld & Nicolson, 1976)

Popov, Dusko, *Spy/Counterspy* (New York: Grosset & Dunlap, 1974)

Ritter, K.F., *Aurora* (Bloomington: Xlibris, 2006)

Ritter, Nikolaus, *Deckname Dr. Rantzau* (Hamburg: Hoffmann und Campe Verlag, 1972)

Sebag-Montefiore, Hugh, *Enigma: The Battle for the Code* (London: Weidenfeld & Nicolson, 2000)

Stephens, R., *Camp 020*, Introduction by Oliver Hoare (London: Public Record Office, 2000)

Tuchman, Barbara, *The Guns of August* (New York: MacMillan, 1962)

Vernon, Doremy, *Tiller's Girls* (London: Robson Books, 1988)

West, Nigel, *MI5: British Security Service Operations 1909-45* (London: Stein & Day, 1981)

West, Nigel, and Roberts, Madoc, *Snow: The Double Life of a World War II Spy* (London: Biteback, 2011)

West, Nigel, *MI5 in the Great War* (London: Biteback, 2014)

Wighton, Charles, and Peis, Gunther, *Hitler's Spies and Saboteurs* (also known in UK as *They Spied on England*) (New York: Henry Holt, 1958)

Winterbotham, F.W., *The Ultra Secret* (London: Weidenfeld and Nicolson, 1974)

Picture Credits

1. Petty Officer Walter Dicketts RNAS, 1915. Source: Associated Newspapers Ltd/Solo Syndication – Image No 5740222.
2. British Mark I (male) tank, named C-15, near Thiepval, 25 September 1916. Public domain. Source: - Wikipedia Commons. Photograph Q 2486 from the collections of the Imperial War Museums (collection no. 1900-09).
3. First World War tank crew splatter mask. Public domain. Source: Wikipedia Commons.
4. Walter Dicketts as a trainee RNAS pilot in 1917, with a Maurice Farman Shorthorn aircraft. Source: Private Collection, Mike Osborn.
5. Phyllis Hobson, Dickett's first wife, whom he married on 13 May 1918. Source: Private collection, Mike Osborn.
6. Captain Walter 'Dick' Dicketts, Dept. A1., Air Ministry (Intelligence) 1919. Source: Private collection, Mike Osborn.
7. Dora Viva Guerrier, Dicketts' first mistress appearing with the 24 Helena Stars, Gaumont Palace, Paris, 1924. Source: Private collection.
8. My grandmother, Dora Viva Guerrier, Dickett's first mistress, 1919–22. Source: Private collection.
9. Dicketts' mistress Dora, with his daughter Effie and Dora's mother Euphemia Smith. Effie was lied to that Euphemia was her mother and Dora was her sister. Source: Private collection.
10. My mother, Effie Dicketts, born on 20 September 1920. Effie changed her name to Tonie Witt in 1940. Source: Private collection.
11. Dicketts' second son, Rodney, to first wife Phyllis, born on 13 October 1921. Rodney's surname was changed to Adair by deed poll. Source: Private collection, Mike Adair.
12. Dicketts' son, Eric, ('Dick' to his first mistress Dora) born on 18 February 1922. With his wife Mary and daughters Susan and Geraldine in the late 1950s. Dick and his sister Effie would never meet. Source: Private collection, Dick Dicketts.
13. Kathleen 'Kay' Mary Holdcroft, Dicketts' second mistress who played a role in his spying activities for MI5 during the Second World War. Source: Brasil, Cartões de Imigração, https://familysearch.org/ark:/61903/1:1:KC65-ZR9.

14. Vera Nellie Fudge, Dicketts' third wife whom he married on 22 April 1933, with his son Richard, born on 18 January 1934. Richard's surname was changed to Tudhope by deed poll. Source: Private collection, Richard Tudhope.

15. Alma Farquhar Wood, Dicketts' 16-year old second wife with whom he eloped and married on 16 April 1929. Source: *Daily Mirror*/Solo Syndication.

16. Arthur Owens, MI5 double agent Snow. Source: Private collection, Graham White.

17. Colonel Thomas Argyll 'TAR' Robertson. Source: John Robertson, Special Forces Roll of Honour, http://www.specialforcesroh.com/gallery.php?do=view_image&id=5183&gal=gallery.

18. John Cecil Masterman, Chairman of the Double Cross Committee. Source: The Provost and Fellows of Worcester College, Oxford, WOR/PRO 10/2/76.

19. Members of the Double Cross Committee during the Second World War. Chairman, John Masterman, with Tar Robertson to his right, and Guy Liddell, Director of B Division (counter-espionage) behind him. Source: The Provost and Fellows of Worcester College, Oxford, WOR/PRO 10/2/77.

20. Lieutenant Colonel Robin 'Tin Eye' Stephens, MI5 Master Interrogator, Commander of Camp 020 and CSDIC Bad Nenndorf, World War Two. Source: Security Service MI5 https://www.mi5.gov.uk/bad-nenndorf, Open Government Licence: http://www.nationalarchives.gov.uk/doc/open-government-licence/version/3/.

21. German agent Gösta Caroli in 1938 – he became MI5 double agent Summer. Source: Tommy Jonason and Simon Olsson, authors of *Agent Tate*, (London, Amberley, 2012).

22. George Sessler, Dicketts' Abwehr bodyguard and escort from Lisbon to Hamburg and Berlin in 1941. Source: Brasil, Cartões de Imigração, https://familysearch.org/ark:/61903/1:1:VRQJ-C4C.

23. Admiral Wilhelm Canaris, Chief of the Abwehr in the Second World War. Source: Wikipedia Commons.

24. Nikolaus Ritter, Chief of Air Intelligence for the Abwehr in the Second World War: Source: Private collection, Katharine Ritter.

25. John Bull magazine, 1957, article showing Dicketts being drugged in Hamburg.

26. Ritter and his wife Irmgard von Klitzing. Irmgard was in involved in Dicketts being drugged in Hamburg in 1941. Source: Private collection, Katharine Ritter.

27. Alfred Naujocks, a major in the SS, was sent to kidnap Dicketts in Hamburg in 1941. Source: Wikipedia Commons.

28. Reinhard Heydrich, head of the Sicherheitsdienst (SD), one of the main architects of the Holocaust. Source. Wikipedia Commons.
29. Dicketts' Brazilian visa on behalf of MI5 in 1941. The strain of war is etched upon his features. Source: Brasil, Cartões de Imigração, https://familysearch.org/ark:/61903/1:1:KC6L-PVG.
30. Dicketts on his boat around 1947. Source: Associated Newspapers Ltd/ Solo Syndication.
31. Dicketts' prosperous period after the Second World War. With his fourth wife Judith Kelman, whom he married on 8 September 1943, and their son, Robert, who was born on 31 August 1944. Source. Private collection, Robert Dicketts.
32. Dicketts on Dartmoor, 1956. Source: Private collection, Robert Dicketts.
33. Mike Adair, grandson of Dicketts' first wife Phyllis, and Carolinda Witt, granddaughter of his mistress, Dora Guerrier. Dicketts was with both their grandmothers at the same time. Source: Private collection, Carolinda Witt.
34. Dicketts' two children to Dora Guerrier: my mother Tonie Witt, who died on 27 June 2007, and her brother, Eric 'Dick' Dicketts. Dick was awarded a Distinguished Flying Cross during the Second World War. They never met in real life.
35. George 'Robin' Graeme Dicketts Adair. Dicketts' first son to Phyllis – he served with T-Force in the Second World War and died on 6 June 2006. Source: Private collection, Mike Adair.
36. Dicketts' son, Robert, to fourth wife, Judith Rose Kelman, born on 31 August 1944. Dicketts' son, Richard 'Dick' Anthony (right), to third wife Vera Nellie Fudge, born on 18 January 1934. Dick's surname was changed to Tudhope by deed poll. Source: Private collection, Robert Dicketts & Dick Tudhope.
37. Dicketts' grandson, Corporal Oliver Simon Dicketts, of the Special Reconnaissance Unit, died in Afghanistan in 2006. He was the only child of Robert and Priscilla.

Index